D0352512

Racism and Mental Health

WITHDRAWN

Book No.   **05212160**

30121 0 05212160

of related interest

Race, Culture and Ethnicity in Secure Psychiatric Practice
Working with Difference
Edited by Charles Kaye and Tony Lingiah
ISBN 1 85302 696 4 pb
ISBN 1 85302 695 6 hb

Meeting the Needs of Ethnic Minority Children
Second Edition
Edited by Kedar N. Dwivedi
ISBN 1 85302 959 9

'Race', Housing and Social Exclusion
Edited by Peter Somerville and Andy Steele
ISBN 1 85302 849 5

Confidentiality and Mental Health
Edited by Christopher Cordess
ISBN 1 85302 860 6 pb
ISBN 1 85302 859 2 hb

Mental Illness
A Handbook for Carers
Edited by Rosalind Ramsay, Claire Gerada, Sarah Mars and George Szmukler
ISBN 1 85302 934 3

Communication and Mental Illness
Theoretical and Practical Approaches
Edited by Jenny France and Sarah Kramer
ISBN 1 85302 732 4

Immigration Controls, the Family and the Welfare State
A Handbook of Law, Theory, Politics and Practice for Local Authority, Voluntary Sector and Welfare State Workers and Legal Advisors
Steve Cohen
ISBN 1 85302 723 5

Racism and Mental Health

Prejudice and Suffering

Edited by Kamaldeep Bhui

Jessica Kingsley Publishers
London and Philadelphia

All rights reserved. No part of this publication may be reproduced in any material form (including photocopying or storing it in any medium by electronic means and whether or not transiently or incidentally to some other use of this publication) without the written permission of the copyright owner except in accordance with the provisions of the Copyright, Designs and Patents Act 1988 or under the terms of a licence issued by the Copyright Licensing Agency Ltd, 90 Tottenham Court Road, London, England W1P 9HE. Applications for the copyright owner's written permission to reproduce any part of this publication should be addressed to the publisher.

Warning: The doing of an unauthorised act in relation to a copyright work may result in both a civil claim for damages and criminal prosecution.

The right of the contributors to be identified as authors of this work has been asserted by them in accordance with the Copyright, Designs and Patents Act 1988

First published in the United Kingdom in 2002
by Jessica Kingsley Publishers Ltd
116 Pentonville Road
London N1 9JB, England
and
325 Chestnut Street
Philadelphia, PA 19106, USA
www.jkp.com

Copyright © Jessica Kingsley Publishers 2002

Library of Congress Cataloging-in-Publication Data

Racism and mantal health : prejudice and suffering / edited by Kamaldeep Bhui.
    p. cm
Includes bibliographical references and index.
ISBN 1-84310-076-2 (pbk. : alk. paper)
    1. Minorities--Mental health services--Great Britian. 2. Raciam--Great Britian. I. Bhui, Kamaldeep.

RA790.7.G7 R33 2002
362.2'089'00941--dc21   2002018448

British Library Cataloguing in Publication Data
A CIP catalogue record for this book is available from the British Library

ISBN 1 84310 076 2

Printed and Bound in Great Britain by
Athenaeum Press, Gateshead, Tyne and Wear

STAFFORDSHIRE
UNIVERSITY
LIBRARY
SITE: SHREWSBURY

31 MAY 2005

CLASS No.
362.2089

05212160

Contents

Chapter 1

Feeling for Racism

Kamaldeep Bhui

This chapter begins the journey of exploring how such a controversial area of study constantly defies thought. Prejudice and suffering for migrant groups are introduced. The motivation for producing a book on racism and prejudice is set out, alongside an invitation to the reader to be challenged by and challenge what follows.

Born in Kenya, and having arrived in the UK at the age of two, most of my childhood influences were in rural Buckinghamshire, where I was schooled and discovered difference and responses to it. Differences of skin colour and culture were inevitably part of the fabric of life, but they were not really at the foreground for me, except in moments of extreme violence to family and friends because of their skin colour and conspicuously different cultural origins. There was always a tension between being ordinary and fitting in and finding myself reminded of my difference from others. I proceeded on a path of being ordinary and passed sufficient academic exams to qualify as a doctor, and then as a psychiatrist in London, a region with a complex admixture of racially and culturally different peoples. Although my fascination with the subject of racism and mental health was born long before I went to medical school in London, this did not really become more real until I saw the experiences of the many validate what I had considered to by my own idiosyncrasy. The curiosity about race, ethnicity and culture arose from two sources. First, from my early experiences of being misidentified. That is, how people saw me, and understood my origins. It was easier to be who I was perceived to be rather than who I was/am. An ongoing interplay between perceived identity and subjective identity is not unique to discourse on racial difference. It is the substance of human relationships in general. Yet racial misidentification seems very significant as it then patterns how others 'see' you.

The second group of influences was encounters with racism. These were raw experiences, that is lived moments rather than considered reflections about prejudicial events. The subjective study of mental distress and well-being must include felt moments as well as any professionalised theories of mind and disease. These two emergent languages capture different facets of the same entity, but then limit the cross-fertilisation and extension of each way of thinking. Subjective experiences are rarely accommodated in scientific understandings as they are considered to be too biased and personal, not in the realms of objectified science, but in the realms of faith and value systems: akin to political or religious thought.

Although I was born in Kenya, to parents of Sikh Indian origin, the confusion around identity was, for me, a mixture of searching for national identity, religious identity, cultural origins and linguistic identity. Racial identity was a convenient shorthand for all of these, but it was used not by me but by friends, teachers and, more importantly, by those who did not know me. I soon learnt that whatever I thought my 'substance' to be, whoever I thought I was, this was always quite different from the ascription with which others invested me. These ascriptions by friends, teachers and other observers usually referred to appearance, and were invested with the meaning that clearly had origins in the mind of the observer. These labels were not just intellectualised names for a category of person, but carried with them sentiments, and hopes, and fears, and excitements about what the 'other' might be. The difficulty was that such ascriptions, at the moment of being applied, were felt to have origins in the observed so as to legitimise the authenticity of the observer's view of my identity.

I discovered similar confusions in everyday psychiatric practice among professionals treating cultural minorities. I was struck by major limitations in all that I learnt and applied in daily psychiatric practice. Yet these deficits, which seemed obvious to me, did not appear so visible to others, including many of my teachers who taught me to think in many other ways. The persistent misidentifications that I saw taking place troubled me more than any involving me personally. It was only when it became clear to me that such misidentifications were crucial to the quality of the relationship between patient and professional that my discomfort with the status quo grew. I was growing more aware of the validity of my subjective concerns about a scientific body of thought, which although valuable, had limitations that did not seem obvious to those enmeshed in its rules for thinking. These concerns were not neutral, as one might notice the time of day, but were more like noticing the shade of autumn leaves or the rotting flesh of dead fox on the road. Such concerns when aired were and still are often met with astonishment, which is driven by blindness and indifference. Thus, not only were they not obvious, but to make them obvious required greater energy and effort than simply pointing out their absence. The emerging research data that black and ethnic minorities were treated quite differently in the health services, and that medical student selection was biased against ethnic minorities, added to a general movement in medicine and psychiatry, a marginalised movement at that, to redress the balance (Coker 2001). Information and awareness combined to organise an endless series of personal observations, research studies, teaching seminars and lived moments telling me how things worked. I witnessed specific examples of physical racist assaults and an endless volley of verbal hostility at family and friends. I recall that somehow I did not understand what I saw. I knew who I was. I knew the reasons for which people inflicted racist violence on others. I knew these reasons were full of contradictions and faulty assertions. Such contradictions and clearly unthought acts prompted me to seek explanations, some of which were rationalisations. Some of my efforts at understanding were tricks of the mind, to distance me from the ferocity of violation. Where I witnessed a similar but more refined activity in my working life, be it between patients, between patient and doctor, or any professional–patient–public encounters, I sought explanations of such behaviour first in people, then in the health service and finally in the fabric of society. It is this endeavour that this book represents.

If only it were that simple. Racist assaults and racist attitudes are but one component of prejudice. Prejudice exists within and between groups that each decide they are 'racially' distinct and distinct in such fundamental ways that they are on different dynastic paths. Thus, an early trip to India between school and college was, for me, supposed to be a rediscovery of a homeland, a place to which I belonged and where my boundaries of identity would be similar to many others. Alas, not only did India not feel like home, but the beliefs systems about Indians who had emigrated to England formed a significant barrier to further discovery. I noticed that 'English Indians', or Indians who were once Indian and who now spend most or perhaps nearly all of their time in the UK, also had stereotypical attitudes about Indian Indians. Therefore, although it is easier to focus simply on race, in a discussion of racism, race is not the only issue. It is a convenient category that lends some illusory context for debate, but by doing so obscures the possibility of real debate that considers people and their attitudes and actions as the issues. It is in the hands of skilled orators and minds, and workers and artists, that racial imagery and discourse is given life. Therefore, any book about racism should also be about people and how they deal with one another.

'Racism' and 'racist acts' generate an enormous amount of puzzling, intense and tormenting feelings among victims, as well as bemusement, paradoxical curiosity and paralysis among observers. The 'motivation' of perpetrators is rarely considered in depth beyond 'gut' reactions of condemnation. On some occasions, there is support for thought about the origins and the destructive impact of racist thought and action. However, this is often obscured or avoided, by moves towards reassuring oneself of one's personal morality, and demonstrating this to others in the form of a public display. In such a manner self-esteem survives accusations of prejudice, whilst the recruitment of support for a particular prejudice soothes away turbulent self-doubt. Part of the difficulty when talking about racism lies in a lack of clarity about what constitutes racism, prejudice, hatred and violent assault.

Why does the colour of skin produce such extreme responses? Is it just the colour of the skin, or is it its texture, its smell, its history of relationships, its way of reflecting light, its softness and its warmth that also fuel the immediate reactions? What is it about difference that produces fear? Numerous scientific analyses have attempted to improve the understanding of racism and of prejudice in general. These analyses have focused on aspects of human behaviour and thinking common to sexism, ageism, homophobia and other emotional states involving fear and hatred of some particular category of human being. Prejudice or violent action or disapproval, whichever of these is provoked, is justified on the basis of diverse physical human characteristics that are invested with monstrous and life-threatening implications. The colour of skin is often considered to be the defining principle that organises racist thought and action. Yet, 'racisms' are invoked in white-on-white, and black-on-black conflict. Where racial appearance is similar, national identity, language, tribe or destiny become the organising principles. Anything, it seems, that justifies applying a scale of worth to human beings can be utilised as a vehicle for the infliction of violence. Thus, black-on-black violence, inter-religious wars and caste-related wars in Indian society all have a different context for explanations of violence and prejudice. But the fundamental elements of hate and violence on the basis of physical characteristics linked to a sense of threat to personal and group survival are recurrent.

And so there appear to be some issues that racism has in common with other forms of violence, be it violent thinking or violent assaults. Both have an emotional impact. The child in the playground may be taunted about the worthlessness of his or her existence because of his or her black skin. This is a traumatic realisation, that black skin and appearance are denigrated. These children adapt, and apply the principles of survival, perhaps exercising for themselves the very prejudices inflicted upon them, and so self-hatred is born. Alternatively, perhaps such children learn that this is the way of the world, and so they take up other prejudices, some shared with their tormentors, in order to salvage some esteem, by boasting the possession of valued physical or cultural characteristics. Denigrating similar but different characteristics in others is a way of saying I'm OK, and you're not; it is a way of being separate; a way of saying you are you, and I am I, and you are not part of me, just as I am not part of you.

Racisms cannot be said to exist as natural entities that are the same the world over, or even the same from one era to another. Elizabeth Young-Bruhl (1998), a psychoanalyst, uses a historical context to identify three types or histories of racism: that located in Nazi anti-Semitism, that located in European colonialism and nationalism, and that involving sexual and homophobic prejudice. Each of these histories has a contemporary legacy.

Skin colour, one of many human characteristics, is a powerful badge that is used by observers as a master label. That is, an observer invests the colour of a person's skin with significance that helps him or her make judgements about the darker skinned person's worth or value and relationship to the observer. This, at one level, is a benign process of human relatedness, whereby individuals in all human societies attempt to investigate, socialise and make sense of their surroundings in order to maximise their rewards and minimise troubles. Clearly these judgements can be faulty and when one derives and attaches 'value' and 'worth' to people on the basis of observed characteristics, the potential of locating the 'other' in a inferior position is immediately generated. The capacity to inflict pain or deprivation on the basis of these judgements is an essential part of racist action. Such a passionate process surely goes on as part of group and interpersonal behaviour, where individuals discover themselves and others during the articulation of a new relationship. The Scottish philosopher David Hume (1711–1776) grappled with this in his *Treatise of Human Nature*. The process of making causal inferences, he argued, is neither rational nor evidential, but rather only psychological, based upon fundamental features of human nature (Popkin 1999, p.456).

> The reasoner thinks that he or she has reasoned correctly and that he or she can ascertain that this is the case…thus the purported independent knowledge claims of mathematics and logic turn out to involve human psychological claims that are less than certain. (Popkin 1999, p.459)

As if to illustrate the very points he made, David Hume's views on other races seem to commit these same errors. His writings are well established as promulgating and setting the foundations for 18th-century and modern racism (see Fernando 1991; Popkin 1999). Hume, alongside Thomas Jefferson and Immanuel Kant, insisted on the permanent inferiority of people of colour:

> there was never a civilised nation of any other complexion than white, nor any individual eminent in action or speculation. No ingenious manufacturers amongst them, no arts, no sciences. On the other hand the most rude and barbarous of the whites, such as the ancient Germans…have all

still something eminent about them, in their valour, form of government, or some other particular. (Popkin 1999, pp.511–12)

White, even if German white, appeared more palatable to Hume. Similarity mitigates towards a more favourable appraisal of worth and diminished perceived threat. One would hope such a crude analysis as this might no longer be relevant, as these writings are dated. I believe such a hope is based on idealistic denial of the capacity of human beings to hurt and despise one another, even in modern Britain. So-called civilisation, or industrialisation, or improving living standards alone do nothing to combat prejudice and racisms.

Hume went on in the *Treatise* to claim that 'reason is, and ought to be the slave of passions, and that passions are open to scientific investigation' (Popkin 1999, p.460). It appears that racism is a sort of passion that can exist despite reasoning, applied intelligence or a good education. Efforts to apply pure logic in order to explain racism, or to draw on reason and common humanity to move towards a more tolerant society, have failed throughout humankind's history. The colour of one's skin is one of the many bases around which prejudice can form. Hatred of other races is also an extremely unique form of prejudice that is always available, as a servant to one's self-esteem, when all else fails. Consider the ease with which a debate or argument or disagreement can be 'racialised' in order to intro-duce a more powerful force into the debate. This 'flexibility' offered by the racialisation of discourse introduces the experience of non-thinking, con-fusion, perplexity and disbelief. The ease with which discourse can be racialised, and stronger emotional forces or passions mobilised, gives racial discourse and the category of race a powerful role in human negotiations. Indeed, it is because it is such a powerful role that racial discourse contin-ues to exist. In states of rageful racialised debate, people of reason are reduced to their 'passions' or to things about which they are most passion-ate. Reason and passion do not mix well. In some instances, passion obscures reason by its very intensity, and in others reasoning itself becomes the victim of the passion. Therefore, any study of racism must include a study of the passions, alongside reasoned argument.

This book begins (in Chapters 1, 2 and 4) with a discussion of racism and mental states in general terms, trying to locate what we mean by racism and prejudice and their psychosocial and psychopolitical origins. Included in this is a need to master the complex and often ambiguous terminology that accompanies such discourse. Edgar Jones (in Chapter 3) writes on how theories of belief formation might assist in understanding racist thinking. In Chapter 5, Frantz Fanon's work is critiqued for its relevance to the debates promoted by the authors of this volume. In Chapter 6 Premila Trivedi illustrates the impact of racism in society on the experiences of people who develop mental illness and then end up contacting mental health services for help. These services compound their problems and add to the spiral of distress. Kwame McKenzie draws on the African-Amercian experience to give depth to our understanding of status and ethnic origin (Chapter 7). Following a brief review of scientific racism (Chapter 8) Bhugra and Bhui address the socio-economic impact of racism (Chapter 9). Later chapters consider 'racism' definitions and associated paradoxes. Theories of racism, ethnocentrism, nationalism and the impact on societies are briefly discussed. Dr Xavier Coll, a child psychiatrist, explores what happens when we are misunderstood and misidentified (Chapter 10). Later chapters consider definitions of mental illness and the validity of measurements of mental disorders across cultural, ethnic and religious boundaries. In Chapter 11 the debate is informed by research data on the presentation and management of mental disorders among ethnic minorities in London. Variations of effective treatments are emphasised before considering possible explanations for these variations. Racism as a form of explanation is discussed in Chapter 12. Chapter 13 outlines some common lessons and thought traps in the form of short essays on some familiar 'statements' that emerge from racialised dialogue. Chapter 14 turns to the future of mental health care, and the elements necessary to deliver appropriate and effective care to all people.

Chapter 2

Race and Racial Discourse

Kamaldeep Bhui

This chapter attends to the difficulties of definition and understanding that arise when different groups use ideas of race, ethnic group, culture and nation state in similar and not so similar ways. Such definitional ambiguity can paralyse constructive dialogue. Without concerted effort at addressing these limitations any debate becomes polarised and fruitless and demonstrates the power of perplexity and confusion to motivate aggression.

What is a race?

Table 2.1 lists some common definitions of terms. These definitions help clarity of thought, yet they can be unpacked with many variations, depending upon particular scenario and context, on particular peoples and their history. As a starting point, these definitions distinguish some core usages to which words are put. Race is now seen as a social construction. Cultural and lifestyle characteristics tend to be shared within particular race categories. This is the common message in race discourse. However, such characteristics show much greater diversity than classical views about racial determinism allow. When definitions of racial difference were historically determined by specific 'encounters' of a particular cultural group (A) with a different cultural group (B), racial differences were held accountable for the noticed cultural dissimilarity. Thus, a patchwork of racial symbolism came to mean many things to many peoples, as if it carried all information about beliefs, lifestyle, religion and relationship.

Table 2.1: Definitions

Acculturation[1]

Incorporating some of the attributes of other cultural groups.

Culture

Tylor (1871): that complex whole which includes knowledge, belief, art, morals, law and custom and other capabilities and habits acquired by man as a member of society.

Keesing (1981): systems of shared ideas, systems of concepts and rules and meanings that underlie and are expressed in the ways that humans live.

Helman (1990): a set of guidelines (explicit and implicit) which individuals inherit as members of a particular society, and which tells them how to view the world, how to experience it emotionally, and how to behave in it in relation to other people, to supernatural forces or gods, and to the natural environment. It also provides them with a way of transmitting these guidelines to the next generation – by the use of symbols, language, art and ritual.

Cultures divide their members into different categories according to gender, age, social class, occupation, able/disabled, kin/non-kin, health/ill, mad/bad...same group/different group, ...same race, culture, ethnicity/other race, culture, ethnicity.

All cultures have ways of moving people from one social category into another or of confining people within the bounds of a category: behaviour, thoughts, access to social groups, access to health care...

Most modern societies are mixtures of many sub-cultures.

Enculturation[1]

Acquiring the same world view or 'cultural lens' of a society by for example growing up in that culture.

Ethnic group[2]

A community whose heritage offers important characteristics in common between its members, and which makes them distinct from other communities...the boundary which distinguishes 'us' from 'them' is recognised on both sides of that boundary.

Ethnic group[4]

An epidemiologist's approach. A social group characterised by distinctive social and cultural tradition, maintained within the group from generation to generation, a common history and origin, and a sense of identification with the group. Members of the group have distinctive features in their way of life, shared experiences, and often a common genetic heritage.

Table 2.1 continued

Ethnicity[2]

Multi-faceted phenomenon based on physical appearance, subjective identification, cultural and religious affiliation, stereotyping and social exclusion…but it is not possible to prescribe in advance what the key distinguishing characteristics might be; the components will be different within Britain compared with, say, Northern Ireland, Belgium, Bosnia, the United States, India or Singapore… So it is important to identify the important ethnic boundaries in any particular society.

Nation[3]

A large number of people of mainly common descent, language, history etc., inhabiting a territory bounded by defined limits and forming a society under one government.

National[3]

Of a or the nation, common to the whole nation; peculiar to or characteristic of a particular nation.

Nationalism[3]

Patriotic feeling, principles, or efforts; policy of national independence.

Nationality[3]

Being national, national quality; patriotic sentiment; one's nation of origin; nation (men of nationality); existence as a nation; ethnic group forming part of one or more political nations.

Race[1]

i) Group of persons, animals or plants connected by common descent; house, family, tribe or nation regarded as of common stock; distinct ethnical stock (as in Caucasian, Mongolian, etc. race); genus or species or breed or variety of animals or plants, any great division of living creatures (human, feathered, four-footed, etc.).

ii) Descent kindred (of noble, oriental, etc. race; separate in language and race).

iii) Classes of person etc. with some common feature (race of poets, dandies).

iv) Race relations: between members of different races in same country; race-riot: outbreak of violence due to racial antagonism

v) Race suicide: gradual disappearance of a race through voluntary limitation of reproduction.

Racialism[3]

Belief in superiority of a particular race; antagonism between different races.

Racism[3]

Theory of human abilities etc. determined by race.

1 Helman (1990)   *2 Peach (1996)*
3 Sykes (1982)   *4 Last (1995)*

A property of racial terms is that they are defined by the context and the discourse in which the term is mentioned. This lends these terms the potential to be used in a multiplicity of ways, and to mean many different things to different peoples. Indeed, it is precisely the 'empty' quality of race as a category that allows racial terms to be misused with ease. Yet race remains important in human relationships precisely because we choose to use race in such a powerful way, and because it is such a core feature of identity, worth and value. It is a way of classifying ourselves and those around us and a way of seeking out the familiar and the less threatening in the apparently unfamiliar and threatening 'other'.

Cultural studies have flourished and definitions of culture abound. Any manifestation of human symbolism, thought, perceptual characteristic and the determinants of human fantasy, which organise relationships, might be considered as 'culture'. This might be signified by behaviour, conversation, art and collective social action or imagination. Internal imaginative constructions of the world are rarely considered as culture, yet clearly beliefs about the world, health, illness, justice and morality all vary across cultures and nations. The salience given to specific arts or actions will vary, just as the valency given to any one activity, in one cultural group, will be different from that given in another. Ethnic groups are no less arbitrary. They might be imposed by law, or they emerge as a consequence of common and agreed rules that define 'relationships' between different cultural and racial groups. The contemporary purpose of ethnic groups arises from the tendency to measure the threat from the other. More contemporary health service and social policy debates promote the use of ethnic categories as a way of monitoring inequality, and institutionalised racist action in public services. This apparently simple concept has given rise to great debate in Britain. Is the British police force racist? The MacPherson (1999) report says 'yes', the implication being that there are deeply ingrained attitudes and practices that have potential to be discriminatory, irrespective of the intention of any one officer to be overtly racist or not. This simple point has caused such controversy because it is interpreted to mean that all people in the police force are actively racist. This is *not* what was meant, but this is what many in the police force feel was meant. It was also the basis of William Hague's, the Conservative leader, attack on the MacPherson report as an incorrect document that undermines police confidence. So here is another example of an attempted remedy to potential prejudice attacked as an aggressive act itself. The response to prejudice is treated as if it is meant to hurt the police. Who is the victim? Who is hurt? Who intended harm? Who can't bear to think about what they do and to whom? In our personal lives such attitudes are, of course, hidden. In public services there must be a duty upon those in powerful positions of authority actively to demonstrate their understanding and ability to perform their duties in the highest professional manner. To feel attacked, and then to attack, is not professional and is not based on thought. It is action based on tribal fantasies of us and them. The tradition of adversarial debate feeds into such niches for prejudicial thought.

Erikson (1993) describes five types of modern ethnicity:

- urban minorities

- proto-nations or ethno-national groups

- ethnic groups in plural societies

- indigenous minorities

- post-slavery minorities.

Each of these has distinct geographical locations and relationship histories to the dominant culture. Globalism is challenging the differentiation that seems so much a part of a psychological need to establish a self and an identity with which individuals can feel comfortable and safe. Each migrant group experiences different tensions whilst trying to establish economic stability and emotional confidence in their survival capacity. It seems the tenacity of racial and ethnic groupings lies in their capacity to fulfil satisfactions for minority groups seeking identity and solidarity. This is by the act of expressing their identity in racial and ethnic terms. Such expressions make groups feel safer at a psychological level, albeit in the realms of the unconscious, by identification with a group and a share in an omnipotent fantasy. This is a much more seductive way of being than to be too fully aware of one's human frailty and isolation. We seek to be in a group and belong, and we choose a group on the basis of shared attributes and interests, of which race is one. Those looking for operationalised and mechanistic logicality in defining racism and its manifestations will be partly pleased, but mostly disappointed. The words in this book sit in the ambiguities and contradictions which are prominently assigned to the realms of unconscious activity, but which surely are just as prominent in conscious interplay of relationships (Lane 1999).

The writings on racism are, to date, incomplete in three essential ways. First, racism is often thought of as a single static entity, a behaviour or an attitude that has firm boundaries and appears in an unambiguous manner. When racism is invoked as an explanation, or it is said to be instrumental in a communication, different players have very different views about what it means. I suggest that racisms are dynamic, adaptive and tenacious constellations of thoughts, feelings and ideas that lead to actions. There are many 'racisms' and any attempt to define precisely a single form will construct one variety to the neglect of others; whilst each may share attributes with others, so each may differ in some aspects. 'Racism' as a word infers a prejudicial act to disempower or disadvantage another on the basis of skin colour and 'racial origins'. The assumption is that there is such a thing as racial origin. Any discussion of race reinforces racialised discourse and reinforces the concept.

There is frequent confusion about 'categories of person' such as race, ethnicity, ethnic group, religion, culture, linguistic groups and nations. Racism and anti-racism, like twins, share identities, by sharing a common chronological evolution. Racism and anti-racism therefore evolve with cultural and ethnic identities as societies change. Thus, children of mixed parentage rarely receive proper consideration; refugees of any background are lumped together and counted as 'other' in classifications and census data. Sub-cultures that define social meaning (consider the Irish in the UK) are also lost in culturally imprecise, colonial and politicised ethnic classifications. The 2001 census introduced a separate 'Irish' ethnic group. A new ethnic group is constructed on the basis of political pressure and recognition of sub-cultures, yet other groups like African-Caribbean, or African or Indian remain anomalous categories that are intended to classify peoples who differ markedly in their cultural, linguistic and religious lifestyles from the dominant governing group.

Racist discourse tends to produce opposite reactions, which service similar psychological functions. Where racism is mentioned there is a tendency to avoid such an unpalatable subject, because accepted unfamiliarity with other races generates apprehension about 'saying too much' or baring, for public display, our own prejudices. On the other hand, some debaters are immediately attracted to disclose their personal commitment to equality (not the opposite of racism of course), and to display their good nature and desire that shared humanity be the organising principle for contesting rights. Such an approach is superficially laudable, but retains the essentialised notion of race, only to under-emphasise its importance. Racial origins should not be important but they are. They are a non-incidental factor in human relationships. There is the truly thoughtful approach that applies intellect to consider the problems of race and race relations, perhaps concluding, as I often do, that the racialised discussion is a vehicle for dialogue about another subject requiring a more forceful argument. Politicians know that racial statements can be powerful mobilisers of shared action and assent. What is certain is that, whichever of these approaches for racial discourse are adopted, there is a distancing from the rather crude and violent and dehumanising aspects of racial discourse and racist acts. Such subtle manoeuvres disguise, avoid, and rein in the passions, whilst allowing a freedom to improve intellectual understanding. The proponents of racist discourse master some of these more contradictory, puzzling and paralysing human feelings that are generated by racialised discourse. The danger here is that what psychoanalytic theory calls psychological mechanisms of defence are heavily invoked to avoid the disturbing feelings which should, in my view, be fully entertained in order to fully appreciate the implications of prejudicial phenomena. This applies not only to perpetrators and victims but to politicians, the public, observers, commentators and policy and law makers. If these groups find racial discourse unpalatable, as something to be avoided or escaped, or even 'rationalised', then critical thought itself becomes a disguise for more fundamental attitudes that set the tone of human interactions.

If one attempts to explore racisms comfortably from a purely intellectual perspective, if one does not mention the 'horrible R word', for fear of acknowledging its place in our world, in order to focus on remedial action through other means, the crucial messages carried by our emotions are isolated from the content of the debate. These affects or emotions carry important information about the impact and origins of prejudicial hatred, and, more importantly, they signal our own agency in the formation and perpetuation of such attitudes. They signal the type of relationship that is configured by racialised discourse. They carry important and vital authenticating information about a subjective form of human experience that no one likes to think about, because it is so disturbing and destructive and murderous in its expression. Helen Morgan, a psychoanalytic psychotherapist in London, wrote a paper called 'Between fear and blindness: the white therapist and the black patient' (Morgan 1998). The title captures the psychological dilemma facing society and the individuals that make up that society. The experience of individuals and groups, when race is on the agenda, includes fear of the unknown. There is a sense of an anticipated witch-hunt, a mass reaction resulting in the demoralisation of our sense of goodness. And so the choice is to acknowledge fear and trust and group exploration of that fear, knowing that a possible outcome is condemnation of self by self, as well as by others, or to be blinded to the issues but to be comfortable and free of self-torment.

Victims of racist thought and action are outraged and increasingly confident about venting their outrage. However, this signalling of an unacceptable way of treating another human being can spill over into anger and a desire to inflict the same torture or harm on the assailant. The assailant, presuming him or herself innocent, is unable to understand the rage in this state of blinded morality, and so the mythology of racist discourse being like a witch-hunt is reinforced.

A contemporary example is anti-racist training in health and social services. This has been heralded as essential to the provision of effective care, yet such training is never a comfortable or popular experience, generating conflict and, in some instances, resulting in the participants feeling hunted. Rarely do people expect their judgements, values and beliefs to be the subject of super-moral collective scrutiny, let alone deconstruction in the form of critical and perhaps itself prejudicial thought. Hence, defensive manoeuvres ensue in order to justify cherished beliefs, which are more than beliefs; they are often our identity, our way of understanding how the world works and what our role in it is. Such beliefs can result in illusory clarity and rigidity of view at the expense of unexpressed ambiguities and ambivalence. This coupled with a universal need to believe in one's morality and goodness generates a fortified state of impenetrable narcissism. Such a state offers comfortable relief and defends against perceived accusation whilst bolstering self-esteem. After all, to consider racist consequences of our actions, or racist re-workings of what subjectively appears to be fair, decent, kind or at best benign deliberations, is extremely worrying. A racialised explanation or interpretation of daily activity means 'racism' exists, is real and is all around us and we cannot even perceive it. But race does not exist – it is man-made. What can be more frightening than such a malevolent force that eludes location even by those considered to have the most brilliant minds that our societies can produce? Paul Hoggett's book *Partisans in an Uncertain World*, quoted by Helen Morgan (1998), grapples with this problem:

> uncritical thought will not simply be passive but will actively cling to a belief in the appearance of certain things. It actively refuses, rejects as perverse or crazy any view which contradicts it. To think critically one must be able to use aggression to break through the limitations of one's own assumptions or to challenge the squatting rights of the coloniser within one's own internal world (p.53)

In Helen Morgan's paper, this quote emphasises how people considering their racist contribution in human relationships must break through states of passive acceptance and avoidance of discomfort. It seems to me that the same is true of the victim who can acquiesce or challenge, risking that the challenge is perceived as destructive aggression or is labelled a 'chip on the shoulder' response. The very response of thinking by the victim is immediately labelled (by the aggressor) as unreasonable and crazy in order to deny any life or power to fresh thoughts. Not only are the victims of racist thought and action considered to carry the aggression, but they are also labelled as being crazy for objecting to the manner in which they are handled in relationships. Perhaps readers will notice such interactive reactions within the contents of this volume, and perhaps they will be able to overcome the sudden clarity and impulsive conclusions which present, to lend a personal clarity at the expense of a deeper thought from which might emerge a self-appraisal and discovery of denigratory attitudes. The deeper sentiments that we each harbour are not readily available for our scrutiny, but consist of complexes of ideas and associated emotions and memories. These are camouflaged as permissible opinion expressed with conviction, clarity and a belief in our moral position.

Extreme acts of prejudice and hatred are common; consider the genocide by Serb forces of Muslim neighbours and one cannot relegate and deny holocaust events to mythology, as some extreme racist groups still prefer, in accord with their 'wished for' record of world historical events. Consider the murder of the black teenager Stephen Lawrence and the world in which many ethnic, cultural and racial minorities live. Racist slogans painted on walls, incessant misidentifications and incorrect assignations of home country (e.g. all brown people are Pakis), verbal threats of assault and equally traumatising physical assaults, dog mess put through front doors, terrified children humiliated by parental fear, and powerlessness are all social realities. Cultural minorities are subject to daily acts of verbal assault and denigration, fears of imminent aggression and anticipation of more unfair and unjust handling by large and powerful organisations including statutory bodies. This is not the foreground of black people's lives, as many minority groups accept this form of daily assault as inevitable, perhaps becoming unaware of its insidious impact on their well-being and optimism. Indeed, many minorities survive and learn to live with being disliked and hated. Nonetheless, it is precisely because this oppressive fabric of life is so easily forgotten and ignored that one needs to bear it in mind. Racist ideology is one avenue to express hatreds and dislikes of many peoples for many reasons. What these have in common is the identification of a conspicuous characteristic of target groups which is a 'core' aspect of identity, cherished, revered, perhaps even worshipped as having sacred or spiritual value. In this light, the attacked characteristic and its meaning is a vulnerability that is created by the attacker. This characteristic is then systematically subjected to a racialised narrative that identifies the characteristic to be a threat and worthy of attack, usually for reasons that include notions of survival even at the cost of murder and war.

This book considers racism both as a theoretical formulation, and from an emotional perspective, in the internal world of our human minds, and in

the external world of social realities. Affective or emotion-based perspectives are included because humans beings are not devoid of an emotional
and spiritual life; human beings are not only mechanistic and logical but
we try to be, and consider ourselves as such. It is because of this very
premise that health and social care agencies have been accused of neglect,
of 'seeing' people as objects, as professionalised reconstructions of essentially human dilemmas and distress (Crawford, Nolan and Brown 1995;
Brown *et al.* 1996). I ask readers to sustain themselves if they discover less
comfortable analyses, and defer immediate dismissals or acceptances of
what follows. A fuller appreciation of racism requires that we participate
and own our personal hatreds, conflicts and stereotypical ways of seeing
the world, and that these are fully appreciated whilst we explore the limitations of alternative ways of seeing the world and of valuing people.

Chapter 3

Prejudicial Beliefs
Their Nature and Expression

Edgar Jones

One approach to exploring racism and prejudice is to consider belief formation as a natural process, and take up prejudicial beliefs as a focus for deconstruction. Dr Jones, Reader in the History of Medicine and Psychiatry at King's College Medical School, explores hateful and prejudical beliefs in their nascent states, following their maturation to their most powerful and devastating consequences.

Beliefs, like desires, are of fundamental importance in determining human behaviour. They govern what we do and the way that we think. It is well recognised how, when subjected to extreme emotions, beliefs can become distorted and sometimes assume a bizarre quality. In the stress of combat, for example, soldiers can acquire beliefs that in their ordinary peace-time existence they would consider untenable. In the First World War, a colonel, worn down by the effects of trench warfare, confided to another officer that he attributed his continuing survival in such dangerous circumstances to 'mystical powers'. He added:

> nothing will ever hit me so long as I keep that power which comes from faith. It is a question of absolute belief in the domination of mind over matter. I go through any barrage unscathed because my will is strong enough to turn aside explosive shells and machine-gun bullets. As matter, they must obey my intelligence. (Fussell 1975, p.125)

Prejudicial beliefs, the expressions of extreme philosophies that commonly run counter to the facts, have something of this character. They often strike the non-believer as extraordinary and at odds with their own experience, and yet they seem to play an important part in the life of the person who holds them. Although individuals may be willing to debate these propositions, they can be maintained tenaciously in the face of convincing opposition. This chapter seeks to discover more about the phenomenal qualities of prejudicial beliefs, their ready appeal to sections of the population and their relationship to other categories of belief.

A definition of belief

Belief has been defined by philosophers in a variety of ways. Gilbert Ryle (1900–76) reasoned that belief is merely a 'disposition' rather than a mental state, and to believe something is simply to suggest a series of conditional statements describing what a person would be likely to do, think or feel should certain circumstances arise (Ryle 1963, pp.116–18). In *The Concept of Mind*, he argued that:

> dispositional words, like 'know', 'believe', 'aspire'…signify abilities, tendencies or proneness to do, not things of one unique kind, but things of lots of different kinds. There are no corresponding acts of knowing, or apprehending and states of believing. (p.118)

Ryle took this position in contradiction to the traditional interpretation of belief, the so-called 'Occurrence Analysis' of other philosophers such as Locke, Hume, Newman and others (Price 1969, pp.19–20). They had each concluded that belief was a special kind of mental occurrence that could be interpreted by the subject in whom it occurs, and hence be distinguished from other mental events, such as the neutral consideration of a proposition without assent or rejection. 'Folk psychology', a development of post-war philosophy, explored the thesis that human behaviour can be explained in terms of beliefs and desires. Accordingly, Dennett asserted that beliefs could be defined as 'information-bearing states of people that arise from perceptions and that, with appropriately related *desires,* lead to intelligent *action*' (Dennett 1989, p.46).

Within the folk psychology framework, Bogdan has offered one of the fullest definitions of belief, which he summarised as:

> a mental form with a propositional content, that is a formal structure of some complexity which encodes some meaningful information that such and such is so and so. This is the sense in which a belief is a mental representation with some cognitive or behavioural business. Belief can be thought of as a function: from a content-encoding mental form to a cognitive or behavioural role. (Bogdan 1986, p.149)

Philosophers have also debated the question of belief formation: what happens to an idea before it can be transformed into a belief? Price considered that individuals entertain rival propositions about an issue until a set of facts allows them to discriminate between them, and they then assent to the one which provides the most confident explanation (Price 1934). Bogdan expanded on this theme and argued that, like a snowball rolled down a slope, a proposition gathers incremental and concurrent information, moulding it until, at some critical mass, it has the power to determine action and thought. Belief, therefore, is not solely a disposition to behave in certain ways should certain situations arise, nor simply an enduring mental state of some kind, and scarcely not a mere stored representation. It is a live entity, drawing on the environment and reacting with it – a dynamic and functional phenomenon. Thus, belief can be considered as a mental state that governs both thought and action. In common with desire, it determines human behaviour and we spend much time trying to fathom what our colleagues, friends and partners truly believe, using this information to predict what they may do in the future.

Towards a nosology of prejudicial beliefs

Prejudicial beliefs are, perhaps, simpler to define by content than by their form. Racist utterances are often designed to shock or incite and their message is rarely qualified or obscure. Although less extreme variants may blur on occasion into beliefs about nationalism or cultural issues, in their most extreme expression they are readily detected.

If prejudicial beliefs can be identified by their content, what if anything is unusual about their phenomenology? Phenomenology here refers to the form that beliefs take, as well as the meaning of the content, and how the content and form together can be interpreted to understand more about the person expressing beliefs, and their mind.

Do they possess the characteristics of culturally acceptable beliefs, or do they have discernible abnormalities of form? As expressions of fanatical philosophies, they are often held with great conviction, to the extent that they can lead the believer into conflict with the law, resulting in a fine or even imprisonment. Prejudicial beliefs are often attached to strong feelings and are considered important by their holders. Given that they are commonly associated with minority groups or factions, do they meet the criteria for delusions? Take, for example, the definition of delusion offered by the *Oxford Textbook of Psychiatry*:

> Delusion is a belief that is held despite evidence to the contrary and is not a conventional belief that a person might be expected to hold given his educational and cultural background... A delusion is usually a false belief, but not invariably (Gelder, Gath and Mayou 1983, p.12).

Although some racist beliefs might satisfy this definition, an important objection to classifying all of them as delusions is their prevalence. In certain political situations such beliefs can become widespread. The Nazi party, an overtly anti-Semitic organisation, more than doubled its membership to 900,000 in two years from January 1931. In the general election of July 1932, it won 13,745,000 votes (representing 37.3 per cent of the total cast) and took 230 seats in the Reichstag to become the largest single party in Germany (Bullock 1962, pp.216–17). It seems inconceivable that such a significant proportion of the population could be regarded as being truly deluded, particularly if delusion is regarded as a key symptom of psychosis. 'Since time immemorial,' argued Karl Jaspers (1883–1961), 'delusion has been taken as the basic characteristic of madness' (Jaspers 1963, p.93). Clearly, a third of the German electorate could not have been suffering from psychosis in the 1930s, however much we may disapprove of their ideology and behaviour.

Are prejudicial beliefs, therefore, more likely to be phenomenologically akin to overvalued ideas? Although clinicians seem to have no difficulty in identifying them, these beliefs have never been defined fully (Jones 1999). Overvalued ideas are the characteristic beliefs of a range of disorders including anorexia nervosa, bulimia, hypochondriasis, morbid jealousy and dysmorphophobia (Sims 1988, p.93). They were first described by Carl Wernicke (1848–1905), who drew on the earlier traditions of the *idée fixe* and *überwertige Idee*. He defined the overvalued idea as 'a solitary belief that came to determine an individual's actions to a morbid degree, while at the same time being considered justified and a normal expression of his nature' (quoted from McKenna 1984, p.579). Wernicke distinguished overvalued ideas from obsessions on the grounds that the latter were recognised by their holders as being senseless whereas the former were always thought to contain an element of truth. The most recent definition, albeit one by exclusion, was offered by McKenna, who argued that the overvalued idea 'refers to a solitary, abnormal belief that is neither delusional nor obsessional in nature, but which is pre-occupying to the extent of dominating the sufferer's life' (*ibid*). He further qualified this by suggesting that the overvalued idea 'seems to combine the unlikely elements of non-delusional conviction, non-obsessional pre-occupation and non-phobic fear' (*ibid* p.583).

A clinical research study of overvalued ideas in anorexia suggested that they have the following characteristics: moderate levels of conviction, a sense of personal importance and repeatedly examined; they exhibit a subjective form of truthfulness but one that would not be regarded as acceptable to the general population. Arrived at gradually, they are the product of rumination and involve use of imagination, together with a lesser input from true perception. Highly emotionally charged, they have considerable capacity to influence behaviour and thought (Jones and Watson 1997, p.385). There appears to be an initial resemblance to prejudicial beliefs as many could be described in this way. An exploration of the function of belief may provide further clues as to their categorisation.

The function of belief

A number of researchers have suggested that delusions fulfil an important role in maintaining a positive sense of self. Psychosis is defined usually by the presence of delusions, hallucinations and loss of contact with reality and loss of insight. Seventeen psychotic subjects with persecutory delusions, matched against depressed patients and normal controls, showed a marked tendency to attribute negative events to external causes, while believing that positive events were of their own making. These beliefs also appeared to be more stable than in the controls, and the deluded group revealed a conviction about the existence of powerful others (Kaney and Bentall 1989, p.196). A further investigation asked deluded subjects to make judgements about short stories describing both successful and unsuccessful outcomes in situations involving themselves. In comparison with controls, they tended to blame others rather than themselves for negative outcomes. These findings support the view that 'persecutory delusions are associated with cognitive biases, which serve the function of protecting the individual against feelings of low self-esteem' (Bentall, Kinderman and Kaney 1994, p.337). Others have argued that, once established, delusions will be maintained by a process of repeated reinforcement and that this may in essence be normal 'in seeking out confirmatory evidence and ignoring conflicting data, but that with delusions these processes are exaggerated' (Garety and Hemsely 1994, p.133).

Furthermore, a study which compared 17 people with schizophrenia holding well-established delusions with a matched sample of previously deluded patients in remission, showed that the latter felt significantly more depressed and found their lives less meaningful than the deluded group (Roberts 1991, pp.23–25). This confirmed the impression that, for some, psychosis is not an unsatisfying experience and that delusion, in certain cases, may have an adaptive and protective role. This research also added statistical weight to Rycroft's hypothesis, based on a study of people with schizophrenia who were in psychoanalysis, that delusions can be 'regarded as attempts to escape from…[a] state of nonentity by some route other than that of insight into the nature of what has been repressed' (Rycroft 1968, p.101). 'Repressed' here means that thoughts and feelings that generate discomfort are removed from conscious awareness; and that, rather than allow such thoughts and feelings to re-emerge, people with psychosis adapt by developing delusions.

Does a similar principle apply to those with overvalued ideas? A major survey of London schoolgirls at risk from developing anorexia showed that:

'Those trying to control weight were more likely to report social stresses, particularly in the areas of social life, home life and having insufficient money. The areas of perceived social stress…[are] understandable in this age group when attempts to achieve greater autonomy and independence from home are being made. (Patton *et al.* 1990, p.392)

Hence, key beliefs about body image or weight in anorexia seem to be connected to a wish for control and a sense of well-being as much as judgements about weight and appearance. It is as if these beliefs serve as general containers for thoughts, desires and fears about the self. Could it be that prejudicial beliefs have a similar function and that they too are designed to give the subject a feeling of mastery and greater esteem? Bullock argued that Hitler's racist beliefs were, in part, defensive and had been intensified as he struggled to survive as an artist in Vienna before the First World War:

often half-starved, without a job, family or home, [he] clung obstinately to any belief that would bolster up the claim of his own superiority. He belonged by right, he felt, to the Herrenmenschen. To preach equality was to threaten the belief which kept him going, that he was different from the labourers, the tramps, the Jews, and the Slavs with whom he rubbed shoulders in the streets (Bullock 1962, p.40).

However, Hamann (1999) has shown that Hitler had a number of Jewish friends and clients to whom he sold his paintings in pre-war Vienna. His virulent anti-Semitic beliefs probably developed when he sought a scapegoat to explain Germany's defeat in 1918 and were intensified by his decision to seek political power.

In his 1939 paper 'Trophy and Triumph', Otto Fenichel (1896/97–1946), the Austrian psychoanalyst, described a psychological process that explained why people seemed to obtain such satisfaction from an association with remote but authoritarian figures. In essence, he identified what is now called 'projective identification'. Individuals feeling a need of power or some other desired quality, observed Fenichel, can at first put themselves in the place of those who are powerful in the external world, eliminating them (actually or in fantasy), or robbing them of their power. If this cannot be achieved, another means is adopted. The individuals allow the powerful beings to remain, but in some way partake of their power — re-introject (or reabsorb or take into themselves) the power they have projected (previously ejected out of themselves into the other). Such mechanisms are thought to play a role in child development, but become particularly powerful if they begin to contribute to non-healthy development. One important way of once more sharing in the lost omnipotence (of infancy) seems, not the fantasy of devouring powerful ones, but of somehow dissolving in them, being devoured *by* them (Fenichel and Rapaport 1955, p.142).

Thus, the patriot can claim 'my nation is infinitely greater than I', that 'God is infinitely greater than the self, yet the believer is one with him'. The supporter of authoritarian figures in general claim that the 'leader is infinitely greater than any single individual of his nation – and yet he himself is a single individual of the nation', each gaining a greater sense of self-esteem as a result (*ibid.*, p.143). As Fenichel practised in Berlin until 1933 and later in Prague (Simmel and Fenichel 1946), it is highly likely that his observations of Hitler's strategy of identifying himself with the desires and ambitions of the German nation contributed to this theoretical understanding. Interviewed in the *New York Times*, Hitler summed up this approach: 'the underlying idea is to do away with egoism and to lead people into the sacred collective egoism which is the nation' (quoted from Bullock 1962, p.402). He presented himself as the heroic leader, who personified the ambitions of the *Volk*. By offering his followers officially sanctioned scapegoats, each Nazi supporter was *freed* to project on to them his own bad parts (denigratory thoughts, feelings and wishes) and the re-experiencing of these feelings provided a fresh impetus for persecutory beliefs and acts of savagery.

A working hypothesis for prejudicial beliefs

Given that the Nazi organisation arose from a popular mass movement, it appears that prejudicial beliefs can assume a variety of forms. Doubtless, a few party members suffered from a paranoid disorder or even schizophrenia and their anti-Semitism was likely to have assumed delusional proportions. This explanation cannot, however, account for the thousands who enthusiastically enlisted in the early 1930s or voted for racist candidates. Swept along by a tide of anti-Jewish and anti-Communist sentiments, together with a nationalistic wish to rebuild Germany as a world power after the ruinous effects of the First World War, the prejudicial beliefs of most Nazis probably fulfilled the criteria of overvalued ideas. These ideas were undoubtedly held with varying degrees of conviction from the fanaticism of party die-hards to the naivety of youth seeking adventure and change. The 'delusion-like idea', a term coined by Jaspers, rather than 'delusion proper', summarises many of the characteristics of these beliefs. They emerge, he suggested:

> comprehensibly from other psychic events and...can be traced back psychologically to certain affects, drives, desires and fears. We...can fully understand the phenomenon on the basis of the permanent constitution of the personality or of some transient emotional state. (Jaspers 1963, pp.106–7)

If this is the case, then prejudicial beliefs may not be inexplicable phenomena but can be understood by employing existing 'categories' and ordinary psychological processes.

It is important, however, to test some of these hypotheses in clinical studies to discover more about the true nature of prejudicial beliefs and the most effective ways of addressing them. They are harmful to society as a whole and are ultimately destructive of the individuals who hold them, undermining qualities of tolerance, openness and the ability to sift and evaluate evidence. The experience of inter-war Germany showed that substantial sections of the population, when suffering from economic hardship and feeling a sense of political grievance, are capable of succumbing to such dangerous ideas. Their simplicity and their ability to transform bad feelings about the self into a personal conviction of superiority and well-being makes them both infectious and potent. Prejudicial beliefs continue to be, therefore, of compelling and imperative interest.

Chapter 4

Psycho-social and Psycho-political Aspects of Racism

Kamaldeep Bhui

This chapter attends to the socially embedded nature of prejudice and illustrates how hatred emerges. Political and social dialogue are an important and popular way of directing psychological violence. Democratic process and high-profile politicians constantly provide energy to racialised discourse in everyday life.

Race:

Sykes (1982) defines a race as a group of persons, animals or plants connected by:

> i) common descent; house, family, tribe or nation regarded as of common stock; distinct ethnical stock (as in Caucasian, Mongolian, etc. race); genus or species or breed or variety of animals or plants, any great division of living creatures (human, feathered, four-footed, etc.)

> ii) descent kindred (of noble, oriental, etc.; race; separate in language and race)

> iii) classes of persons etc. with some common feature (race of poets, dandies, etc.).

Race relations:

Relations between members of different races in the same country.

Race Riot:

Outbreak of violence due to racial antagonism.

Race suicide:

Gradual disappearance of a race through voluntary limitation of reproduction.

Democracy and prejudice

Descent, heredity and transmission of attributes are included in general understandings of 'race' terms. 'Race' labels suggest natural origins of the categories, assuming that meaning exists for these categories when applied to human populations, rather than exploring why humans need to apply such categories and why some groups of humans need to apply race, and dictate to others groups the sort of terms applied. At a broader level of abstraction, any category of person can be used to signify a special group, of which race is one such categorisation. Racial categories are quick and easy terms through which differences between groups are explained. Many other cultural or lifestyle characteristics are neglected. Thus, where there is conflict between groups, the conflict is explained all too often in terms of racial difference. 'Race relations' is then invoked as an activity to manage a *natural* problem, that of inevitable conflict between races wherever races mix. Successive British governments have brought in legislation for the sake of 'good race relations'. It could be argued that the implicit message is that hatred, aggression, war and denigration are necessary natural and inevitable responses whenever races mix – therefore, by resort to racialised explanations, antagonism and violence between socially defined groups are assumed normal because the conflict is considered intrinsically racialised. Such a notion was at the roots of Enoch Powell's 'Rivers of Blood' speech advocating a restriction of 'aliens' entering the country, as otherwise 'race relations' would be damaged (20 April 1968, cited in MacArthur 1993):

> As time goes on the proportion of this total who are immigrant descendants, those born in England, arrived here by exactly the same route as us, will rapidly increase. Already by 1985 those born here would constitute the majority. It is this fact above all which creates the extreme urgency of action now, of just that kind of action which is hardest for politicians to take, action where the difficulties lie in the present but evils to be presented or minimised lie several parliaments ahead… The answers to simple and rational questions are equally simple and rational: by stopping or virtually stopping further inflow and by promoting maximum outflow.

> Those whom the Gods wish to destroy they first make mad. We must be mad, literally mad, as a nation to be permitting the annual inflow of some

fifty thousand dependants...it is like watching a nation busily engaged in heaping up its own funeral pyre. So insane are we that we permit unmarried persons to immigrate for the purpose of founding a family with spouse and family whom they have never seen.

This example illustrates a proposed political and social policy, which is restrictive and oppressive. Yet it is presented as a just and necessary measure for the common good. The premise upon which action is condoned and marketed as a reasonable action serves only to forge notions of colony, empire and conquerors. Conquerors do not adopt the customs of the conquered. Powell talks of falling onto one's own funeral pyre. This ritual, which is practised among the conquered (Indian sub-continent groups), emphasises the distinction of 'us' and 'them'. A psychological separation is offered and on this basis a preoccupation to promote the interests of the 'us' group inexorably follows. The elements of a racist ideology are captured by references to 'alien', 'survival', invoking 'God' and 'madness' of the nation as an explanation for the 'evils' to be witnessed. These appear not to be logical or reasoned assertions but passionate exclamations in response to deep-seated fears motivated by an imagined threat to survival. Perhaps even Powell had not realised the power of racist ideology to infiltrate the minds of the public, to resonate with other forms of prejudice and to seek expression by influencing the destiny of black and ethnic minorities. Powell put forward recommendations in a manner that suggested his solutions to be in the best interest of the minorities as well as the majority; the colonial tendency to save immigrants from themselves allowed no room for a debate with ethnic minorities, but appealed to the majority to act on behalf of both parties. Indeed this approach developed as a good currency in racial debates, whereby good race relations were put forward as policy objectives. The notion of new boundaries, or new identities and of letting go of a historically worshipped British identity appeared not to be available to Powell. The prophecy that 'in 15 years' time the black man will have the whip hand over the white' has not been a reality, but moreover it is not what black British people, 'alien descendants', actually want. Powell busily projected his own fears of a lost identity and loss of power as a perceived loss of the national identity to 'alien descendants' who were feared to hold the same colonial aspirations as did the British in an earlier era.

Was this simply a dated phenomenon that can safely be renounced as having historical importance but no real importance in the modern world? After all, we tend to be critical of much that was once fashionable and the ethical standards by which a society judges its actions with hindsight are not the same ethical principles governing its actions at times when atrocities are being committed. This historicisation is, I believe, a part of a neutralisation, a distancing oneself from thoughts, actions and feelings of which we are all capable. A similar situation as this arose recently in Australian politics. Australia has a different admixture of cultures and ethnic groups from Britain, but it is a rich mixture. Because of Australia's geographical location, much of its business depends on trade with Asia. Pauline Hanson, in her maiden speech in Parliament, asserted that she wanted the Australian immigration policy reviewed, and the policy of multi-culturalism abolished (Webb and Enstice 1998). The language was telling and strikes a similar resonance to that of Enoch Powell's speech.

> I believe we will be swamped by Asians…they have their own culture and religions, form ghettoes and do not assimilate. Of course I shall be called a racist, but if I can invite whom I want into my home, then I should have the right to say who comes into my country. A truly multi-cultural society can never be strong or united. (Webb and Enstice, p.275)

The battle of morality and righteous causes was fought out in the media, and so Miss Hanson released a book in which similar views were expressed. On direct questioning she distanced herself from many of these views, although it could be argued that she was posturing with subtlety to maximise the political gains whilst not damaging her media image of a person who has concluded after reasoned thought that her views were in the national interest. The equation of her words with national identity again resonates with Enoch Powell's performance. One million people, 10 per cent of the electorate, voted for Miss Hanson. What impact has this had on the many Australian immigrants and second-generation communities who had contributed to the economy of Australia? After all, this is a form of threat to those immigrants, who fear a racist party coming into office each time there is an election. Does democracy really work if, through its actions, whole groups of society are considered expendable for the democratic principle? In such circumstances minority groups are faced with verbal attacks on their entitlement to exist. They hope that a balanced view will emerge to ward off 'extremist' activity. However, such attacks give life to racialised discourse and have several consequences. Racist words feed racist discourse in society generally. Prejudicial attitudes are kindled and become embedded in national causes and national identity. Second, such verbal assaults disempower the victim by attacking the emotional well-being of minorities. To be told you are not welcome in your country, because of your appearance, and that you are a threat, demonstrates how the majority hold you and your kind as less worthy. *You* are inferior and *we* will eject you from this country. This is not nurturing but neither is it neutral in effect. It is harmful to the well-being of individuals. It can be nothing other than destructive and a form of civilised aggression. Democracy allows this, and yet no one has been able to promote a more successful approach to organising society. Perhaps there is no alternative. Edgar Jones, in the previous chapter, asserts that prejudicial beliefs serve functions in human societies and racism is one form of prejudice through which atrocities against humankind can be committed. We all recognise its violence, but we are powerless to extinguish it.

Pauline Hanson's 'One Nation' party's policy attacked those with a different appearance, and those with different cultural lifestyles, from the idealised and imagined homogenous culture of party members. Pauline Hanson's righteous tone resonates with Powell's delivery. The meta-message is that such views are reasonable, natural even, religiously justified, and understandable: 'what else am I supposed to do when under this (imagined) threat?' Perpetrator becomes victim. Victimhood is a more justifiable position from which to launch an attack. Heritage is always part of racialised discourse, but heritage itself is subjected to selective interpretation. Some people's cultures and beliefs, their heritage, are relegated as superstition or magical anti-God ways of living. Aboriginal peoples, the native custodians of Australia, for example, are dismissed. Their rich heritage and the culture of a spiritual life in harmony with the world, a philosophy that in a modern political form is winning votes in the USA and the UK, is entirely dismissed as an inferior and less developed way of living. The rationalisation is that of social Darwinism, that the fittest, strongest, richest and inevitably the most destructive can rule, so why should they not take over as that is promoted as their natural destiny. The Aboriginal people have a very different world view with a spiritual existence that dominates their actions in the world. One must not romanticise or popularise poverty and starvation, and a way of life that some of the younger generation of Aborigines may not wish for. However, the traditional ways, when studied in full context, leave one humbled by a richness of spiritual connectivity with mother earth and nature that is neglected in the popular portrayal of an exoticised culture (see Elkin 1994; Bell 1998). Diana Bell, an anthropologist, described Aboriginal women fighting to sustain their 'way of life' in accord with spiritual sanctions and taboos that must, by convention, be confined to women. This sacred knowledge could not be communicated to the public, even if they were ordered to do so in a court of law. Courts of law considered whether these women could be compelled to disclose sacred information. If they did not they might have been 'in contempt' of court proceedings and the law: the law, of course, being a largely white version of law with no place for laws of peoples other than those in government. It is an example of modernity trying to have its way despite common lay cultural principles and laws which are so close to religious doctrine and heritage that to defy them is to wound a people and a way of life.

Who are the ancestors? Pauline Hanson and colleagues seem to deny them a right to exist or have an opinion. Democracy is a cherished virtue, but here is the uglier side of it. Democracy sanctions the verbalised assault on peoples because of their skin colour, their physical appearance, their cultures, and their capacity to survive and make successes of hopeless situations. Perhaps that is what is attacked by racist ideology, the capacity to survive and demonstrate humility and acceptance as a response to hatred. To ingest and digest and survive hatreds, but then to remain uncontaminated by hatred and to remain true to one's own morality. Gandhi in India, during the last days of British rule, discovered a way of dealing with oppression which allowed perpetrators of violence an opportunity to experience, feel and see the uglier side of their acts. Was Gandhi's approach only a form of non-violent protest? Violence was still done. Starving oneself to near death and allowing your tormentors to punish and inflict wounds are forms of violence, only violence to the self. They actualise, in a visible and bodily form, the emotional violence felt by victims. Deliberate self-harm is not an ordinary act: it develops out of self-hatred, be it self- or other-motivated. Gandhi took control of hatred and turned it on himself and his people in order to emphasise and thus bring to conscious awareness the effects of the British presence in India. Irrespective of whether approval is justified, the point was made and the world sentiment grew that there must be some other solution. Such sentiments might otherwise be lost if the victim also took up arms and demonstrated aggression. This is the more human thing to do, to defend oneself. In essence, what passive resistance in India did was to deny a common antecedent of war by not allowing the projection of aggression from the perpetrators to be given a life in the mind of the victim. This is not an easily achieved task, as it requires sacrifice, courage, great tolerance, reflective intelligence and an ability to think about assault under the most intensely vulnerable and painful circumstances. The capacity to survive emotionally and to draw strength from adverse experiences appears incomprehensible and envied by the observing perpetrators. This capacity appears to threaten perpetrators of racist ideology as they cannot fail to notice that the hatred is theirs, and that there is a discrepancy between what they expect and how other cultural groups actually behave. As long as the oppressed group behaves in the 'expected way', fulfils the stereotype, then all is well as the racists remain untroubled and unaware that their actions are a form of hatred.

Sequential spirals of suspicion and fear, coupled with organised attack, are not easy to unravel. It is clear that 'race riots' are the non-thought outcome of frustrations that amount to aggression as a result of the absence of 'capacity' to tolerate hatred and deprivation. Unemployment, harassment and social exclusion amplify the frustration. In such instances, aggressive solutions are brought closer to realisation and intensify in the internal battle for esteem and entitlement. A parallel form of thinking is created in both victim and assailant. As long as this parallel thinking persists, each can continue to play his or her role in the unsatisfactory but unambiguous drama. Frantz Fanon (1986), a French doctor and psychoanalytic thinker, wrote a book titled *Black Skin, White Masks*. In this book he talks of the black man and the white man being trapped in their respective skins. Each a slave to the other. Such a co-operative relationship requires this parallel form of thinking to persist.

Today we can still notice hatreds that focus on skin colour and difference. Racist political parties in Britain have the right to voice their opinion and stand for elections. They may distribute material promoting their views, although carefully edited or targeted so as to avoid prosecution. This is democracy. A democracy supports non-democratic teachings as part of a hope that the majority 'reasoned' view will always moderate extremists. At what price? The cost appears to be the victim's rights to be who they are without condemnation and fear of hatred. This makes no sense to a victim of today. Thus, morality and prejudice are inextricably intertwined. In the name of a higher morality, many destructive deeds are committed and the perpetrators consider themselves to have a moral right, perhaps even a divine destiny, to protect certain aspects of their lives. Such people are entirely sane and intelligent, and fulfil many highly skilled functions. Aggression, and racist aggression, is not a simple function of poverty or of a lack of education. Differential poverty, and differential levels of education and privilege and access to wealth seem to be more important. That is, the juxtaposition of two groups in a situation of threatened access to limited group wealth, and with clear differences in levels of wealth, are common substrates for the racialisation of difference. Its contemporary form in Britain may be different, more subtle, more rational. The impact is identical – a denigration of 'other' on the basis of the dominant group's imagined hierarchies, which are given expression in social structures and social policies.

There is now an increasingly complex but fascinating body of data on differential poverty, and extremes of poverty, trust in the local community, participation in one's community and collective action in a community (see Chapter 7). In the USA, neighbourhoods that have fewer of these virtues, called 'social capital', have higher homicide rates, poorer health and more crime. Extremes of income appear to promote the use of aggression to contest one's basic needs, and to promote esteem by acquisition of what is otherwise denied. Through aggression, the imagined boundaries of worth are demolished. The victim and assailant share in something through aggression. They are both the same in one way whereas before they were different. Whether the aggression arises from perpetrators of prejudice or from the victims, it seems the origins are similar. Anna Freud writes on similar processes in the normal development of children calling it an 'Identification with the Aggressor' (Freud 1986, p.110). She writes that a child will internalise criticisms, but these criticisms are turned on the outside world. As such, the child protects itself against blame but also seeks proximity to the aggressor. Differences of culture and belief vanish whilst aggression is expelled to generate a fusion of some sort, be it an unhappy one, and on occasions a fatal union.

Identity as process

Victims subjected to racism and sexism as well as other forms of prejudice share the tendency to attract labels of deviancy. The perpetrator of prejudicial beliefs locates within the victim group aspects of behaviour and lifestyle which are not condoned and may even be prohibited by the supposedly like-minded majority. There is nothing novel in this, as decades of prejudicial treatment of racial minorities have been accompanied by fears about their capacity to breed, about the size of their genitals, their physical prowess and their connectedness with deeper more primitive layers of the psyche which are feared by the 'civilised' (Fanon 1986; see Fernando 1988; Young-Bruhl 1998). These acts of ascription can be understood in psychoanalytic writings as 'projection'. Thus, feminine men attract criticism from 'masculine macho' men. Feminine men who are black are especially suspected by macho heterosexuals who fear finding femininity and blackness in themselves. The criticism of the loathed then reaffirms one's distinction from the loathed (see Young-Bruhl 1998).

Avtar Brah (1996), a sociologist, asserts more definitively that gender politics and race politics are inseparable. That is not to say that black men share experiences of the same oppression as black women, or women generally, but that behavioural and emotional dynamics of power relationships are similar, as are the behaviours and intricate justifications by perpetrators of prejudicial behaviour. Thus, cultural politics and racial politics take on a more nebulous and shared life. Indeed the concepts of 'race' and 'ethnic group', a more palatable and supposedly less racist term, are similar in that they are not rigidly defined. Such terms are capable of generating powerful motivations and fears; the very flexibility of the boundary between the safe in-group and feared out-group allows ethnic and racial labels to be ascriptively mobilised to a mutually satisfactory stability where in-group and out-group appear to co-operate in order to create an illusory clarity about mutual identities. One cannot exist without the other, but the dominant out-group has access to reifying machineries such as the media, and control over the written word and dominate the process of identity manufacture.

Gupta (1995), an anthropologist in India, outlined how 'ascriptive mobilisation' of identity was enacted when the Sikh militant movement in the Punjab consolidated into a protest/terrorist group to demand a separate state. Hindu and Sikh peoples who had shared households and cultures and languages soon re-grouped as adversaries. Even Hindu and Sikh families in the UK, families who were geographically removed from the conflicts in India, began not to be able to neglect their allegiance for survival of their 'own'. Of about a million Sikhs abroad, over three-quarters live in just three countries: Britain, Canada and the USA (Tatla 1999). 'On 3 June 1984, in a meticulously calculated operation code named "Bluestar", the Indian Army stormed the Golden Temple in Amritsar, along with 37 other Sikh shrines in the Punjab…From a self confident religious community, the Sikhs rapidly acquired many characteristics of a persecuted minority' (Tatla 1999, p.1). The emergence of demands for a Sikh nation were expressed by a worldwide movement in which Sikhs shared notions of homeland and nationhood, and shared a cultural identity such that the term 'diaspora' is now applied to them (Tatla 1999). Despite the academic arguments for and against such forceful retention of national and ethnic allegiances, there is no doubt that individuals, and social groups, find these meta-identities comforting, and prefer to find their identity closely tied to one or another national and ethnic grouping. Misidentification, to be considered not to be who one believes one is, to be denied preferred identities that are precious, are akin to psychological mutilation or annihilation. Identity is cherished, even at the expense of it being illusory and temporary. The emergence of 'ethnicity' as a subject is correlated with restructuring of traditional kin and tribal loyalties in urban settings. It is a part of transitional cultures. The promotion of one language or the demand to retain minority languages are also forms of ethnicisation that enliven ethnic and racial discourse in order to meet a need to belong and have a place (Werber and Ranger 1996).

Ethnic and cultural categories as political process

The 'New Commonwealth and Pakistan' ethnic category reached its expiry date when it became obvious that it no longer allowed an accurate description of *the labelled* in their colonial identity. That is, the coloniser learnt that the colonised did not group themselves in the way the coloniser imagined. Other census categories were introduced. Ethnic groups are, therefore, just as great a social construction as are racial groups and cultural groups. These limitations of the categories or 'classes of person' are often neglected when statistical data are interpreted to favour the political or racial ideology of the interpreter. 'People draw on beliefs about race as they draw on beliefs about nationality, ethnicity and class as resources for cultivating group identity' (Cashmore 1988, p.294).

Charles Darwin demonstrated that varieties of life adaptively changed, and that the terms 'race' and 'sub-species' could be applied to humans if groups were isolated from one another. This isolation does not really exist for humankind. Race assignments follow social rules rather than zoological ones; there is now less isolation of so called 'races', if these are distinguished by physical characteristics. There is now more sharing of the gene pool than is appreciated and racial categories should, therefore, be scientifically meaningless as a determinant of biological influences on health. But there is evidence in the USA and UK that racial categories are associated with different levels of public service delivery (Bhopal 1998). Therefore 'race' retains significant power as a determinant and explanation for variations of health care in delivery. Racial categories are invested with a 'mission', albeit a religious one or a national or other prophetic one, where the category is invested with unspoken 'survival' urgencies, imagined dynastic futures or continuities with a noble past. Therefore racial classification takes on a new life. It is re-invented each time by the circumstances of its resurrection (Arnold 1999). Such is the raw material of racist ideology, to draw on basic human motivations and fears in order to mobilise unthought action whilst de-humanising the casualties of a 'just' cause. 'Race' terms are polysemic and decipherable only through social discourse from which the rules of membership can be understood and/or modified to serve a more practical purpose (the census, for example). The purpose to which racialised discourse is put actually defines its precise meaning during its expression.

Nation and identity

Nation is often muddled with ethnic grouping. Some argue that an ethnic group with a political ideology constitutes a nation, or a desired nation (Edwards 1994). Nationalism is defined as an ideology or as a national sentiment. Nationalism, many believe, emerged in Europe after the French revolution when sovereignty, autonomy, fatherland and belief in unity found more forceful expression (Cashmore 1988; Edwards 1994). In the 20th century, it expanded throughout the world. 'Nationalism' is distinct from national sentiments (Cashmore 1988), where there may not be a coherent ideology, but there is a solidarity maintained by geographical boundaries. Cultural boundaries and ethnic boundaries might coincide with, or be at variance with, national boundaries. If conflictual, the proponents redefine their allegiances in other terms, to clarify opposition or alliance. Nationalism and the movement to define ethnicity itself may be a reactionary response to lost identities due to globalisation, multi-nationalism, or multi-culturalism. Each person seeks identity at a time when there is a mixing of peoples, cultures and values. Cultural flux itself may account for the search for identity and our increasing fascination with it. At times of transition, each social group fears domination by another, and therefore seeks to define its boundaries whilst propagating action to retain autonomy and power. For example, the very development of the Transcultural Psychiatry movement in Britain might be understood as a redefinition of a group of people (ethnic minorities), in order to give them a greater political role in their treatment (see Littlewood 1993). Such a thesis supports the view that racialisation of discourse and politics serves an important function, one of defining and redefining group boundary in the redistribution of power in social exchanges.

Language as identity

Language is one mediator of identity. Edwards (1994) writes about language being the basis of nationhood and ethnic identity: the continuing power that resides between nationhood and ethnicity lies in the bond that can survive the loss of tangible and visible markers. Language is one such marker that might persist as a distinct characteristic where skin colour and culture are similar. Consider the Welsh in the UK; they are highly motivated to sustain their language. Consider Sikhs in the Punjab, wanting a separate state which returns part of Pakistan to them, and for such a state to have predominantly Punjabi and Sikh teachings. Neither India nor Pakistan will realistically consider this, yet similar, although less separatist, forms of devolution are manifesting in the UK, where Scotland and Ireland are reclaiming a separate identity, and religious schools are flourishing.

Language offers one set of rules that give meaning and form to experience (Davies 1999). The use of language in the construction of identities to which all relate has a long history. Language constructs our world and lends depth and qualitative accent to otherwise limited communications. Clearly the dominant language in any society presents as a dominant force for propagation of views held by the linguistically dominant group. And so minorities, where language preferences differ, are silenced and immediately located in a position of non-thought and mind paralysis until they master the linguistic skills of the dominant group in the hope of an equal footing in political debate (a process that can actually take generations). Is such a level of equality realisable? Yes, but only if racism were a single, definable, consistent and concrete phenomenon that attracted broad agreement about its origins and manifestations. After all, Caribbean 'immigrants' share the same base language as English natives, yet social and economic opportunities and representation at all levels of society are still generally poorer for them (Skellington 1996). What of the Irish community? They hold geographical proximity and a long and shared history, as well as shared physical characteristics with the English. One would expect their access to employment opportunities in Britain to be on an equal footing. In reality the Irish fare badly when it comes to healthcare, unemployment and social opportunities (*ibid.* 1996). The more we consider the concept of race, the more apparent it becomes that race is actually a non-concept; it is not a natural given as is implied in dictionary definitions, but it is a social construct, and its persistence and resilience as a thought-patterning force owes much to its chameleon-like properties. The concept of race is especially attractive in 'border' territories – this means borders that are imagined and real, and not just those over which there is current political controversy and conflict.

Empire and racism

Equal weight is often given to the concordance of 'racism' definitions generated by the in-group and out-group. Yet, where there is a dominant racial group, dominant not always in terms of numbers but at least in the articulation of varieties of power relationships, then the dominant out-group's appraisal of racial types, race relations, racial motivations and hatreds are more likely to be reified to further oppress the in-group's freedom to define themselves. The racially powerful, historically predominantly white Caucasians from Europe (and the USA), set the political agendas not only in their own countries but also across the globe by the historically celebrated infrastructure called 'Empire'. This role is partly superseded by modern global economies, but most of the world's wealth is 'stored' in industrialised and Western nations.

The British context of racism usually locates the debate in an anti-colonial paradigm, limiting the discussion of racism in other contexts (Miles 1993, p.86). The countries from which racial minorities 'originate' already bear the hallmarks of oppression which continue in global economic terms. Such a picture has historical relevance and is now altering as the Asian economies escalate. 'Arrested development' of the natural progression of pre-colonial societies that were colonised is but a romantic concept of how things might have turned out had empires not existed. The purpose of empires was not to colonise and reap benefit to the countries and peoples being colonised, but was simply one of profit and wealth for the colonisers. Anything that made economies more profitable and rewarding to 'mother country' would be pursued, and obstacles overcome by diplomacy, war and tribal re-configuration. This reality often escapes debate about colonialism. The human factor of mixing of value systems, ways of living and subordination of anything not condoned by British or French or whatever colonial influence, barely features in the strategies of political powers unless profit was threatened. Miles (1993, p.90) links the emergence of racism to that of prejudicial treatment of different classes, and a period when superiority of one class over another was also assumed, and lent racialised discourse a model of explaining the natural order of humans and this just happened to support profit-making enterprise (Fenton 1999, pp.82–83). Even today, a commonly expressed reason for dislike of ethnic minorities is competition for jobs, and the economic stability of the 'host' populations (see Institute for Public Policy Research 1997).

British Immigration Acts have aimed to limit non-white immigration rather than white immigration from the USA and other 'white' countries (Skellington 1996). The recent trend in Britain, of harsh responses to white refugees from Europe has been extraordinary. The language of 'floods' of refugees was reminiscent of Powell's speech that invoked images of domination (Jones 2000). The United Nations High Commissioner accused Conservatives of breaking the spirit of the all-party agreement not to use racist language, whilst Labour accused Liberals, and Conservatives accused Labour, of focusing on race rather than policies (Shrimsley 2000). The churches and charities recognised the dangers of such discourse going unchallenged, and so a response was launched and the language used to describe refugees was labelled as 'racist' and 'disgraceful' for a civilised society. Violent attacks on refugees were becoming increasingly common (Herbet 2000; Foster 1999). An atmosphere for hatred saw the National Front plan a protest against immigrants and asylum seekers that, fortunately, was banned under the Public Order Act of 1986 (McEllroy 1999). The arguments presented by nationalistic racists were economic in nature, but fuelled by notions of racial difference and tense 'race relations'. We do not talk of gender-relations conflict or class-relations conflict in the same way. Race has a special place as a way of explaining conflict between groups.

Inter- and intra-racial group prejudice

The complexity of racialised activity, thought and action is not only of a white vs. non-white polarity. Interracial hostility has been known for many years and persists today. Slavery, for example, existed as early as 8000 BC. Slavery and racism share a history. Each holds similarly disparaging views of subordinates, in relation to masters. The Romans and Greeks made use of slaves, as did the African empires, and the colour of the slave was an irrelevance (see Thomas 1997 for a definitive history of slavery). Thomas (1997) writes that in the sixth century the Greeks and Romans were unprejudiced on grounds of race: they were quite insensible as to whether someone with black skin was superior to someone with white skin or vice versa. This reassures us that hatred is not 'naturally' monopolised by the politics of skin colour. Plato, Aristotle and other learned thinkers accepted slavery as a natural form of existence (see Popkin 1999). Cicero argued that 'all inequality (hence slavery) could be explained by degeneracy, that the reduction of conquered people to slaves was legitimate if the people conquered were unable to govern themselves' (Thomas 1997). This view is commonly expressed to justify the colonisation of peoples across the world. A paternalistic attitude of saving the slaves from themselves and a wise parental right to govern shine through.

Thomas (1997) asserts that specific religions also have not been free from prejudicial responses. Just as Christianity condoned slavery in the 17th Century, so did Islamic rulers in Turkey, although the laws of Islam were a little more specific and benign by not separating slave children from parents, and condoning respectful handling of slaves. 'Slaves were not to be treated as animals, and slaves were free men in the eyes of God' (ibid., p.37). Every age has its own social climate and set of ethical principles, so one might argue that the time came when people were more able to accept similarity to themselves in those 'apparently' so different; to identify aspects of themselves in the 'other' without fears of annihilation. But this could only happen if the ruling race was reassured and protected by institutions that preserved their status (Fenton 1999, p.78). And so arose democracies that excluded a specific group, producing 'a master race democracy' in which black and white could not even begin to live side by side until they shared other attributes of wealth, power, language and education. The time taken for black people to position themselves in situations of financial security ensures that any recovery from being colonised is a slow one. Does colonisation of the mind take as long to escape from as colonisation of land? This is the subject of Franz Fanon's works, some of which are explored in other chapters in this volume.

Racism exists in other non-European cultures and nations. Fenton (1999, p83–6), writing on Chinese views of early European settlers, concludes that all groups throughout history construct views of themselves and others in which others are relegated to lower status. The recent influx of East European refugees adds a further dimension: white-on-white prejudice is less often explored. European refugees arriving in Dover were reported to be in conflict with local peoples such that they would be dispersed across the country perhaps in detention or reception centres, in order to diminish the concentration of 'other' and to diminish the economic burdens openly publicised by local government (Rufford 1999).

The Institute for Public Policy Research survey (1997) illustrated how Caribbean, African and Pakistani groups are the ones who consider themselves, and are considered by others, to be the most under racist threat. This survey also paints a more complex picture. In response to the question 'do you think most white people in Britain would mind or not mind if one of their close relatives were to marry a person of African-Caribbean origin?', a third of white and Asian respondents and approximately half of African-Caribbean and Jewish respondents said they would mind a lot. To the question 'would you personally mind?', 13 per cent of white, 32 per cent of Asian and 29 per cent of Jewish respondents said they would mind a lot. When similar questions were asked about white people marrying an Asian, 34 per cent of whites, 46 per cent of African-Caribbean, 34 per cent of Asian and 42 per cent of Jewish respondents said that most white people would mind a lot and 13 per cent of white, 10 per cent of African-Caribbean and 27 per cent of Jewish respondents said they would mind. When the marriage was to be to someone who was Jewish, 12 per cent of white, 23 per cent of African-Caribbean, 16 per cent of Asian and 24 per cent of Jewish respondents said most white people would mind, and 5 per cent of white, 10 per cent of African-Caribbean and 30 per cent of Asian respondents said they would mind personally. This is just one type of example, whereby prejudice breaches white/non-white boundaries. Religious groups as well as whole lifestyles can come under attack.

Very few people of any ethnic or religious group said that there was no prejudice or racism in Britain (6% of whites). Immigration was a concern of many, and up to a third disbelieved that those claiming to be refugees were genuine. In some instances, people believed immigration of the same ethnic group to which they belonged needed tightening up. Identity alters following immigration and immigrant groups are known to go through a process of acculturation, assimilation, marginalisation or isolation. Identifications with host country might explain the view that one's ethnic group should be prevented from entering the country. Sources of concern were the survival of white identity and economic crises. The survey concluded that there were four groups:

- *The Die Hards*: their racism is strong and freely expressed. It appeared to be rooted in economic fears. Yet this was the group most likely to feel uncertain about their own future.

- *The I'm not racist buts…*: 'I don't care what colour someone's skin is but they can't come over here and get more than we do.' This group rationalise their feelings, claiming not to be racist.

- *The comfortable liberals…*: 'I didn't learn about racism at school, but just having a good education has enabled me to see how stupid racism is.' This is a group of educated professionals who are anti-racist but do not feel racism is remediable.

- *The young optimists…*: 'Racists are stupid. How can you judge everyone by their skin colour?' This is a younger and more racially integrated group. Their idealism and anti-racism is instinctive. This group would have great difficulty appreciating the destructive aspects of racism.

Each of these groups would have difficulty understanding the others' view. The first two groups tended to interpret data about the contribution to industry and economy made by ethnic minorities as a deprivation as if *their* jobs' were being 'taken over'. These are the very views that are harnessed by politicians such as Powell and Hanson. Overestimating the numbers of immigrants is common (Coker 2001) and this adds to the sense of being dominated, swamped and mentally annihilated. These fears are never realised.

Racism as desired and imagined worlds

The delicate language used to motivate and propagate racist ideologies is not easily recognised, but the consequences are often very clear to the oppressed minority. The language that carries hate messages might be one of survival, economic limitation, poverty, unemployment, immigration as a drain on resources, nationalism, dignity, imagined past dynasties or a higher morality for the good of the majority. Prejudice may be propagated in the service of religion, king and country. Irrespective of the virtues seen in these seductive and highly motivating causes the outcome is one of oppression of racial minorities and powerless racial groups. After all, why do people die for king and country and for causes like racial and religious wars, rather than for charities or for their local hospital? The source of such powerfully destructive motivators is to do with a less logical aspect of the human mind. Some would argue that the motivating centres of the brain are the most primitive parts of the human mind, and no wonder our emotional lives are so difficult to appreciate and understand in a logical, intellectual and objective manner. It is known that human beings of all races share more of their genetic material than not. Yet racist research looking for genetic explanations for differing abilities among racial groups persists.

Racial theories and racist research are full of contradictions, paradoxes and selective interpretations of data to support favoured hypotheses. Race categories are immutable, and as anti-racism gathered momentum, explicit race-related research became unfashionable. Thus, racialised research was re-invented in the form of studies that propagate racist ideas, include racialised hypotheses and racialised interpretation of research data. The scientific community might wish to excuse itself for such acts of journalistic appeal, but again the responsibility for the use of research findings and for the rebuttal of misinterpretations must lie with the researchers. Passive dismissal of adventurous interpretations of research findings is no longer an acceptable stance. These supposedly benign and ill-informed acts perpetuate race-related ideologies. History is peppered with figures who appear to 'believe' in racial inferiority of black and ethnic minorities, and proceed by whatever means to prove and publicise this 'fixed belief'. The urge to have their belief sustained is so great that it is not amenable to reasoned debate (see Chapter 3), even though they might engage in what might be broadly termed 'democratic debate'. How can a democracy tolerate the propagation of views that advocate the hatred and destruction of citizens whose skin colour or country of origin is different from the white majority? How can successive British governments accept that the BNP, and its sophisticated and intelligent propagation of hatred, are compatible with a democratic society in which a significant proportion of British citizens are fearful of their lives? The difficulty might lie in accepting claims to British citizenship of an Indian-born immigrant having equal value as say a white, English-born subject. Similar disparities are more evident when Britain entered a war to protect white British citizens in the Falklands. This re-invigorated 'Englishness' or 'Britishness' (Miles 1993, p.74). Margaret Thatcher's task was to sustain and redirect this positive sense of national identity, attained through military conflict, in order to reorganise civil society and correct economic decline. Her speech explicitly connected the contemporary with the past in order to identify a future project for an entity whose social identity was reconstructed as a result of threat' (Miles 1993, p.75).

This vision was that of an Island race and a white history. In contrast, Britain neglected Chinese citizens in Hong Kong when they were under similar, although politically more complex, threats. Of course, the debate has to be more complicated, with a variety of legal precedents, and 'proper' sanctioned actions. Nonetheless, to an innocent Chinese-origin Hong Kong citizen, it seems somewhat irregular that his or her life is worth less than a white Falklander. Similar incongruencies of justice arose in the Stephen Lawrence case (MacPherson 1999). None of the police officers in the Stephen Lawrence enquiry were successfully prosecuted, but a supporter from the 'Nation of Islam' movement who was supporting the Lawrence family was imprisoned for disturbing the peace. This picture of justice must raise serious questions. But this is precisely the strength of racist ideology. It lives in the contradictions we create in our societies, in legislation and in 'reasoned' thought about legal justice rather than what is judged as just, alongside who makes the judgement and according to which value orientations.

British society after all keeps producing leading figures who can seem deeply suspicious of the 'Britishness' of ethnic minorities in the UK. In April of 1990 Norman Tebbit suggested that members of British Asian and West Indian communities should be judged on who they supported in sport (Millward 1999). This preceded criticism of multicultural Britain, views that received public rebuke from William Hague (G. Jones, 1997). At the same time the Queen, whilst touring in Pakistan, celebrated the identity of British Muslims, finding this healthy (G. Jones 1997). The Pakistani cricket players' allegiance questioned by Tebbit did not include a consideration that intelligent thought allows human beings to shape their allegiances and to play by different rules in different social groups, of which race is one. This seemed unavailable to Tebbit. To conclude that a Pakistani cricket player playing for England has not the integrity or capacity to play for England again draws on ideas of essential differences between peoples of different skin colours. It repeats David Hume's description of errors of causality and inference and appears to originate in a passion rather than a reasoned and informed mind. Does Tebbit really believe that individuals can have many influence and allegiances, and that they can shift between these and remain loyal to their particular team? The whole debate centres around the perceived fixity and dynastic nature of British identity. To Tebbit, British is about being white and English, or so it seems from his statements. To Tebbit, this is irreconcilable with being Pakistani.

> I am asking people to accept that in a society you have one language, one standard of ethics, one history. If asked where you stand, you stand on your country…if one is living in a Christian country, it is Christian law that overrides Muslim Law. (Tebbit 1997)

Technically, prejudices can be positive or negative but, in race-relations terminology, negative and destructive impacts are emphasised. How do these beliefs continue to be professed in such frankly prejudicial ways when it is clear that society no longer publicly tolerates such beliefs?

Elizabeth Young-Bruehl (1998), an American psychoanalyst, explores racism and generates a classification that includes 'ideologies of desire'. These are considered to be regressive prejudices, which resonate with fantasies of idealised epochs that are sought after. Young-Bruehl (1998) distinguishes *obsessional* prejudices from *hysterical* prejudices, using psychological defence mechanisms and their defensive function to explain the persistence of such prejudices, and to explain the form that they take. At risk of oversimplifying the matter, she creates a typology and asserts that societies can be obsessional or hysterical in their functioning. Prejudice is defined as a negative attitude to socially defined groups and their members. The hysterical form is that where the unconscious prejudice is to act out forbidden sexual and aggressive deeds. The victim is not destroyed, but is needed for satisfaction of these desires. The in-group needs the out-group to help define itself at a time of confusions about self-identity. These fluxes of thought may have different valencies, ranges, intensities and degrees of conviction. The *ideology of desire* form of prejudice uses prejudice to order selves, secure identity and groom a wished-for state. She asserts that hysteria is an eroticisation of a past and that it has nationalistic consequences. Conformity and competitive societies are described as leading to obsessional conflicts, and outbursts against authority result in deregulation and anarchistic societies. Young-Bruehl's classifications attempt to rid society of simplistic and bounded classifications of racism, but in suggesting a typology, she ends up particularising and reifying fragments of informative experiences into a structural model.

Young-Bruehl (1998) distinguishes ethnocentrism from ideologies of desire. Ethnocentrism, she says, denies the role of emotion and desire. It is a group hatred of, and claims to supremacy over, out-groups, although its use has been broadened to include inadvertent judgements and outcomes, which arise from a particularly in-celebrating and outward-denying world views. In contrast, ideologies of desire are pseudo-scientific hopes of a destiny, so that all experience is seen through such a perceptual filter. The world becomes as it is wished. She argues that ethnocentrism finds the world as it is expected to be in view of past failure to sustain an ethnic heritage. Furthermore, ethnocentrism is considered to have gradations, whereas ideologies of desire are dualistic and evolutionary, and the conflicts last longer and touch the deeper layers of the psyche. Ideologies of desire also deny similarities of humanity and spiritual existence. In ethnocentrism, contradictions in the society's own rules are ignored. The dominant ideology must be sustained: for example, the co-existence of Christianity and slavery and the inherent contradiction never reached consciousness to the extent that the contradiction resolved in the real world rather than in the public mind.

Ideologies of desire generate guilt, whereas ethnocentrism is expressed in shame. The shame reflects a world stage on which to play out the past. This model asserts that guilt, associated with ideologies of desire, is repressed by the prejudice which is itself repressed partially. Its emergence into conscious awareness threatens the self in such a way that the threat is experienced as arising from 'other' and is streamlined with fears of annihilation. This makes a conscious awareness of the prejudice extremely difficult as this would be accompanied by distress and a change in self-image, where conscious guilt requires the acknowledgement of hateful action. Self-reproach and feelings of unworthiness are projected, whereas in ethnocentrism the aggression is displaced onto other groups. The former attacks the mind of the victim and induces perplexity, whereas the latter expresses an opinion of the other, but this opinion, being given an authoritative licence, is 'floated' as acceptable, disavowing the destructive elements. 'Ethnocentric displacement' and 'desirous projection' may appear identical to the observer, but the processes and experiential quality for the victim are different. An admixture of the two may also exist.

It would be difficult to locate Enoch Powell or Norman Tebbit in either of these frameworks, yet elements of their speeches are recognisable in both. Ethnocentric prejudice is naturalised as a defence against something dangerous and risky; it is presented as a rational act of self-interest. Enoch Powell's speech might be considered in this light. Norman Tebbit's sporadic thoughts might be consistent with an Ideology of Desire (IoD), a passion in David Hume's philosophy; this includes a preoccupation with the future. Indeed, those who fit an IoD pattern of prejudice may well adopt ethnocentrism as a more acceptable facade.

Prejudice and the capacity to think

A common feature of prejudice is its capacity to silence victims and destroy the 'capacity to think'. This arises partly because of the juxtaposition of a trusted 'like-self' individual suddenly being transformed into the source of 'self-attacking' convictions. Confusions arise in the mind of the victim; thinking is disrupted. Attacks on the capacity to think and link thoughts have been described in the psychoanalytic literature as a function of psychotic process, a projection of destructive 'breaks' into someone else's mind in order to paralyse and prevent them making sense of what is being done, not to them as a physical person, but to their mind. Melanie Klein and Wilfred Bion considered psychotic process to be a function of the environment and the personality. Bion's preconditions for the development of psychoses were: (1) a predominance of destructive drives to the extent that love is readily transformed into sadism; (2) a hatred of internal and external realities, extended to all that makes one aware of these realities; (3) a dread of imminent annihilation; (4) premature and precipitate formation of object relations (Bleandonu 1994). I am not suggesting that racism is like psychosis (see Chapter 2), but that the impact of racist thinking on individuals, victims and perpetrators resembles the attack on thinking processes found in psychosis.

Bion's criteria refer to psychotic-type personalities rather than psychosis characterised by hallucinations or delusions that are found in conditions such as schizophrenia. Thus, reality testing is distorted and there is an investment in not being able to think or to question the self's perception apparatus. Reality is too ridden with conflict because of the threatened awareness of destructive impulses. This view is concordant with prejudice serving as a form of extreme defence. This process of destroying thinking, or 'attacks on linking thoughts', as it is more commonly known, is a common experience in psychotherapy. This is a disturbing experience. I liken it to the moment in which a racist comment is made, or a victim is attacked, physically and psychologically. The response is shock and perplexity. One minute predictable safety and certainty and the next an assault. The verbal form, especially when delivered with eloquence by respected people considered to be guardians of a wider ideology for the safety of society, further compounds the incomprehensible aspects of it. As the prejudice is repressed or projected to protect the speaker from guilt or shame, so it is terribly difficult for the speaker actually to come to know their hatred, or the impact of their words, which seem rational and self-sustaining. The victim is outraged, his or her intellect defeated by the cold obsessional aggression and clear convictions of a better future that are used to justify racist 'action that must be taken'. Thus, racist statements will be supported by 'scientific truths' or subtle and complex scientific theories, which scornfully dismiss opposing opinion.

Chapter 5

The Legacy of Frantz Fanon and Contemporary Representations of Racism and Mind

Kamaldeep Bhui

Franz Fanon's work on racism and states of mind using psychoanalytic thought is well known. This chapter distils the essential elements of some of Fanon's work, alongside other high-profile authors, in order to convey the mechanisms of racist thought and action at the microscopic level. This chapter draws on traditional psychoanalytic writings to explore ways of understanding why society demands that racists and victims of racism continue to exist.

It is 27 August 2000 – the beginning of the Notting Hill Carnival in North London. This is a carnival that celebrates freedom from slavery. It developed in London in the 1960s. As Britain explores the freedom and diversity of its society, for orators of racist ideologies it is business as usual. Dr Liam Fox, the Conservative Party's shadow health secretary, has announced that the English language ability of many doctors from abroad is inadequate and constitutes a public danger (Sunday Times August 27, front page; see Coker 2001). Echoes of Enoch Powell and Norman Tebbit are difficult to silence. On television news, his statement was a little more liberal: 'Language and skills' were deemed inadequate among doctors from abroad.

The British health service is known to have a substantial number of doctors from the Commonwealth countries and, more recently, from South Africa and Australia. However, in line with previous restrictions on immigrants, Dr Fox is not referring to doctors from white English-speaking countries, despite their radically different healthcare systems and national language. Foreign doctors, usually of Indian sub-continent origin, have made up for a shortfall in skilled expertise in the British health service for decades; they usually do so in junior positions, rarely getting the opportunity to seek and be granted promotion. This glass ceiling is well described. Discrimination from entry to medical school to the granting of discretionary points for consultant grades is no secret (Esmail 2001; Gill 2001). The large numbers of foreign doctors who work in the British health service is a legacy of colonial domination of labour markets in Commonwealth countries, but Dr Fox fails to acknowledge the 'authors' of a situation that he now attacks. There is already a language test in place, but rather than explore the parameters of the language test, and other differences between health services in other countries and in the UK, Dr Fox, in the hope of appealing to the racist self of British white peoples perpetuates a sense of threat from other, darker-skinned people. He seeks to win public acclaim for a statement that turns figures showing a disproportionate number of GMC actions as a form of institutional racism into one that for him represents inferiority of others who are racially and culturally unlike him. A solution he suggests is to offer remedial English classes. This is a gift to all black doctors from Dr Fox. He wants to help the inferior other, a non-white and non-English speaker who he sees as a 'danger to public safety'. He wants to help them lift themselves up to better standards defined by him – to standards that subjugate non-whites as if they were once again colonised citizens.

Dr Fox and the Conservative Party must be counting on a social niche for fostering such views. The assumption is that the public includes people who welcome these thoughts. The implication is that a racist politician, working for a racist party, hoping to win the racist vote promotes his views to nurture a racist society. Carnival or not, MacPherson or not, British society still harbours racist thought and action. The Conservative Party have scored yet another racist goal for a racist team. But they do not mind as this wins votes.

Frantz Fanon (1986) wrote *Black Skins, White Masks*. In this he discussed colonial domination and the survival of racist ideology in the mind of the white. He raised some pertinent associations between racism, sexism, aggression, domination and individual identity development. He did so using psychoanalytic thought and process as the tools for unearthing the racist in us all. Fanon considered racism to exist independently of prejudice, and that it came before the creation of racial category. As if to emphasise this point, Fanon used racial categories in his analysis. A unique contribution was the description of the interdependence of the racist and his or her victim. The victim of racism, created by the racist, finds difficulty continuing a meaningful existence without relating that existence to racist action. This, Fanon asserts, partly relates to the 'dependency complex' of colonised people, the internalisation of decades of inter-generationally transmitted knowledge about how to behave in a world of differences in which the black skin, the non-white skin, is inferior. Inferiority as a complex, Fanon stated, was emergent where there were different peoples, receptive to being labelled as 'other'. Amongst minorities, inferiority claims its victims through glass ceilings, non-achievement and labels of deviancy and social exclusion. Here Fanon begins to develop how the inferiority of the dominated correlates with the superiority of the dominating. There is a relationship whereby black people are trapped in their skin just as white people are trapped in theirs. The skins are inherited symbols that carry with them knowledge of historical events and relationships between peoples who differ. This is not simply intellectual knowledge, inherited in some mechanical way, but emotive knowledge passed on through symbolic cultural transmission. 'It is the racist who creates his inferior.' The need to label, categorise and make sense of others, of different peoples, is the preoccupation of the racist, who perceives threat through contact with the other.

At times of cultural flux, where a minority is exposed to other cultures, shifts in the minority's cultural attitudes and behaviours take place. Acculturation is the term used to describe the process whereby the cultural beliefs and lifestyles of immigrants and their descendants tend to change, and approximate closer the beliefs and lifestyles of the host population. The retention of original beliefs and attitudes is variable, thus leading to bereavement at loss of culture. The notion of how host beliefs and life-styles adapt is rarely considered but is certainly evident wherever cultures interact. How can we measure acculturation? Some have argued for a single dimension from being culturally integrated with the host popula-tion to being strongly identified with an ethnic minority group of origin, or at least with the group to which one self-assigns belonging. This, almost certainly, is far too simplistic as it implies that one can only be strongly identified with the host community or one's community of origin. An alternative view proposed by William Berry in the USA is that there are two dimensions and people can show strong or weak identifica-tions with each. Thus, those with strong identifications with the host and one's own cultural group are considered 'integrated' or 'bi-cultural'. These individuals are deemed the most functional. Those with weak identifica-tions with each of these are considered marginalised. Those only with strong host identifications are considered assimilated with loss of identifi-cation with culture of origin; and those with strong own group identifica-tion only are considered 'separated' and perhaps unable to be as functional in the community as is possible, although still enjoying some psychologi-cal protection. This model has been developed to suggest that those in intermediate stages of identity development are more vulnerable. That is, where individuals have not explored their identity and have not estab-lished an identity, or have established an identity without personal thought about their sense of belonging, are vulnerable to psychological distress. Within this shifting morass of identities, individuals seek an identity that best represents them as individuals, that best protects them and that best avoids conflict with other identities. However, each of these models does not do justice to the fluid nature of identity at critical periods such as adolescence and at times of migration; nor do these models consider that any one individual can have multiple identities that flow in and out of each other to develop new identities that move away from both the original and the host culture to form new identities.

When racists create and give birth to their inferiors, certain identities are placed on the market. Adopting an identity given by the fantasised superior is better than having no identity or an identity in flux that risks receiving an identity that does not confer protection. A superior-made identity, if adopted, will at least receive the sanction and protection of the fantasised superior. So a deal is done between the newly made inferiorised dominated mind, and the self-made superiorised dominating mind. These ideas are echoed in Joel Kovel's book *White Racism* (Kovel 1988). Kovel specifically explores patriarchy, the development of the superego (the seat of morals which according to psychoanalytic theory are internalisations of parent figures) and the Oedipus configuration. That is, in order not to damage the father, the patriarchal figure and the source of threat, the mind of a child (or of the infantilised adult) seeks protection through accepting the given identity. This resolves the threat, and gives the child a legitimised place in the order of things; however, the given identity will not quite match the subjective sense of self, and there is always a cost experienced as being misunderstood. Kovel and Ivan Ward, in the introduction to Kovel's book, both emphasise patriarchy as a source of racialised hatred and prejudice. They explore how the deeper layers of the mind, the id, the seat of irrational and raw aggressive and unprocessed impulses, seeks expression of ideas and actions through the civilising ego, whilst subject to the moralising influences of the superego. Their conclusion is that the racist, in order to avoid castration anxiety of the oedipal situation, attacks a sibling who is inferiorised: the black, or the non-white or the other. Thus, one of Kovel's central theses is that aggression or relational violence are expressed through racial hatred, whilst racism also exists at a collective level to shape the expressions of violence in a form that is acceptable to the different layer of the racist's mind. This only leaves the black person the choice of becoming white in order to achieve equality, yet with each step towards equality, there is a destruction of the black self, and greater intolerance of the remaining differences between black and white. Lose oneself, lose one's identity or persist with domination. That is the choice made on a daily basis in acculturative identity changes.

One way of understanding the hatred of black or Jew or Indian is that racists project their own desires onto them, and then act as if they actually had those characteristics. Kovel and Fanon have both described their assertions in relation to psychoanalytic concepts, which for the majority of the public remain obscure, tentative and subject to criticism on the grounds that several influences are thought to act on the conscious mind, and that psychoanalysis reduces these to internal events in the realms of fantasy whilst being unable to verify assertions. In Sigmund Freud's writing, effort was expended at linking cultural and societal acts and fantasy to that of individual psychic survival (Freud 1923; 1930). Psychoanalytic thought is a way of thinking that brings to bear the collective experience and knowledge of the workings of the mind.

Informed by psychoanalytic perspectives, Kovel gives three categories of racist. The first type the dominative classically prejudicial person of the American South, who promoted racism as an economic and political system within which black life was to be the responsibility of whites. This sort of racist openly seeks to keep black people down and is willing to use force. This is now a rare sight, although in any democratic society fascist parties continue to exist and keep alive the sentiments expressed by dominative racists. It is not uncommon in European politics for shifts to the right to be marked by more powerful statements about immigration or that national threat from a new 'other'. Asylum seekers in the UK have become the latest victims of this mentality; and it is not just a lynch mob of non-thinkers responsible for such actions. Politicians and the intellectuals in society also play a major role. Kovel's second type of racist is the aversive type. This is far more relevant a typology of today's white liberal or silent racist who takes no action against racist activity, but silently pleasures in the world of the unconscious by the observation of racial hatreds. An intra-psychic battle between racist sentiments and conscience proceeds, sometimes to the effect that the individual takes part in anti-racist action. On the other hand, aversive racists try to ignore the existence of black peoples, try to avoid them, to be polite, correct and cold in dealings, to promote the intellect over emotional disgust and hatred. Kovel argues that if such racists come into contact with black peoples, there is internal dis-harmony and their personality organisation can be disrupted to react in a dominative manner. The third of Kovel's categories is the meta-racist, who does not express racist tendencies except through participation at a group unconscious level, in which black and white relations are organised at a collective meta-level to disempower the blacks. This type is at the forefront of technological advance, and as it is the least visible, it continues to exist through power relationships that are not obviously racist. Thus emerges a racism through technocracy and without need for psychological conscious motivations. Economic justification alone is sufficient for a variety of other technical reasons for the existence of a particular dyad of dominated and dominator without overt reference to race. Those who fare poorly are those that society labels as 'other', that is those without the same stake in local communities, society, capitalist success and notions of having a 'safe home'.

There will be individual instances of black-on-black prejudice on the basis of different origins in terms of continents, countries, religions, tribes; similarly within Indian society the caste system affirms a separatist and hierarchically structured set of relations. However, at a meta-racist level, white developed countries dominate world markets, have promoted capitalism as a dominant way of existing and, because of the historical inheritance, have shaped unconscious collective fantasy with content that is saturated with symbolism of the inferiority of black, of otherness, to white-developed symbols of power.

To summarise the arguments so far presented on unconscious fantasy and identity or personality organisation, I draw on a way of representing internal worlds developed by Anthony Ryle at St Thomas' Hospital in London. Ryle was the founder of Cognitive Analytic therapy, a movement that promoted an eclectic brief form of therapy that engaged the patient in a dialogue that spoke to the person in their own language of distress. As part of moving to a more digestible form of therapy, Ryle promoted the use of pen and paper diagrams to capture, in concrete and digestible chunks, what psychoanalysis leaves at audible sense impressions which might be lost in their transience. Pen and paper representations of different states of the mind allow scrutiny of how transient mind states relate to one another, and their predominant characteristics. Although the following diagrams are not as complex, and do not fulfil the function of representing complex internal states of mind, I summarise, using similar diagrams, some of the main findings of Kovel's and Fanon's analysis of unconscious fantasy. Using Freud's clarification of superego, ego and id, Figure 5.1, adapted from Ryle's diagrams, represents some of the relationship-sentiments experienced at each of these levels.

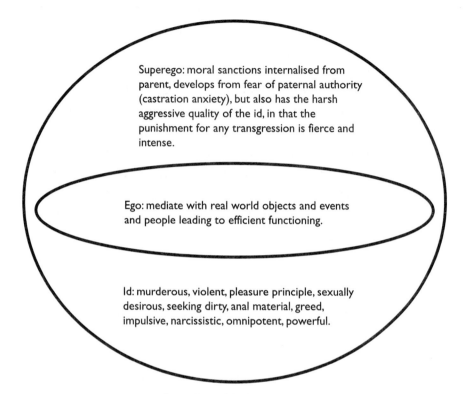

Superego: moral sanctions internalised from parent, develops from fear of paternal authority (castration anxiety), but also has the harsh aggressive quality of the id, in that the punishment for any transgression is fierce and intense.

Ego: mediate with real world objects and events and people leading to efficient functioning.

Id: murderous, violent, pleasure principle, sexually desirous, seeking dirty, anal material, greed, impulsive, narcissistic, omnipotent, powerful.

Figure 5.1 A representation of Freud's model of superego, ego and id (adapted)

Collective id fantasy is projected into or onto blackness. White behaves as if black has characteristics which white tries to repudiate. Although these arguments are presented in black/white terms, in my view, a more accurate rendering of these is to use self–other distinctions. So where there are mixed marriages, a not uncommon reaction among relatives of the couple is to fear the unknown, to have reservations, to explore fantasies of sexual promiscuity or of different norms of sexuality, child rearing, morality, industriousness, commitment. Colour of skin is most obvious but a recognition of that alone is not what reveals racist unconscious fantasy.

A five-year-old boy recently said to me out of curiosity, 'how long have you been brown for?' He, in his innocence, knew only of white as a condition of existence, but explored why white was not as pervasive as he expected. Somewhere along the line, his expectation was that brown was defined by the loss of white. Already there is an organisation of relations into superior and inferior, permanence and transience, normal and abnormal. Through images of white domination, such a child will further internalise more powerful images, and other non-white children will also internalise representations of their own inferiority and degradation. Thus, the unknown 'other' becomes a receptacle for the search for the expression of id fantasy. This, at one level, is as racist as the often-quoted Jungian equation of the black with the infant, and the white with the adult. Jung's analyses fell foul of the very projective process he was trying to unravel. Just because the self identifies the other with id fantasy, that does not make the other into the self's fantasy. However, this is what the racist perceives and communicates in such a way that the victim, the other, has to unravel who he is from the projected fantasy.

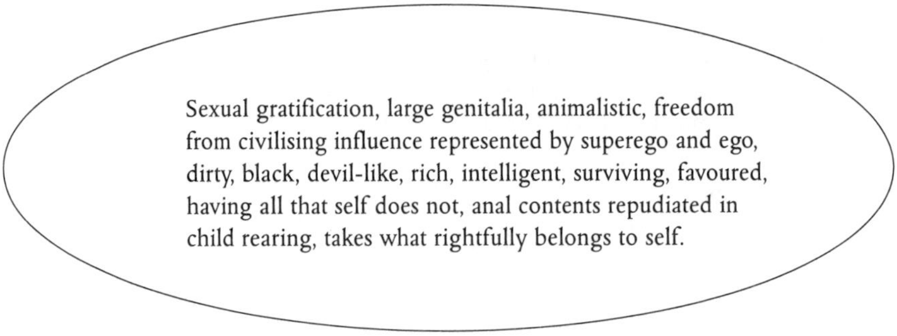

Sexual gratification, large genitalia, animalistic, freedom from civilising influence represented by superego and ego, dirty, black, devil-like, rich, intelligent, surviving, favoured, having all that self does not, anal contents repudiated in child rearing, takes what rightfully belongs to self.

Figure 5.2 Race and projected fantasy

The matter becomes more complicated when one considers why such fantasy is given life through an 'other'. The repudiated aspects of self (see Figure 5.2) are given life in the other and so some satisfaction is granted to self. Furthermore, if the repudiated fantasy is then attacked, the full might of superego harshness is released on the other to give further expression to id aggression under a legitimised campaign. Thus, the fantasised racial other is in fact created by the racist as part of the self; the 'other' is needed to define self-superiority. Edgar Jones, in his chapter on beliefs (Chapter 3), touches on this process as expressed in nationalistic fervour.

The self seeks the other, seeks proximity to another that is not known, but which allows some expression of id. Seeking experience of being another is not something humans do well. At one level, we give expression to racial hatred; at another, giving some of the 'forbidden fruits' expression is part of normal development. That is why teenage sexuality, drinking and rebellious activity is so common in societies that foster the individual rights to freedom of expression as being more important than group prohibitions. This proximity-seeking allows an act of intimacy, without recourse to conscious pleasure of intimacy, whilst not defying the parental superego authority. Thus, racial hatred is like a form of aggressive exploration and conquering, whilst repudiating that the fantasised other is desired and exciting, and that the triumphant moment of colonisation is secretly celebrated. Yet, accompanying a pursuit of relations, there is also initial fear and excitement. Fanon's dissection of motivations behind white rapists of black women does more justice to this subject.

I return to Dr Fox's statements, and here I could quote many statements made every day by many public figures, showing how popularity for such assertions is never far away. The public complaints that led Dr Fox to express his views were related to communication, to sharing distress, to sharing pain and the perception that the 'other' does not understand the 'us', that 'the black other does not understand, and therefore is defective', rather than 'we create the black other as a non-understanding defective'. Dr Xavier Coll (Chapter 9) outlines how the black professional can be on the receiving end of these projections. When, as a medical student, I visited a man to take a blood sample, the following morning on the ward round, this man stated to the consultant: 'a black doctor came to see me yesterday to take some blood, but he was good though'. I had not been recognised from one day to the next; I had been understood as being black (not white and non-self from him), and there was a statement that I was 'good though' as if this mitigated against my blackness and my non-understandability. A denial of me and a relief that I was adequate. The complaints of Dr Fox's constituents were probably fuelled by dissatisfactions with inadequacy of the professional in a shared communication. Is this a real inadequacy, or is there an element of expected inferiority which is fuelled by cultural distance, and so the other becomes a vehicle for the patient's own sense of powerlessness against their illness? To some extent, this is a natural process that, in this instance, has sought expression through cultural and racial difference. So the role of black doctor, someone who momentarily might be considered to be symbolically powerful, is reversed into someone who is disempowered through being made to feel inferior and a 'public danger'. A failure of sharing, of knowing the other, emerges. Doctor–patient encounters are particularly vulnerable to frightening feelings of patients seeking a parental, authoritarian superior to deal with fears about illness and bodily integrity. They seek similarity in order to better share ego content, but failing this, if there is sufficient frustration, under such circumstances of cultural or linguistic mismatch, the other is held to account for the failed communication. In Dr Fox's case these are GPs who are 'other'; not a real other but a fictionalised other that suits the politics. Kohut (1971) in *Analysis of the Self*, writes that empathy declines the more dissimilar is the patient to the professional. This empathy relies on cultural experience and a shared understanding of the rules of social communication. The absence of such empathy can feel like an act of abandonment, of punishment, of fear of the unknowable, and it is to this end that cross-racial encounters, with failed empathy, can have disastrous consequences. Racists, after all, have no empathy with the victim's pain, indeed they feel justified in exercising oppression whilst hating any representation of their own actions, and the associated desirous id fantasies. Fanon puts this another way (p.231): superiority? inferiority? Why not the quite simple attempt to touch the other, to feel the other, to explain the other to myself?

Racists need victims, and victims need to resolve the assault, but cannot do so without the racist. The response may be individual but the forces are more collective, and diffuse. An exit strategy requires such a diffuse collective, and yet powerful, raising of conscious awareness. Conscious and unconscious, individual and society, social and biological, love and hatred all converge in the moment of such acts, and must also be harnessed for a solution. The solution might simply be bearing the impossibility of the task, but persisting in the search for understanding, coupled with action at a social and institutional level. Within such a context, care of the mentally ill in our society can then be addressed more specifically.

Chapter 6

Racism, Social Exclusion and Mental Health

A Black User's Perspective

Premila Trivedi

'To oppress a race and then label its reaction as mental illness is not only morally wrong; it is criminal and a fraud'

Equal opportunity policies, strategies for valuing diversity, charters for anti-discriminatory practice, training programmes in cultural competency, the setting up of ethnically sensitive public services, the Government focus on social inclusion – all feel-good developments that, together with an increasing reluctance to use the 'r' (racism) word, serve to reassure us that we live in an equitable and caring society that is truly committed to upholding every individual citizen's rights, no matter who the person is or how different he or she may be. In this world, it is as if difference is accepted and valued, with a capacity to encourage unity in diversity so that individuals, groups and society-as-a-whole all benefit. At the same time it is as if there is a clear acknowledgment of similarities and a wider common interest and humanity which provides the basis for an ethic that overcomes discrimination, exclusion and injustice (Brown 1998).

However, as a black[1] person who has grown up in Britain, I know that life is not like this and, in a society in which difference on the basis of skin colour routinely attracts discriminatory behaviour, racism is rife. My experience (and probably that of the vast majority of black people) shows that difference is only accepted as long as it fits in with the dominant group's world view, with some differences (e.g. the exotica of saris, samosas and steel bands) being acceptable and even desirable, while others (e.g. our free expression of emotion, some of our family structures and manifestation of our religious beliefs) are much less easily tolerated. So for many of us, it is as if our acceptance and inclusion into society as black people is dependent on the will of the dominant group and if we are to be socially included we must to a certain extent learn to be what they want us to be, e.g. not too loud or too quiet, too aggressive or too passive, too rich or too poor, too successful or too unsuccessful and above all to know our place as black people in society. But altering our behaviour to satisfy others can have damaging effects on our psyche, especially when that behaviour is culturally determined and forms an essential and integral part of our identity and sense of self.

In this chapter I consider how racism can lead to marginalisation and social exclusion and some ways in which black people may respond to this. In particular, I use my own personal experience to focus on those of us who seek to cover up or eliminate our cultural differences in an attempt to be socially included, sometimes with serious consequences on our emotional and mental health. Finally, I consider how contact with mental health services can often, rather than helping our problems, actually exacerbate them, partly because the racism that caused our distress in the first place is reproduced and concentrated within mental health services (Sashidharan 2001) and partly because we now (by virtue of being mental health service

---

1   In this chapter I have used the term 'black' in a political sense to denote those who are distinguished and discriminated against on the basis of their skin colour. All of the issues discussed may also apply to other ethnic minority groups but my brief is to write from a black perspective.

users) become subjected to society's negative and oppressive attitude to those they see as mentally ill.

Racism and social exclusion

Prejudice, discrimination and oppression, together with the 'inability of our society to keep all groups and individuals within reach of what we expect as a society and the tendency to push vulnerable and different people into the least popular places' (Power 2000, pp.47–51), all contribute to the way in which certain individuals and groups become marginalised and socially excluded from mainstream society. Racism in particular has always served as a powerful weapon to keep black people in disadvantaged positions and even in this day and age, when there is a general acknowledgement that racism is unacceptable and the majority of individuals aspire to being fair-minded, just and inclusive, racism still very significantly affects most black people's lives and their position in society.

This is almost certainly in large part a result of the prevalence in our society of institutionalised racism, in which discrimination on the grounds of 'racial' difference is so deeply enshrined into the systems within which we live that even those who are fair-minded and just somehow become separated from their own personal beliefs and instead get drawn into 'processes, attitudes and behaviours which amount to discrimination through unwitting prejudice, ignorance, thoughtlessness and stereotyping which disadvantages...ethnic minority people' (MacPherson 1999). Such institutionalised racism arises because institutions and organisations (which carry the power and influence in society) are deeply imbued with the (racist) dominant group's values and work to serve that group's vested interests so that its power structure is maintained and the status quo undisturbed. Unlike personal racism (which is blatant and relatively easy to identify and condemn), institutionalised racism is subtle and hard to pin down and (because it is considered to be unthinking and free of personal prejudice or intention) is too often discounted or ignored. Thus, it continues to go largely unchecked, with widespread and pervasive effects on black people's social, educational and employment opportunities, their economic situation and the way they are treated within public services.

This results in significant numbers of black people being pushed to the margins of society, where socially they become isolated and often live in fear of abuse or attack, economically they are restricted to low-paid work and unable to afford quality housing, food, clothes, heating and other things that make up a decent standard of living, culturally they may be prevented from being who they really are, and politically they are unable to influence their destiny or get the back-up they need to improve their situation (MIND 1999). They may also at the same time come to be seen as 'a problem' rather than as the recipients of society's problems, and thus become even more marginalised, deprived of their citizenship (Miller 2000) and disempowered.

Some responses to racism and social exclusion

For many black people, racism and being socially excluded are just a 'normal' part of life. In recent years, dealing with social exclusion has become a key part of Government strategy, and many social inclusion policies have been introduced to draw the excluded back into the mainstream. But for many, this means joining a mainstream that largely demands conformity and a diminution of those differences that it finds difficult to accept. So the choice seems to be either to retain those differences and remain socially excluded, or to modify those differences in the hope of being more easily socially included. Of course the situation is never this clear-cut, and the choices people have will depend on many different factors, including their internal and personal resources, their political will, their family and community supports and the sort of opportunities they have to influence their own position.

Below, I give some very simplified examples of the ways in which black people may respond to being marginalised and socially excluded on the grounds of cultural difference. Each response is presented as a separate entity but in reality people may vary in their response and move from one to the other at different times in their lives to suit their situation and serve their needs.

Counter-response

Those with a strong sense of self, a high degree of self-esteem and the political will may be very clear that their cultural differences are an absolutely essential part of who they are. They will therefore present themselves to mainstream society with these differences intact, certain that they have the right to do this and ready to deal with any negative consequences as they occur. Many will, at the same time, work to raise awareness of the impact of racism on the person and society as a whole and try to bring about some positive change.

Accepting response

Others may also decide that they need to maintain their cultural differences in order to preserve their identity and sense of self, but may lack the confidence to present these to a mainstream society that essentially seeks to exclude them. They may therefore retreat into their family and community, which is often the only place where they can feel strong and secure in who they are and where they can develop a kind of psychic envelope that strengthens their self-identity and sense of oneness to a belonging group (Rouchy 1995).

Adaptation response

Some with a more pragmatic approach may decide that, while their cultural differences are extremely important, they are willing to modify them if this allows them to be socially included. They may therefore constantly juggle their identity, covering up or diminishing their 'unacceptable' cultural differences while in mainstream society in an attempt to be socially included, but retaining them within their own family and community in order to constantly reinforce and validate their true individual and group cultural identity.

Assimilation response

Finally, some (perhaps with a weaker sense of self and/or poor family and community links) may consciously or unconsciously come to the conclusion that, since their cultural differences are what cause them to be rejected by mainstream society, they should cover them up or diminish them and assimilate in order to increase their chances of being accepted and socially included. Perhaps of all the responses, this is the most worrying since it can, in some cases, lead to a dangerous loss of cultural identity and sense of self and as a result give rise to severe emotional and mental health problems.

The dangers of assimilating in order to be socially included

Assimilation involves two parallel processes, a modification or elimination of those cultural differences that the mainstream deems to be unacceptable and an adoption of the mainstream's values, attitudes and practices, including its racist attitudes and practices. While both processes will lead to a lessening of cultural identity and sense of self, it is the latter that may be particularly damaging because in adopting the racism of the mainstream we may internalise it and (as labelling theory suggests) come to see who we are only by the (negative) way others respond to us (Goffman 1963).

Such internalised racism means we may start to dislike and despise who we really are, at the same time feeling guilty for being so despicable and part of such an unacceptable cultural group (Anonymous 1999). So we may try to deny who we are and distance ourselves from our family and community. But our black skin will always remind us (and others) of the truth of our being and we will know in our hearts that we will first and foremost always be seen as black and may never be accepted on truly equitable terms. This may result in feelings of confusion, vulnerability, powerlessness and hopelessness, with subsequent emotional and psychological distress often accompanied by self-destructive feelings and (in some cases) psychotic disturbance (Hickling and Hutchinson 1999). This may then lead us (voluntarily or involuntarily) to mental health professionals who, rather than understanding our distress in its true context, too often try to define it simply as biological mental illness. This effectively confines the problem to us and may increase our distress and self-hatred (Anonymous 1999) and drive us into a spiral of oppression (Figure 6.1) from which it can become almost impossible to escape.

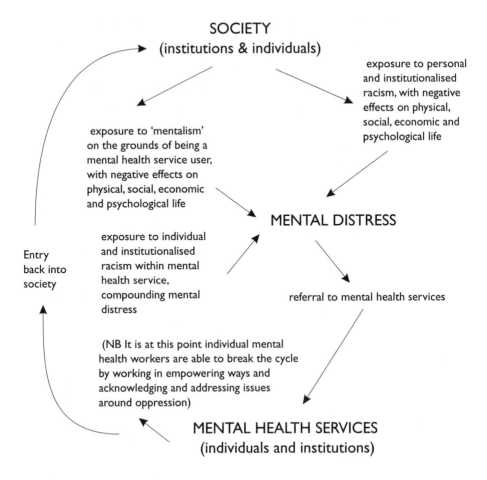

Diagram to illustrate the spiral of oppression that may be experienced by oppressed groups in society when they come into contact with psychiatry and enter the mental health system. Personal and institutionalised oppressions in society on the grounds of difference (e.g. as racism, sexism, classism, ageism and homophobia) can have a negative effect on the physical, social, economic and psychological lives of individuals, and may (in some) cause emotional distress and sometimes mental health problems. Society's response to such distress is to treat it within mental health services in a system of medical and social care that rather than understanding and challenging oppressions that give rise to mental distress, reinforce them with their own oppressive attitudes and practices. This results in even more distress, driving the individual even further into the mental health system and into a vicious circle of society's oppression – distress – mental health services' oppression – more distress. At the same time, individuals may, by virtue of having contact with mental health services, become subject to the oppression of mentalism since society (and mental health services!) has such a negative attitude towards anyone who has a psychiatric diagnosis. Thus it continues, leaving users of mental health services within a spiral of oppression that perpetuates oppression and discrimination.

Figure 6.1 Racism and the spiral of oppression

Racism, mental health services and the spiral of oppression

As already described, black people in society may respond to racism in different ways, e.g. by countering it, accepting it, adapting to it or internalising it. All of these may to a greater or lesser extent cause emotional distress, e.g. in the first case because of constantly having to challenge racism often with seemingly little effect, in the second because of being excluded from the benefits of mainstream society and made to feel inferior, in the third because of constantly having to juggle identity in order to be accepted and in the fourth because of having to deny cultural identity with a consequent fragmenting of the sense of self. How we deal with such distress very much depends on our internal and personal resources and our life circumstances. While many will somehow be able to manage it well, some of us (particularly those who internalise racism) may not and may go on to develop psychological problems and diagnosable mental illness. This may then take us into the mental health system, which (because it is a product of society) reproduces the individual and institutionalised racism of society, often exacerbating and compounding our distress as, for example, we get defined in terms of Eurocentric norms and our cultural differences (in particular our culturally determined expressions of emotional distress) get pathologised. This may then drive us into a vicious circle of racism, distress, more racism, more distress, which is only likely to be broken if the true issues are acknowledged and addressed.

This is where, in spite of institutional racism, individual mental health workers may be able to have an influence, by working with their patients in empowering rather than disempowering ways (Table 6.1). But too often this does not happen and the real issues, particularly those related to racism, are minimised within mental health services. In my case I was almost completely blind to the issues until I got into psychotherapy with a down-to-earth (white) therapist who enabled me to see beyond my despair and confusion. As my issues, particularly those around my internalised racism, became clearer I became more convinced that I needed to work through these further. But I knew that, in spite of my very positive relationship with my white therapist, I would only feel safe to do this with an appropriate black therapist – so I decided to explore further. Maybe my biggest mistake, though, was to raise this with my consultant psychiatrist.

His immediate (to me almost triumphant) response was 'Oh, so you'd rather be white?' and while I suppose the issues could be reduced down to this, I felt such simplification completely denied the complexity of what I was trying to say. Furthermore, my consultant went on to tell me that I was very unlikely ever to find anyone who would work on these very specific issues with me and while I acknowledge that there may not be many therapists (and even fewer psychiatrists) out there who work with issues of internalised racism, surely that should not stop us from looking for those who do? But I was left with the impression that I should not even bother to think of finding such therapy and just bury the issues again.

Luckily, I later contacted others who were much more aware of the issues and, through various activities (including finding therapy and even writing this chapter), I have been enabled to try to begin to make some sense of my feelings about my blackness. In particular, I am beginning to see how racism (both external and internal) contributes to my mental distress and, while this may not deny any internal problems I have in dealing with that distress, it certainly helps me to see patterns and gain a better understanding of the wider picture. I hope that this will enable me to take more control of my own responses to racism, perhaps by learning to challenge it rather than internalise it.

Table 6.1 A black user's view of how mental health workers empower and disempower mental health service users

IN GENERAL

you empower when	*you disempower when*
• you recognise we are people first and patients second	• you see us only as psychiatric patients
• you treat us as equal human beings	• you assume you are somehow better than us
• you treat us with dignity and respect	• you let your power make you act in authoritarian or paternalistic ways
• you value our skills and talents and the areas of our life where we are doing well, and acknowledge our mental health problems are only one part of our jigsaw	• you see us only as a set of pathological signs and symptoms
• you explain to us why you do what you do, take on board our views and allow us properly to share in formulating our care	• you act in high-handed ways and assume we have no insight into our distress or what will best help us
• you share your perception of us with us and are open to amending your views of us	• you discuss us behind closed doors or write copious notes on us which are never verified or amended by us
• you allow us time to talk through our distress/crisis/psychosis (if that is what we want)	• you assume we don't wish to know what we have been like when we are distressed and have no memory of that
• you make sure you provide us with accessible and useful information, including information about complementary therapies	• you provide only the information that you think is relevant for us
• you allow us to laugh as well as cry and above all to hope and dream for the future	• you assume we are in distress all the time and this is the only way we can ever be
• you learn from us – we are the experts on our own self, our individual identity, our culture, our values and our 'madness' and what we think will help us	• you think you are the expert on us and know what is best for us

WITH SPECIFIC REFERENCE TO RACE AND CULTURE

you empower when	*you disempower when*
• you acknowledge and value our cultural differences	• you use our ethnic and cultural differences to pathologise us
• you allow us to express our culture and spirituality in our own way	• you let your fear of the unknown force you into action that blocks out our necessary cultural and spiritual modes of expression
• you recognise and acknowledge that personal and institutionalised racism is a very real feature of black people's everyday lives	• you assume we have a 'chip on our shoulder' if we talk about racism and the racist attitudes and behaviour we have encountered
• you take responsibility for challenging racist behaviour and comments, whether from staff or other patients	• you ignore or make excuses for racist behaviour and comments or think that it is not important if we do not complain
• you recognise institutionalised as well as personal racism within psychiatry and how it affects black users	• you don't acknowledge or understand how institutionalised racism operates and how it oppresses and invalidates black people and their experiences
• you recognise and acknowledge that some of our anger at oppressions within the psychiatric system (e.g. being sectioned, forcibly medicated) is very justified and a healthy response to injustice	• you never listen or ask us to explain why we are sometimes angry and violent
• you make it your business to find out about culturally appropriate services in the hospital/community /voluntary sector and help us to access them practically	• you have no knowledge of what is available outside (or even inside) the statutory sector and/or are reluctant to refer us to other services
• you recognise the importance of our family and community to our mental well-being and our inter-dependence with them	• you pay lip service to our family and community links and/or consider us to be over-dependent or over-involved

Conclusion

The views expressed in this chapter may be considered to be very simplistic and naive. But they are derived from my (and other black users') experience of racism, social exclusion and mental health services and may therefore need to be seriously considered. To me, social inclusion means being an integral and valued part of the whole, with enough money, good housing, satisfying employment, sufficient leisure time and activities and proper meaningful relationships. Having access to such resources and feeling a useful part of society are essential for good mental health. But for many black users of mental health services, personal and institutionalised racism within society and mental health services and the negative and stigmatising attitudes to people with mental health problems mean that for many of us proper social inclusion may only ever be a dream.

The stigma of mental illness is a heavy one for us to bear, sticking like glue and often blinding those around us to the causes of our distress and to any hope of our recovery. It is as if we, as black users, are branded, losing all of our often rich and valued past as we become just psychiatric patients, with little realistic hope of ever again being socially included. If however we were seen as the people we really are, maybe vulnerable at times but full of creativity and potential, our lives could be transformed to the mutual benefit of ourselves and society-as-a-whole. But it is for society to decide whether it truly wishes to include us. If it does it requires a real change in attitudes and culture, in social as well as mental health policy. Perhaps now is the time really to acknowledge the social causes of much mental illness and tackle them, rather than leaving the largely biological discipline of psychiatry to deal with the casualties of social inequalities and injustices. The current approach to mental health, which essentially adopts a 'sticking plaster' approach and perpetuates stigma and prejudice against those with mental health problems, will never address many of the true issues and will only ensure that for most black users social inclusion will continue to remain a far-off dream.

This chapter is dedicated to my brother Vinod Trivedi who died as this book was going to press. Vinod always worked determinedly to retain a sense of self and could never fathom why that presented such problems for me but always made sure he stood by me.

Chapter 7

Understanding Racism in Mental Health

Kwame McKenzie

Dr McKenzie searches for a fresh approach. Using the African-American experience, he shows how racism can take many shapes, and how oppression among black peoples is a product of the people and the environment in which they live. Presenting data on health and mortality, African-Americans appear to be in dilemma of identity and belonging. The contrast and shared problems with British black people is absorbing and raises questions about why and how we need race as a way of understanding health, disease and death.

Racism is a fundamental cause of disparities in health. Its myriad effects and links to other forms of social stratification lead to it being both obvious and masked. Its boundaries are indistinct because it is internal as well as external, individual as well as ecological, and shunned while being an integral part of dominant culture ideology. Its investigation is important and yet part of the spider's web that traps the best thinkers of ethnic minorities in contemplation instead of action and this brings us to the final paradox – understanding racism is a prerequisite of beating it.

Some may argue that it would be better to investigate the forms of social stratification that are linked to racism or the tools through which racism exerts its effects rather than to try to study racism itself. But racism is more than the sum of its parts. Disaggregating its effects may tell you less about its nature than conceptualising it as a distinct entity. Moreover, an acknowledgement of its existence and its nature is necessary for its extinction.

Below I will try to investigate the nature of racism borrowing heavily on the plight of African-Americans. Despite their long history in the USA, only 7 per cent of African-Americans marry white Americans. Segregation is rife and increasing. And though disparities in health between African-Americans and white Americans have been acknowledged by governments since the 1980s they have been getting worse rather than better.

Fundamental causes and health

If it is possible further to understand the nature of racism by outlining its processes, the fundamental-causes hypothesis is a good place to start. This hypothesis tries to explain why disparities between rich and poor with regards to rates of illness remain despite the fact that there have been effective interventions against the most potent risk factors for disease.

In the 19th century, infections were the major cause of death for the poor. Immunisation, sanitation and antibiotics have decreased the risk of death or long-term illness from infections, yet disparities in health between rich and poor have remained. The fundamental-causes hypothesis states that this occurs because as some risk factors are eradicated, others emerge.

There is data to support this. Infectious diseases are no longer the reason for disparities in health between rich and poor; chronic diseases such as cancer and heart disease have taken over and the differential likelihood of encountering risk factors for these (such as stress, smoking, alcohol, low levels of exercise and poor diet) maintains class differences in rates of illness.

These class differences and the mechanisms that maintain them are fundamental causes.

> ...fundamental causes are linked to resources like money, power, prestige and social connections which strongly influence people's ability to avoid risks and to minimize the consequences of any disease which emerges. (Link 1996)

Fundamental causes are particularly important in periods of change. New diseases, new environmental hazards, new knowledge of risks and new treatments are all the currency of fundamental causes. In a dynamic system, fundamental causes are always important. Those who have more access and power will be less afflicted by disease.

If disparities are to be decreased, research and interventions would need to focus on fundamental causes.

Racism and segregation can be viewed as fundamental causes. Their effects are meted out partly through discriminatory social policies, social institutions (such as healthcare), business and individual and community responses to perceived racism. They impede the ability of ethnic minority groups to avoid risk factors, to access new ideas for prevention and to avoid new diseases. They also produce new hazards – for instance, crack cocaine, HIV or the availability of low-cost high-calorie food leading to heart disease.

Interventions to decrease disparities which aim to do this by targeting the effects of fundamental causes are balanced by the production of new hazards. Because of this, though there may be a general improvement in life expectancy and infant mortality in a country (as in the USA over the last 20 years), the health gap between ethnic minorities and ethnic majority populations has usually increased.

Researchers have been able to differentiate between the fundamental cause such as racism or other forms of social stratification and the process by which its effects are realised such as economic status. Potent effects of perceived racism on health when economic factors have been taken into account have been described. Patho-physiological effects of racism, which are independent of poverty or social class, have been demonstrated. The argument that racism is not important and that class and money can be substituted for it cannot properly account for disparities in health or explain the reasons why particular ethnic groups find themselves in the lower social classes often with poorer access to healthcare. Nor can it explain why this issue is still a matter for debate despite the fact that there is clear evidence that racism exists, that socio-economic status does not account for its effects and that conceptually socio-economic status is merely an objectified proxy measure for perceived social stratification when racism is a direct measure of social stratification.

Racism and health

Racism is associated with increased rates of a number of cancers, with chronic diseases such as diabetes and hypertension and with low birth-weight babies (with all the long-term consequences that this brings). However, it is unclear whether this is due to the effect of racism at an individual, institutional or ecological level, or whether it is a mixture of all of these.

Racism as an ecological variable[1]

Racism as an ecological variable is associated with adult mortality rates. An illustration of this comes from US researchers who measured racist attitudes in each of the States by weighted answers to the question:

> On average blacks have worse jobs income and housing than white people. Do you think the differences are?

1.   mainly due to discrimination

2.   because black people have less inborn ability to learn

3.   because most black people do not have the chance for education that it takes to rise out of poverty, or

4.   because most blacks do not have the motivation or will power to pull through?

The percentage of people who answered yes to questions 2 and 4 where calculated for each US State. A higher percentage was said to denote high 'racial disrespect' in that State and a lower percentage low 'racial disrespect' (Kennedy *et al.* 1998).

Racial disrespect was strongly correlated with the all-cause, age-adjusted mortality rates for self-assigned 'blacks'. It was also correlated with mortality in 'whites' – though less strongly. A 1 per cent increase in the prevalence of those who believed that blacks lacked innate ability

---

1   Ecological variables describe groups of people or areas, not individuals.

was associated with an increase in age-adjusted black-mortality rate of 350.8 per 100, 000.

Such work argues for a community level effect of racism that goes beyond the individual. Racism can be seen as having an effect on the whole society and the disunity that is reflected by it decreases all-cause life expectancy for all sectors of society. Clearly, cross-sectional studies like the one just featured do not prove cause and effect. Racist attitudes could be more likely to thrive in areas with high levels of distrust and disrespect. Racism may be an effect not a cause. However, it is unclear how societies that are divided can work together to improve their health.

At an ecological level, frustration and disillusionment of individuals could have community effects; they could lead to alternative economies and lifestyles which undermine the family and are associated with low social cohesion. This would also decrease the social buffers and level of social organisation needed to promote health.

Features of social organisation that facilitate co-operation for mutual benefit, such as civic participation, norms of reciprocity and trust in others, can be thought of as social capital. Social capital is an ecological variable which could be said to have an individual-level counterpart in individuals' social networks. Social networks have been linked to clinical outcomes in diseases as diverse as depression and breast cancer.

State-level variation in social capital (controlling for poverty) is related to mortality. The link between income inequality and mortality state by state may be explained by changes in social capital (Kawachi *et al.* 1997).

The gap between rich and poor affects social organisations and communities. The resulting damage to the fabric of society may have profound implications for the public health.

The 'Roseto effect' is widely cited as evidence for the positive effects of social cohesion on health. Roseto, a town in Pennsylvania, is populated predominantly by people of Italian origin and has been studied since 1962 because of its low level of cardiovascular mortality compared with other towns nearby. Roseto at that time was characterised by high social cohesion, close family ties, social homogeneity and good community relationships. A sharp increase in cardiovascular deaths and total mortality between 1965 and 1974 was associated with a decrease in social cohesion.

A recent study in Chicago has shown that high collective efficacy, defined as social cohesion among neighbours combined with their willingness to intervene on behalf of the common good, is linked to reduced violence and decreased mortality. Associations between concentrated disadvantage and residential instability with violence are largely mediated by collective efficacy (Sampson, Raudenbush and Earls 1997). Levels of collective efficacy are often low in inner-city areas.

Studies testing associations between social cohesion, collective efficacy and health in minority groups are underway. They may build on the work of LaViest (1992, 1993), who showed that 'relative political power' or the proportion of black Americans on the city council, divided by the proportion of blacks in the voting age group, was a strong negative predictor of black (post-neonatal) infant mortality rates in US cities with populations over 50,000.

Individual level effects

Individual experience of racial discrimination has been shown to affect health. It can raise blood pressure and has been linked to hypertension. Laboratory-based experiments of witnessed discrimination have been shown to produce physiological changes including raised blood pressure. Self-report levels of experienced discrimination and the experience of frequent frustrating social interactions of a racial nature (micro-aggressions) have been linked to hypertension.

The effects of racism on health are complex; both socio-economic class and psychological coping style affect the association between high blood pressure and the experience of racism. Added to this, the experience of racism is not uniform for different members of an ethnic minority group. It depends on residential area, socio-economic class and skin colour. Darker-skinned individuals are more likely to experience racism than those who are lighter skinned. There is also an interaction between skin colour and socio-economic status; darker skin has been shown to be associated with the experience of more racism in lower socio-economic groups but not higher socio-economic groups.

Studies have not linked the direct experience of racism aetiologically to specific psychiatric illness. If there were a link that had been missed this could be due to difficulties in measuring racism or in illness categorisation. The perception of racism depends on the individual and also the process through which it works. Institutional racism is subtle and often occurs with no individual racist act, though its effects are clearly discriminatory.

Parker and Kleiner (1966) have demonstrated a relationship between thwarted aspirations and psychological stress in African-Americans. More recently, the persistent, prolonged struggle and failure to overcome difficulties of blocked opportunities (John Henryism) has been linked to a decrease in psychological well-being, though not as yet to operationally defined mental ill health (Neighbors *et al.* 1996). A discrepancy between occupational status and an ability to maintain the appearances of a successful lifestyle has been linked to depression in young African-Americans. A link between internalised racial stereotypes and depression and alcohol abuse has been described.

Neighbors *et al.* (1996), in their review of racism and mental health in African-Americans, give the following summary:

The writings…emphasize the following points

1. the importance of striving for upward social mobility among African-Americans

2. the importance of racism as manifested in discrimination that block opportunities for advancement among blacks

3. the stress that results from inconsistencies between lifestyle and economic resources, and differences between aspirations and expectations

4. the importance of values like hard work, strong individualism and persistence in overcoming barriers to racism, and

5. the health risk of persistence and prolonged striving in confronting the difficult realities of institutional racism.

From the above it is clear that racism has individual, community and societal meanings and correlates. Though the majority of researchers have concentrated on the effects of racism on individual African-Americans, others hypothesise that minority group failure is important for the self-esteem of African-Americans but may be more important in increasing the self-esteem of white Americans.

Institutional racism

Even the more conservative governments such as the US Republicans in the 1980s accept that there are pervasive and persistent racial differences in healthcare in the USA (AMA Council on Ethical and Judicial Affairs 1990). US whites are more likely to receive coronary angioplasty, bypass surgery, chemo dialysis, intensive care for pneumonia and kidney transplants, even after adjustment for severity of illness, income and insurance status. Similarly comprehensive studies in the UK have not been undertaken but what evidence there is concurs with the US work.

There is demonstrable difference in access to preventive care for majority and minority ethnic groups. This is partly because the structure of the health services is often cast in the dominant culture's mould. Access to care and benefits often discriminates against ethnic minority patients. The USA again can be used as an example – the life expectancy of African-American men is 64.9, which is lower than the age for entitlement to the government-paid medical insurance programme, Medicare. Within Medicare there are demonstrable differences; more money is spent annually per white Medicare recipient than is spent per African-American recipient. Moreover, the whole system makes care more difficult for African-Americans to access. There are fewer doctors and hospitals in African-American neighbourhoods than white neighbourhoods. African-Americans are less likely to have a primary care physician than whites. African-Americans are more likely to be uninsured than whites, and employed African-Americans are less likely to have health insurance provided by their job.

For 'African-Americans in the USA' one could substitute a number of different ethnic groups and countries. Where racism exists such disparities are common. The true institutional nature of the racism comes not only in the fact that disparities exist but also in the fact that there is rarely significant widespread action to close the gap.

The concept of institutional racism in medical care is useful in analysing the reasons for differential service provision. The institutional racism paradigm:

1. helps to distinguish between actions of individuals and institutions; individuals may act in good faith, not harbour racist attitudes, but perpetuate discriminatory practices because of the systems set up by the institution

2. targets the results of practice rather than the intent; rather than discussing whether service providers have racist ideology it concentrates on proved differences in services and attempts to discuss reasons for these

3. acknowledges that medicine acts in a social world which may be discriminatory and that connection to other social systems may be important in producing the discriminatory practices – e.g. poor educational provision to some minority groups limits the proportion available for entry to medical school

4. takes into account the history of institutions – e.g. resistance of the medical profession to de-segregation plays a role in attitudes of African-Americans to the medical profession in the USA

5. leads to recommendations for fundamental changes in inequalities and processes in health

6. acknowledges other forms of social stratification and their effects – e.g. gender and social class

7. acknowledges the fact that racism is dynamic and changes with time and the type of institution

8. identifies the problem as an ideological problem and states that effects are not brought about only by culture, class and socio-political forces external to medicine.

Institutional racism may explain one of the paradoxes in African-American mental health. The factors that predict poorer physical health in African-Americans would be expected to predict poorer mental health as well. The elevated levels of morbidity, premature deaths, social stress and life events would be expected to cause higher levels of psychiatric morbidity in African-Americans when compared with American whites. However, though earlier studies had consistently shown increased levels of distress in African-Americans, recent epidemiological studies have shown lower levels of psychiatric illness in all categories except phobias and agoraphobia.

Of course, African-Americans could have lower levels of mental illness despite higher levels of social stressors but there are other hypotheses which could explain this phenomenon. It may be accounted for, in part, by the fact that surveys often do not sample inner-city areas, those who live in institutions and the homeless – these are all groups with a high proportion of African-Americans and a high percentage of people with mental illness. Also, the dominant culture's model of mental illness is used to define illness in African-Americans. Because of this the degree of dissonance between the behaviour and language of distress in African-Americans and that in white Americans is an important factor in making the correct diagnosis. Recent studies have shown that the language of distress used by African-Americans differs greatly from that on which structured diagnoses for DSMIIIR are based. This could lead to an underestimate of levels of distress and anxiety in African-Americans.

The mental health of African-Americans has not been defined by the community and neither has mental illness. It is unclear whether current estimates of illness properly reflect that which African-Americans would call mental illness.

Use of the institutional racism model helps to further highlight other aspects of the problem:

- *Institutional discrimination not individual*: As just stated, DSMIIIR, which has been produced to standardise diagnoses, has been shown to not properly sample the language of despair of African-Americans. Hence, diagnoses made using it and surveys based on it may be flawed. Doctors using DSMIIIR may make diagnoses in good faith, yet act in a discriminatory way because they are using tools that do not work as well for African-Americans as whites. Similar validity problems are found in other diagnoses and may lead to an over-diagnosis of schizophrenia and an under-diagnosis of affective disorders in American blacks.

Inappropriate treatment due to erroneous diagnosis will have a poor outcome. This, and what the community see as a lack of understanding of their problems, will undermine confidence in the services.

- *Connection to other social systems*: An ability to use the language of distress sampled by DSM is linked to social class and racial group. The lack of an African-American perspective in psychiatric diagnosis may be in part due to the historical lack of African-American doctors in positions of influence and the continued under-representation of African-American doctors in academic positions.

- *History of institutions*: The under-enumeration could also be due to the distrust of research and researchers. The Tuskegee Affair, in which Government-supported scientists denied African-Americans treatment for syphilis in order to document the natural history of this often fatal disease, has seemed to confirm their long-standing suspicion of medical research. African-Americans' views of the medical profession may still be suffering from the American Medical Association's resistance to de-segregation.

- *The culture of medical research*: This may be an impediment to improving the measurement of distress in African-American patients. There is a need for ethnographic research to rectify this problem but grant-giving institutions have difficulty funding such research because of its 'soft' nature. The fact that this research can take longer than bio-medical research can mean that it is expensive.

Institutions that may want to do such research – such as the historically black medical schools – have difficulty in getting funding for research because they are considered not to have sufficient research capacity. Their staff have heavier clinical loads because of the levels of morbidity in the poor areas in which they are located. Because of this they have less time for research. Money is not forthcoming to build their research capacity properly and it is considered fair for them to compete with richer research-based institutions for funding.

- *The ideology of medicine*: Though social factors may be important in the genesis and the perpetuation of depression, there is relatively little current research on this, or on specific therapy models for African-Americans, and so treatment for the depression may be less than comprehensive.

- *Fundamental changes*: Community-informed diagnostic rubrics may better describe mental illness in a community and so better inform treatment modalities. Money for research-capacity building and academic partnerships between historically black universities may increase the research undertaken on this subject. More flexibility in the grant-giving process at National Institutes of Health, for instance, to lengthen the funding cycle and promote more qualitative research may help. Even more fundamentally, the medical professions would need to embrace the concept of social forces as an aetiological factor and so a treatment opportunity in order to offer equity of care to disadvantaged groups.

Institutional racism and fundamental causes can be tied together in an analysis of the situation thus: the fundamental cause of disparities is institutional racism but because action rarely targets this, little changes.

Mechanisms

Before we go further we will need to explain how such social forces change individual health and rates of illness in a community. There are a number of hypotheses which aim to explain how racism causes illness.

The fundamental-cause hypothesis links differences in health between groups to money, power, prestige and social connections which strongly influence people's ability to avoid risks and minimise the consequences of any disease that emerges. Institutional racism and differential access to services are organisational expressions of the fundamental social-cause hypothesis. The increased exposure of ethnic minorities in the USA to carcinogens, toxins, poor quality housing, poor quality food, pollution and infectious agents may all increase their rates of illness. Income inequality may lead to poor health in a number of ways such as individual frustration, under-investment in human capital or under-investment in social capital. Political marginalisation and segregation allow disparities to persist as the will and the impetus to produce effective remediation may be lacking.

Despite the multitude of possible mechanisms, most research on mechanisms through which social factors influence health has concentrated on 'stress'.

Stress

The physiology of stress is complex. Stress is a neuro-endocrine reaction involving multiple systems including the adrenomedullary hormonal system, the sympathetic and parasympathetic nervous systems and the hypothalamic-pituitary-adrenal axis. As well as the direct neuro-endocrine 'stress' effects, other neurotransmitter systems are affected.

Severe or recurrent stress may lead to long-term changes in neuro-endocrine modulation systems which may make the body more sensitive to stress and make other neuro-endocrine pathways more sensitive. Prolonged stress leads to a number of physiological changes which produce ill health. There are documented effects on the immune systems, cardiovascular systems, renal system and the brain.

The perception of threat and the level of control are important in the production of stress. Both are influenced by personality, history, culture, social buffers, the media, the place of the individual in the social strata and the type of threat.

Control may be exerted by action to get rid of the stressor or by adaptation. Adaptive responses may decrease stress in the short term but may lead to harm in the long term.

Stress can produce a number of behavioural changes including drinking alcohol and smoking, and these behaviours can have effects on the individual and society. Stress is important in defining self-efficacy, self-worth and the ability of families and communities to act cohesively. Current biomedical reductionist theories rarely acknowledge that stress is more than an individual response with a physiological correlate. The community-level effects argue for hypotheses in which stress is conceptualised as an ecological variable.

Social disorganisation

Explanations of geographical differences or increases in mental health often use the disorganisation model. Here bonds are broken between individuals and their societal guy ropes; there is stress, anxiety and social pathology.

Change and adaptation can make a society vulnerable to crisis because cultural guidelines for coping do not work, so new types of behaviour are tried. New behaviour clashes with old culture and undermines the stability of culture, and change defines the culture as opposed to the culture defining itself. Because society is in flux it is difficult to produce consensus and trust; this leads to socio-cultural flux and decreased social cohesion/efficacy.

Social disorder has proved difficult to study. There may well be disorganisation as a result of low socio-economic status in inner-city minority areas in the USA with little residential stability, but there are also co-existent high levels of sub-cultural order. Inner-city African-American women are resilient and resourceful in getting what they need for their families.

Some have argued that anomie may be the cause of high rates of illness and mental illness. Anomie and disorganisation may co-exist and be part of a complex long-term process acting on different families at different timescales with different end-points.

However, not all the associations can or should be explained at an individual, or even family, level and there are pitfalls in doing so. Offering mechanisms based on the individual to explain group effects is called the ecological fallacy. For instance, whether one gets an infection depends not only on the individual's susceptibility but also on herd immunity – the level of susceptibility in the general community and the amount of disease that is therefore present in the general community. There are links between the two but they do not explain each other. They have different mechanisms of action and work at different levels.

Complexity

There are links between macro-social, community and individual level variables. Culture and community can be a response to macro-social pressures as can the size of a family and the nature of family ties. Hence, social support, an important buffer to the effects of macro-social forces such as planned levels of unemployment, will depend on the history of the effects of such forces on the culture and the community. The level of social support is likely to be low in an inner-city community in which re-structuring of the labour market and decreases in fire surveillance and sanitation have led to urban decay and highly mobile populations. But the levels of resilience to outside pressures may be high in communities where there is a history of oppression.

When investigating links between illness and societal factors, researchers have often taken a uni-directional approach and tried to elucidate causal mechanisms, but it is likely that there are a multitude of links between factors which may not be causal, and if there is causality there is also reverse causality.

There are important caveats to this work. More often than not, work has been cross-sectional, though most adult diseases have long courses of development. Most prevalent environmental hazards such as tobacco smoke and atmospheric pollution take decades to exert their effects. Also, the fine social distribution of mortality argues for cumulative effects with a dose response relationship rather than short-term biological or socio-economic factors.

There is often not a sharp health divide but differences in risk, and these seem to be cumulative or additive. Short-term changes can be important especially for the young – who die from violence, become addicted to drugs or are victims of accidents – but mostly one has to think of long-term social and psychological hazards. This is important in that it makes social processes difficult to measure adequately. An understanding of lifetime trajectories is important.

For instance: poor kids are more likely to fail at school, find poor work, experience early unemployment and produce lower birth-weight babies. Low birth-weight babies are more likely to have problems during childhood and an increased risk of chronic disease in middle-aged life. These trajectories are amplified by social strata and macro-political forces. And in concert they help to shape the social and psychological environment in which people live. Such lifespan effects call for long-term research and solutions.

Conclusion

Racism demonstrates the variety of levels at which social forces work to produce disparities in health between groups of people, and how these different effects are linked. Segregation and political marginalisation compound the effects of fundamental social forces such as power and money.

Discriminatory social policies have an impact on the individual, the community and on health. Poorer access to education decreases the number of ethnic minority physicians and so their views are not reflected in dominant culture illness models, in research or in preventive strategies. Poorer health and poorer public health policy may be a consequence of this marginalisation.

Political and economic marginalisation have direct effects on the physical and social environment but may also lead to frustration and alternative economies and lifestyles. Alternative lifestyles may produce new health hazards themselves or through the response of the dominant community to them – such as a crackdown on drugs, which may undermine communities by incarcerating large numbers of their youth.

The perception of self and the perception of community may affect an individual's self-esteem, and their ability to live a healthy lifestyle and to support others in a health-promoting life-style.

The experience of ethnic minority groups is varied. For some, the impact of racism on their mental health may be minimal but for those in more marginalised communities, social factors may be of the utmost importance to their physical and mental well-being. Racism, through social factors, works at a number of levels, over different time spans, and can have generational effects. Their effects on the individual may have an impact at a family and community level. They may affect available family support, social cohesion and efficacy. The effects on the social environment may increase the chance of experiencing life-events while, at the same time, decreasing the ability of an individual or a community to cope with them. The perception of belonging to a community with low efficacy can lead to low self-esteem for an individual while predicting further political marginalisation by the majority population. Marginalisation can lead to poorer healthcare provision and poorer public health interventions.

The need to do something about community reactions to their marginalised place in society can lead to policies which further undermine those communities and decrease social buffers – as in the case of imprisonment for possession of crack.

The fact that ethnic minority communities and particularly black groups are more likely to experience most of the social forces that have been linked to poorer physical and mental health is due to racism. The variety of social forces involved, their complex inter-relationship and the fact that they may have their effects over years may explain why these factors, though clearly important, are not well researched.

Racism is the root of disparities in health. Its mechanisms may be more easily understandable social factors but looking at these and making cross-sectional associations between them and health indices does not help us understand why they exist. If we are to improve disparities in health we have to conceptualise racism as discriminatory forces that mould both the psychological and physical world of the individual; that have an effect on the structure and functioning of cultures, communities and States and that have effects in the here and now as well as into the future. It is this complexity with which we will need to grapple if we are not to fall into the trap of trying to cure the results of racism rather than racism itself.

Chapter 8

Scientific Racism

Kamaldeep Bhui

History shows that scientific endeavour, although promoted as a noble activity, has perpetuated racist thought and action to damage non-white minorities for generations. This chapter looks at some of the works that might be considered racist, and explores why scientists continue blindly to ignore their responsibilities to all peoples while lending respectability to racist thought and action.

Making sense of prejudice and racism

Scientific attempts to understand racial prejudice and racist ideology have focused on notions of illness or pathology or faulty reasoning of the racialist (see Chapter 2). Romantic notions of ridding society of such evils to yield a more just society neglect the pernicious and complex nature of prejudicial beliefs which survive at all expenses and in the form of layered psychological compromise formations. Racism has a history which, on occasions, aligns with historical developments in science.

'Who is not racist in psychology?' (Howitt and Owusu-Bempah 1994). These authors promulgate the view that psychology and, by inference, psychiatry and other disciplines or professions, were crystallised in the very fabric of racist societies and, therefore, they reflect racist ideologies in their theories of mind, science, relationships and in a revered body of knowledge known as 'research'. Research is regarded as the epitome of objective fact-finding, but usually this is without recourse to a consideration of epistemology. Thus Howitt and Owusu-Bempah assert:

it is a white view of racism serving white people's purposes...academic discussions of race have frequently been incorporated into sweeping and draconian social policies which serve white people's interests, at the expense of black people.

This has been the emphasis given to much of the research in Britain on mental health. However, this is not an accident but follows in the footsteps of a whole history of scientific endeavour to understand human diversity and difference and learn something of the white person's fascination for the black person. I believe, at a more generic level, this fascination is also about learning something of the *other*, who is separate and different from *self*. This fascination with the other is a tortuous endeavour as it holds many fears and fantasies of the 'aliens'.

Alien: adverse, contrary, conflicting, foreign, inappropriate, incompatible, incongruous, not native, not naturalised, opposed, outlandish, remote, repugnant, separated, strange, unfamiliar, foreigner, newcomer, outsider, stranger. (Collins Thesaurus 1986)

Once psychiatrists were even known as Alienists. The use of the term 'alien' is no coincidence in book titles and sub-titles such as Littlewood and Lipsedge's *Aliens and Alienists* (1989) and Webb and Enstice's *Aliens and Savages* (1998); the 1914 immigration bill was called the British Nationality and Status of Aliens Act, followed in 1920 by the Aliens order (see Skellington 1996). 'Alien' carries the fantasy of extreme unintelligible difference as if from another planet, perhaps dangerous but certainly unknowable, with connotations of disgust.

These unspoken and unthought influences emerge when we are confronted with unfamiliar peoples, and we emphasise the difference rather than notice similarity. In emphasising difference, the other takes on attributes of all that we consider different from ourselves, and this includes parts of self with which we are uncomfortable. Thus, it is easy in scientific endeavour to replicate this process, and to generate a whole host of theoretical 'truths' upon which social behaviour pivots. In the realms of mental illness and psychiatry, a subject founded on subjective impression, conversation and perceptual distortions, the dangers of over-determined scientific theory are even more marked.

Suman Fernando has spent many hours writing and talking on racism and its endemic influence in psychiatry (Fernando 1988, 1991, 1996). I discuss the evidence for this at a later stage, but Fernando's volumes are renowned for their public accessibility and frank discussion. They are given much sharper criticism from academics who, for better or worse, still determine what is considered rational and digestible within the realms of the psychiatric profession. This criticism, of course, does not take on a crude visible form, but a more refined balletic quality, which enacts the sense of indignity felt by any good soul doing their best and accused of some monstrous act. These feelings and motivators are often not readily available for inspection. When we humans, black and white and others, encounter accusation of wrong-doing, immorality, or dreadful demeaning treatment of others because of their skin colour, it is a bitter pill to swallow. It is as if the individual who feels accused, or perceives racist accusation, is the victim of an injustice. However, the messengers of the disturbing message, the people who bring to light the hidden racism, themselves come under attack. The form of defence taken by the accused appears to be rage, or frank denial, or indeed an absence of acknowledgement that their words might be hurtful and emotionally damaging. Richard Norton-Taylor's (1999) edited transcripts of the Stephen Lawrence enquiry demonstrate this. Jamie Acourt is asked if the video in which he is seen using racist language was shocking to him (p.137). The answer is simply 'no, I ain't shocked, it's nothing to do with me.' Yet the language, which I do not reproduce here, clearly reflects a deep hatred which manifests as a talk of cutting, mutilating, wounding and killing, and insufferable dehumanisation of people simply because their skin colour is different. An alternative response is the reasoned one which denies that there is a problem beyond the individual. So Police Commissioner Condon's initial refusal to accept the possibility of institutionalised racism reflected the assumption that racism is about conscious prejudice and hatred, and institutional, to him, simply means it exists throughout an organisation. This blindness to a daily social reality for ethnic minorities is astonishing for a leader in a public service.

Racism is pretty much endemic to the human condition, however, where racism pervades public institutions, and where these institutions are invested with power then there is potential for systematic bias in the way particular non-represented groups are handled by these institutions. The MacPherson report attempted to define institutionalised racism to overcome this hurdle, yet it is clear that an acceptance of this appears, to those in the police service, to be an accusation of blatant hatred. The subtlety of the point, that racism is a human failing that requires careful thought, escapes. Police officers surely felt damaged by the publicity, but the whole notion that racism is invisible and can survive conscious good will seems implausible to many, such that it is denied.

Racism is not a reasonable business, and the strong primitive urges to leap to one's defence or ridicule someone's comments as being less that scientific may appear to be reasonable to the untrained eye, but they serve to silence and sustain a status quo. In such a climate, one can imagine how racist ideology flourishes. The revelation of new information, or new radically different ways of thinking have never been a welcome activity among intellectuals. On Charles Darwin's *The Origin of Species*:

> The origin is the most important book of the last century…it became a popular sensation and transformed attitudes to God, and to the human race, that it was invoked as a justification by Capitalists, Communists and National Socialists, and that its author was once described as the most dangerous man… (Burrow 1968)

Burrow argued that Darwin's writing would destroy the myth of racists, that we could be different and belong to the same species, and yet the popular evolutionary line taken by racist ideology readily draws on Darwin's revolutionary scientific ideas to justify its preconceived notions of difference and hierarchy. Thomas Malthus (1766–1834) is considered as the founding father of scientific racism (Chase 1977) when he advocated the extermination of the poor, the sick, and the 'unfit'. Indeed he argued it to be against the laws of God to interfere with poverty (Howitt and Owusu-Bempah 1994). Similarly Herbert Spencer (1820–1903), Edward Thorndike (1874–1949), Arthur Jenson (1923–) and Eysenck (1916–) (*ibid.*, p.5) have all played in the familiar area of searching for scientific truths – oblivious, it seems, of the dehumanising impact this has on the poor, and the victims of the scientists' intellectual pursuits. It is as if intellectuals, by virtue of their intellect, deem themselves to be the fittest and, therefore, suitable to make history and naturalise their findings as if they were objective truths. This echoes Gramsci's Marxist interpretations of the ruling classes that gave rise to the concept of 'hegemony', that a select group of intellectuals or the bourgeoisie dominate the political, economic sphere as well as the social conscience of society (see Cashmore 1988, p.157). Eminent intellectuals believe they have the right to proclaim on the future well-being and very existence of others on the basis of experiments which they revere with an omnipotent fantasy of moral truth.

Marek Kohn (1996), in his book called *The Race Gallery*, suggests that anti-racist science is not nearly as ready to meet this intellectual challenge as it likes to make out. It will not be ready unless it treats modern race galleries (collections of art, artefacts and scientific displays that illustrate racial difference and invest it with hierarchical meaning, which are to be found across the western world) with the seriousness they deserve.

Howitt and Owusu-Bempah (1994) explore these ideas in detail; they conclude that scientific thought is far from objective; it takes place in a particular era, with a particular sensibility of the rights and wrongs of the world. When science, having grasped the moral high ground, argues for some natural justice in sustaining a social order as if it fulfils some pre-ordained destiny (see Eysenck 1975), then it becomes not dissimilar from the worst of religious doctrine that justifies intolerance and no acknowledgement of common humanity. Science is not a passport to neutrality, and these ideas of race, difference and threat are so powerful that responses akin to self-preservative actions appear inexorable and easily obscured if one is preoccupied by behaving in accord with the very conventions that limit truly free thought, which is the business of science. And so Hitler's own ideas about saving the 'superior races' were rationalised and marketed so as to become common knowledge and action, without there being a common and prominent capacity for the ideology to be challenged. In many countries of the world, ethnic cleansing and race riots are promoted with 'crusade'-like motivation to destroy the other. Race, ethnicity, religion and national status are mobilised to subserve the desire to dominate and subjugate. The racialisation of the conflict not only adds a repugnant quality to the conflict, but it also serves to armour the perpetrators emotionally, as it gives them an illusory cause and illusory channel through which their imagined future and glorious past are brought a little closer. It gives them the experience of triumphant victory over the imagined unidentified dread so readily located in effective carriers of 'otherness'. Racism finds ever-new strategies to justify racial inequality.

Biological doctrines are expressions of racist views disguised as critiques of defects and pathologies in the social organisation of black communities and families (UNESCO 1967). The psychological process, the emotional interplay and the illusions necessary to sustain racist ideologies are subjects of interest but are neglected. It is, after all, in the emotional, the personal and private arenas of self-esteem and entitlement that racism has its most pernicious effect.

Paradoxically, much of the research into prejudice and racism has tried to do the opposite, that is, to seek some objective reason for prejudice and, in so doing, it promotes and develops the very methodologies from which racist ideologies are justified. A closed system of enquiry ensues and supports its basic premises. Some statistical techniques and methods of analysis were developed especially to study the racial differences in intelligence (Howitt and Owusu-Bempah 1994). Thus, the search for racial difference has been couched in methodologies designed specifically for that pursuit, rather than being located in any independent body of thought.

Theories of racism are advanced to attempt explanation of a diversity of historical moments and practices under a single over-arching principle deploying logic and extrapolation. The events of Nazi Germany, eugenic science, the nationalism evident in Europe recently, and other forms of prejudice such as sexism and homophobia are deconstructed in order to find common elements with which a rational mind can come to understand how racist beliefs and practice can survive, and survive successfully, despite antipathy to common notions of humanity, dignity and justice. Race does not stand on equal footing with gender, or age. Race is an imagined construct, which is either defined in scientific endeavour (often poorly) or is assigned by delicate social negotiations in real-life experiences. But where hegemonic process raises race to a more important role in consciousness, invested with faulty generalisations, then racial discourse takes on a more pernicious role in sustaining legitimised disadvantage.

Research and scientific racism

Genetic theories about human populations emerged initially because of the relentless search for racial differences in intelligence, height, cranial cavity, emotional life, morality, sexuality (see Fernando 1988, 1991; Littlewood 1993; Kohn 1996; see Chapter 4 and Chapter 9). One might, of course, relegate prejudicial research to the efforts of academics attempting to discover the 'true' properties of human ability and that naively these 'great minds of civilisation' believed the 'truth', if a racist one must be known and shared. Alas, such findings in science have, for generations, been portrayed as realities beyond question. Indeed, some argue that science supersedes religion in managing our morality and in dealing with uncertainty in an increasingly secular world. Can science be interrogated on its propagation of racist ideologies? An appraisal of scientific discovery and race soon highlights that scientific thought originates in humankind, and the culprit is not some charitable noble activity for the good of all humanity, but specific individuals who appear to show no humility or reverence when dealing with the generation of knowledge that potentially humiliates, hurts and oppresses people. Researchers consider some people sufficiently different as to warrant the pursuit of theories of inferiority. If one thing is clear from our histories, in whichever continent one chooses to locate our studies, there are scientists, politicians, members of the public and great world leaders who propagate racial hatreds, and justify racial persecutions.

Fernando (1991) outlines three distinct origins of these views about ethnic minorities:

1. In the 18th century, Rosseau's concept of the 'noble savage' gained popularity. Savages were considered to be free of the civilising influence of the developed worlds, and were thus considered to be spared mental illnesses as these were thought to be products of a higher developmental level of mind. These theories gained favour with Daniel Tuke in the UK, Esquirol in France, and Benjamin Rush in the USA.

2. Aubrey Lewis drew attention to a prevailing view that freedom of mental illness was considered to arise because of freedom from 'cultures' of the developed world.

3. Finally, epidemiological studies in the USA were used to justify slavery as a state in which blacks were free of worry and mental illness, but 'they become prey to madness when set free' (Thomas and Sillen 1992). At this stage, preoccupations with race and colour precluded any thought about cultures, as cultures could only become of relevance if the slave could be 'seen' to be more similar to white American society than was 'permissible' by the predominant American consciousness. In Lewis's terms (1976), by appropriating the term 'race' they seek to invest these cultural stereotypes with a unique finality and metaphysical value, implying that culturally patterned behaviour is genetically determined.

A further example of a scientific racist ideology serving the economic and emotional needs of the powerful are Cartwright's (1851) writings on Dysaesthesia Aethiopis, a condition of the mind that only afflicted free slaves; Drapetomania was described as a condition peculiar to slaves propelling them to run away (Fernando 1991). It was not only the enslaved that suffered exoticisation by oppressive societies. 'Medical pronouncements seem to have articulated coercive measures, serving perhaps more personal justifications rather than any coherent ideology' (Littlewood 1993). Thus, observers continued to be called in as experts of exotic unknown peoples that were fascinating but were also feared. The possibility of developing shared understanding with people of a different race could not be entertained. For example, J.C. Carothers (1953) was asked by the World Health Organization to help with understanding African mental illness. He concluded insanity was rare in 'primitive peoples'. He concluded an absence of particular genes, on the basis that primitives lost these genes through natural selection (warping the time scales required for such an effect), and that there was no place in Africans for the European virtues of self-reliance, personal responsibility and initiative (Carothers 1953). This work was extremely influential and was even quoted by

African psychiatrists as a testament to their own incapacity to think freely and independently.

Racism and anti-racism may only have developed as a body of knowledge, theory and practice to counter moral objections to domination based on technical superiority, armed forces or religious expansions (Littlewood 1993). The colonial legacy has certainly a 'crude bigotry' in language that was used to sustain prejudicial hierarchies among human populations. Scientific investigation appeared to lead the assault, as science took over from the Church and religion as the guardian of truths to which all must adhere (Wilson 1992). Progress, persistently understood as an evolutionary activity in line with Social Darwinism, was sought by all. Thomas and Sillen (1992) were the first to write a textbook devoted to racism and psychiatry. In it, they describe Carl Jung's return from Kenya with the idea that cortical organisation was akin to societal cultural development: 'living with barbaric races exerts a suggestive effect on the laboriously tamed instinct of the White race and tends to pull it down'. Jung has come under a great deal of close scrutiny for generating hypotheses which liken the minds of blacks to those of a child, to be akin to the unconscious, and of Indian minds to be incapable of thought, but only capable of perceiving the thought like a primitive (Jung 1921, 1930). These theories echo a persistent attempt at celebrating the 'innate' intellectual capabilities of the white civilised societies, and re-affirming the degeneracy and helpless state of 'inferior' non-whites, who came to represent earlier stages of white development in a linear evolutionary model. Self-definition arising through a definition of 'not-self' is not uncommon in the history of racist thought. Yet Jung touched on some important and perhaps, to the white majority, unspeakable aspects of the unconscious. Jung identified the disparaging attitudes of whites towards blacks as a function of the shadow in the unconscious terrain of whites, projected onto blacks. This attribute of the unconscious is not, in my view, confined to whites, but actually constitutes the shadow in unconscious life of each human being, and in the collective consciousness of groups. Levy Bruhl's work on collective representations in groups seems to feed this idea (Adams 1996, p.60). Adams (1996), who is more sympathetic to the elephant-traps faced by Jung, explores the world literature, which persistently demonstrates white to be symbolically superior to black, even in black societies (*ibid.*, p.24). This might be a Jungian legacy, but from my own experience of Indian social discourse, it is not uncommon for darker-skinned brides, for example, to be less sought-after than lighter-skinned ones. Yet such an idea may itself be the legacy of generations of colonial rule, and an internalisation of values belonging to those 'perceived' in the colonies to be superior; namely the white rulers. Dalal (1988a, b) raises similar concerns about modern practices in psychotherapy, if Jungian in flavour, as Jung advocates that the modern black is like the prehistoric human, that modern black consciousness is like white unconsciousness, and that is like a white child.

Early pioneers in research conceptualised racism as an individual activity, thus shaping future research efforts to emphasise racists as abnormal from the majority, suggesting they could be identified by questionnaires (Howitt and Owusu-Bempah 1994, p.87). Gordon Allport (1958) promoted such a view, that racism was a faulty attitude and if racists could be shown their faulty assignation of values, then they would cease being racist. This again assumes a singular type of racist, and one who would accept his or her views to be distressing, or a form of belief that might be incorrect. Such presuppositions do not do justice to the diversity of racisms, not only in degree but in kind (Young-Bruhl 1998). If racism is conceptualised as a manifestation of a pathological psychological defensive mechanism (*ibid.*; Sherwood 1966) then distress is absent, as the psychological defensive mechanism serves to exclude from conscious awareness anything that is distressing. One theory is that there are vulnerable spots in individual personality development, and that at times these vulnerabilities led to racialised exchanges of attitude (Sherwood 1966). The emergence of identity confusion in adolescence, and at times of immigration, are regarded as the stimulus to faulty 'projection' of particular attributes into others, and then receiving similar distortions back from them. How do white policemen respond to accusations of racism? What does this do to their development, or should we be preoccupied by the victims only? Sherwood's analysis of cycles of misidentification suggests that the two are linked; that racial misidentifications serve to perpetuate sequential projection which triggers counter-projections. If this is an unconscious activity then the defensive denial of any 'conscious' prejudice is the usual response following any accusation.

Adorno *et al.* (1950) examined prejudice as a function of an authoritarian personality. Adorno identified ethnocentrism as a mediator of racist ideology, perhaps through hegemonic practice. This raised concerns that society itself promoted racist views by facilitating the emergence of particular styles of relating that, although not intended to be prejudiced, were vulnerable to develop into racist practices as expression of this vulnerability. This was a potentially valuable contribution, as the emphasis on societal values addresses the prejudicial attitude in society as a norm. However, there was fierce debate about methodology. These patterns of science challenging any small movement in any direction other than findings consistent with accepted premises, persist into modern-day debates about how to tackle mental health issues (see Chapter 10). Science is not objective, it is value-laden, but rarely do scientists consider the racist potential of research. Science can help us consider the impact of race on mental health, it can even help us explore how racism impairs mental health, but most importantly scientists must ensure that racism does never again masquerade as science.

Chapter 9

Racism in Psychiatry

Paradigm Lost – Paradigm Regained

Dinesh Bhugra and Kamaldeep Bhui

We explore sociological and social-anthropological lessons for thinking about racism and distress. This chapter shifts the focus of the reader's journey to the practical provision of mental health care to black and ethnic groups. Specific treatment modalities and service structures are considered for their cultural competency (reproduced by kind permission of Taylor and Francis from International Review of Psychiatry 11, *2/3, 236–243).*

Introduction

Racism has played an important role in the subjugation of ethnic minorities in certain societies and cultures. Sometimes it has been linked with the historical, social and economic contexts in which ethnic minority groups have survived. In addition, psychiatry has often been seen as a tool of the state, and psychiatrists encouraged to detain people who appear to be a threat to themselves or others – thus being 'saved' from themselves or 'saving' others. In psychiatry, more than in many other disciplines of medicine, 'prejudice' is asserted to explain variations in the management of ethnic minority patients.

Although diverse cultural groups mingle in various social, political and spiritual contexts, for example through trade, migration or conquest, the benefits of any one group's cultural advantage do reach others eventually. However, this passage to equality of opportunity is hard won at many levels of society. Therefore, racism in its functionality, and existence in its entirety, cannot be treated simply from a single theoretical perspective, or from a simple individualistic approach.

Historical and economic contexts are important. The structures of society play an important role in the development and maintenance of racial prejudices and racism in society. All pervasive state regulations that structure social and economic processes have to be taken into account. When comparing psychological and cultural variables across cultures, Bagley and Verma (1979) reported that although personality factors such as neuroticism, psychological rigidity and poor self-esteem were contributing to prejudiced attitudes in Britain and the Netherlands, prejudice was in overall terms much less prevalent in the Netherlands, which the authors attributed to a lack of a cultural tradition of racism in that country. In this chapter, we link individual and group factors that contribute to the emergence and persistence of racism. We then go on to study these in relation to psychiatry and we conclude by identifying the practical, clinical and research implications of racism.

Definitions

Race and the use of this word have multiple meanings and are often emotionally loaded. A distinction between biological and social concepts of race muddles the issue further. Even though racial characteristics should be seen on a continuum, race is defined as a socially defined group for which membership is based on a combination of cultural heritage, historical circumstance and/or the presence of distinguishable physical features such as skin colour. It can be applied to nation states, languages, families, tribes and minorities, and is seen as a phenotypically distinct group. Often, race itself is used as a derogatory term – identifying groups that may be seen as economically or culturally vulnerable.

Racism

Racism is as old as humankind itself. Cicero (100 BC) had advised Atticus not to get slaves from Britain because they were stupid and incapable of learning. Racism can be described as an ideology or belief that helps maintain the status quo and, more specifically, it refers to the belief that one race is superior to other races in significant ways and that the superior race is seen as being entitled, by virtue of its superiority, to dominate other races and to enjoy a share of society's wealth and status. These advantages are related to healthcare, education, employment, wealth and power, hence there is resistance to change society's institutionalised ways of doing things. Rex (1983), while defining racism and race prejudice, suggested that the concepts of race used by biologists have no relevance to the political differences between people and sought to indicate problems of race relations. He proposed three elements:

- That it was necessary, but not a sufficient condition of a race relations situation, that there should be a situation of severe competition, exploitation, coercion or oppression.

- That this situation occurred between groups rather than individuals, with only limited possibilities of mobility from one group to the other.

- That the inter-group structure so produced was rationalised at the ideological level by means of a deterministic theory of human attributes, of which the most important type historically had been based upon biological and genetic theory.

UNESCO, following a meeting of biologists and social scientists, concluded that race as a taxonomic concept is of limited usefulness as a means of classifying human beings, and probably less useful than the more general concept of population. The former term is used to refer to 'groups of mankind showing well-developed and primarily heritable physical differences from other groups' and the latter to refer to 'groups whose members marry other members of the group more frequently than people outside the group' and hence have a relatively limited and distinctive range of genetic characteristics. Rex (1983) summarises their observations as:

- It is agreed that observable human characteristics are, in nearly all cases, the result of biological and environmental factors.

- Various characteristics commonly grouped as racial are, in fact, transmitted either independently or in varying degrees of association.

- All people living today belong to a single species and are derived from a common stock.

- It may not be desirable to deny a particular national group as a race, but rather to affirm that it is not justifiable to attribute cultural characteristics to the effects of genetic inheritance.

- Human evolution has been affected to a unique degree as compared with evolution of other species, by migration and cultural evolution.

As Rex (1983) concludes, taking into account all of the above, the concept of race as used by the biologists has no relevance to the political differences between people.

Types of racism

The persistence of racism in society can be understood at different levels and in different categories. Richardson and Lambert (1985) identified three associated aspects of racism: ideology, practice and social structure. Racism may operate through overt beliefs and actions of the individual (active racism) or through less conscious attitudes in society as a whole, for example, not offering housing, education or care to ethnic groups (aversive racism) (Dolan et al. 1991). The aspect of racial actions taking place, in an 'unwitting' manner, has recently been given credence in the UK by the enquiry into the murder of the teenager Stephen Lawrence. Yet, such an accusation produces not rational thought but narcissistic rage.

Rattansi (1992) argues that racism must be distinguished from racial discrimination. The former is restricted to discourses about grouping human populations into 'races' on the basis of some biological signifier – for example, 'stock' – with each 'race' being regarded as having essential characteristics or a certain essential character (e.g. the 'British' character, or in attributions to races of laziness, rebelliousness or industriousness) and where inferiorisation of some 'races' may or may not be present. Such views may shade off into ethnocentrism – where ethnic groups are defined primarily in cultural terms and are regarded as having essential traits. Nationalism therefore can be seen as a form of ethnocentrism in which cultural groups and their essential characteristics are defined by nationality and cultural attributes of one or more nations are regarded as inherently superior or inferior. Nationalism may also contain racial elements in so far as particular nations may be regarded as deriving from specific racial stocks, and biologically defined communities may be regarded as the prime source of cultural characteristics.

Institutional racism can be defined as enforcement of racism and maintenance by the legal, cultural, religious, educational, economic, political, environmental and military institutions of society – racism then becomes an institutionalised form of (personal) attitude. As Feagin and Sikes (1994) suggest, the majority of whites appear to view racism as 'racism in the head'. The majority of whites, in response to African-Americans, see serious racism as the prejudices and actions of extreme bigots who are not considered to be representative of the white majority. These authors assert that the whites can thus see these attacks of racial discrimination with detachment, which makes it easier for them to deny the reality of much of the racism reported by blacks. Racism, therefore, is a combination of prejudices and discrimination and recurring ways in which white people dominate black people in every major area of the society.

The economies within the capitalist system were political and not national economies and such economies went on to shape the capitalist system. The enslaving of Africans and Asians, and the particular forms of racist ideologies constructed to rationalise such activities were embedded in earlier forms of organisation of labour within European societies. Giddens (1986) argues that the employment of immigrant workers from poorer countries in the affluent societies of western Europe has led to ethnic oppression. The differences in the way in which European and African migrants to the USA were treated have led to differences in assimilation which, according to Feagin and Sikes (1994), reflects the differences experienced by middle-class African-Americans. Such ethnic oppression is not exclusively associated with capitalist systems but in the context of understanding such expressions, historical and economic factors are important. It can be argued that the British efforts to recruit Asian and African-Caribbeans to fill the low-paid menial jobs, and the lure of working for the mother country were nothing less than an over-oppressive act to colonise the minds of the economically disadvantaged.

Racism has been classified into several types – a mixture of prejudice, power and identity. It can be dominative – where hatred is turned into action and the stereotype of racial bigot is met. It could be aversive racism, which accepts the superiority of the white but cannot act on it and avoids conflict by avoiding any kind of action. It can be regressive. Other types of racism that have been identified have included pre-reflecting gut (fear of strangers and need to feel superior to others), post-reflecting gut (rationalisation and justification), cultural (leisure, social customs, manners, religious and moral beliefs), institutional (already discussed above), paternalistic (white majority decide for black) or colour-blind (acceptance of differences is seen as racially divisive). New racism is the variety where as a symbol it is couched in values like individualism in the USA, where affirmative action is objected to, special favours are criticised and ongoing racism is criticised on grounds of present achievements.

Psychiatry is reflecting dominant social values, discriminating these values in the pervasive form of so-called scientific statements and providing an asocial image of human beings which portrays individuals as essentially independent from their socio-historical contexts. Racist experiences of patients affect help-seeking, diagnosis, compliance with treatment and attitudes towards mental illness, psychiatry and the psychiatric profession. They impinge on the clinician's attitudes, the way help is provided, diagnosis and management. It affects society by inducing feelings of rebellion, alienation, poor membership and the need for increased resources.

Institutional levels of racism pertain to 'establishment' which, at a macro level, decides on the values important for society and members of the society. Thus, patterns of language-use including use of grammar and accent, and educational systems which stream pupils, causes misalignment, inculcating feelings of superiority on the basis of some artificial factors. The legal system by virtue of class, upbringing, background and symbolised and invested powers means that the system encourages individuals to set themselves aside. Thus, the police, political systems and financial services form an 'elite' that less familiar ethnic minorities have to negotiate. On an individual level, the notions of racial superiority are then subliminally expressed and sanctioned, although racist thoughts may not translate into racist attitudes and behaviour. Yet, at some level, there occurs a transformation (see Figure 9.1).

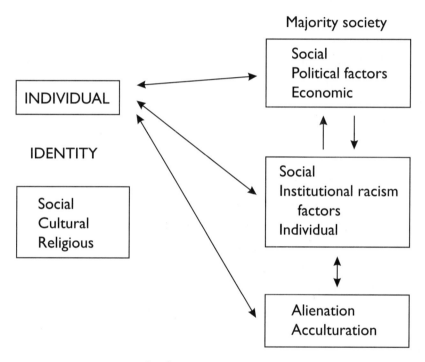

Figure 9.1 Factors associated with racism

Why racism?

Racism in society plays a role in allowing the majority to identify 'the other' who can thus be pitied, looked down upon, hated or marginalised. Such a concept makes the majority society feel pure about itself. This set of 'skills' allows one group to identify factors which give it a sense of superiority and survival. Two caveats must be borne in mind: first, that such differences are often institutionalised and the individuals may not see it as a problem; and second, that such views are not static. Despite prevailing 'social science' approaches that depict people as creatures of their surrounding environment, or as victims of social institutions immediately impinging on them, both emigrants and conquerors have carried their own skills and behaviours – their cultures – to the farthest regions of the planet in the most radically different societies, and these patterns have often persisted for generations or even centuries (Sowell 1994). The concepts of racism often involve the conqueror and the vanquished.

Immigrant workers in all the countries concerned generally share the same basic position: they have the poorest and lowest status in every social sphere, are furthermore highly concentrated in a limited range of occupations and industries and are over-represented in the lowest categories of socio-economic class. They experience great difficulties in obtaining housing which then reflects in serious health problems (Castles and Kosack 1973). This proletariat is also a focus of nationalism, where the employers (or the majority society) tend to control the housing, health, education, legal standing and other institutional aspects of control. The central location of such institutions deals with the majority whereas immigrants, ethnic minorities or 'the other' identified by sexual orientation, gender, skin colour, religious values are on the periphery. The central value system has primary and secondary values and legitimises the existing distribution of roles and rewards to persons possessing the appropriate qualities, which in various ways symbolise degrees of proximity to authority. The central institutional system therefore is legitimised by the central values. Although there may be a sense of consensus in maintaining the central institutional system, this emerges from the majority who have a vested interest in the status quo. There is of course a limit to consensus and it can never be all-embracing. Although Rex (1961) proposes that central values are dictated by central conflict, the balance of power within such conflict does not always shift rapidly. The 'other' is therefore required to maintain a control and balance of power and is associated with keeping the outsider out, just in case he or she becomes a threat from within. While the 'other' is outside, such an individual is far easier to define and identify. Thus, from this necessarily brief discourse, it would appear that if psychiatry is at the periphery of the medical society, the psychiatric patient too is at the periphery. To complicate things even further the ethnic minority mentally ill patient is at the periphery of the mentally ill patients, bearing the weight of double jeopardy.

Ethnic and cultural identity

The word 'identity' is fraught with difficulties – it often means different things, depending on how it is conveyed. It may include the self, religious identity, sexual orientation or occupational identity. Psychologists have long been aware of the highly complex process of identity formation and of the critical role played by race and ethnicity in this process. Early research was grounded on the assumption that out-group orientation as measured by doll preferences and other paradigms was interpretable in terms of psychopathology. At the level of adulthood, outgroup-identification, self-hatred and psychopathology were conceptually merged and interpreted in the historical context of slavery, segregation and the cultural disenfranchisement of the Negro in America (Harris, Blue and Griffith 1994). The self-hatred gave way to pride and positive identity during and after the civil rights movement. Group and individual identity comprise functionally distinct domains within the individual (Cross 1991). Cross (1978) has developed a multi-stage model of identity development that analyses the psychological process of coming to terms with one's racial identity. Racial and ethnic identity is not static and is in a constant state of development and reworking in the adult.

Racism in clinical situations

The impact of racism and its influence on the institutional practice as well as individual diagnostic patterns can be investigated at the one-to-one level in clinical encounters.

- *Misdiagnosis*: Psychiatric diagnostic systems deal with categories which have been developed with Western nosological categories in mind. This means that individual differences get lost in the diagnostic encounter. Although ICD-10 and DSM-IV have both started to take the impact of culture into account, day-to-day interactions may not be affected at all.

Individual diagnostic patterns and impressions of interactions contribute to the therapeutic encounter. Chess, Clark and Thomas (1953) had highlighted the deterministic nature of behaviour within a group membership, thereby reflecting different psychodynamics in individuals' functioning in different situations and in individuals from different cultural backgrounds. At the other extreme, there is often a temptation to make sweeping generalisations concerning culturally-determined differences in behaviour patterns which are not backed up by evidence but are arrived at by apparently rigid preconceptions of the author. The fact that such a discrepancy may reflect lack of ability on the part of the diagnosing physician or clinician to bridge the culture gap is often ignored. Both under-diagnosis and over-diagnosis are often a result of ignorance and are a result of the observer's lack of effort in making any attempt to understand the cultural norms and gaps. The whole concept of diagnosis in psychiatry and its stability has to be looked at again (see Clare 1973 for some of the arguments).

- *Under-diagnosis*: For a long time it was considered likely that if depression existed in Africa and in India it was of a fleeting nature and the stereotype of the noble and happy savage persisted, ignoring the clinical evidence and relying on rather inadequate epidemiological data (see Bhugra 1996 for a review). The psychological conflicts of the Negro group seemed of a more simple, elementary nature, resulting in the less complex type of symptomatology typical of sociopathic behaviour, emotional instability, inadequate personality, simple maladjustment and temperamental unsuitability. The tortuous, intricately structured mechanisms typical of psychoneurosis seemed to be less common. There appeared to be a conspiracy of collective conviction among psychiatrists who, having believed that depression was rare among savages, did not care to look any deeper or anywhere else, relying on epidemiological data collected in psychiatric hospitals rather than from the community. The possibility that this difference may not be a real or significant one but rather a reflection of a lack of rapport and understanding between the two participants in the therapeutic encounter did not appear to occur to the clinician.

- *Culture-bound syndromes:* Culture-bound syndromes are a classical example of Western methods of looking at the esoteric, exotic and the rare, sometimes ignoring the social and cultural contexts altogether. The ongoing debate between Simons (1985) and Kenny (1985) on the concept of *latah* is an excellent example of the divide between the anthropologist and the psychiatrist and between the universalist and the relativist positions. There is also an underlying question about the validity of such syndromes. The whole concept arose out of social anthropological discipline which is blamed on the colonial administration in the UK at least. The exotic and slightly crazy native who had to be sorted out by the colonial master is reflected in the criteria for diagnosis and also legal changes the colonial administrators brought in to deal with these syndromes (e.g. *amok*). The development of these syndromes and the maintenance of such categories is linked with diagnostic environments and has to be seen in that context.

- *Management:* Clinical management in psychiatry reflects that prevailing clinical practice and it can be argued that where there is a pressure to be colour-blind in managing psychiatric conditions, an underlying racist streak exists. Such clinical practices may be encouraged and endorsed by the establishment.

  - *Medication:* There is plenty of clinical evidence to suggest that people from ethnic minorities are often given higher doses of medication without clear indicators and also for longer periods (see Bhugra and Bhui 1997b for a review). Not only are the ethnic minorities more likely to be treated compulsorily, they are also more likely to be given ECT and higher doses of neuroleptics, minor tranquillisers and anti-depressants. Limited research data is available on pharmacokinetics and pharmacodynamics of these drugs in ethnic minority groups.

- ○ *Psychoanalysis:* Freud developed his theories of psychoanalysis in 19th-century Vienna and, although universally accepted, adopted and applauded, they remain tied to the culture of a specific period. Psychoanalysis itself has been branded racist on the grounds that some analysts have adapted it blindly for application to other cultures and groups ignoring the advice of many authors including Chess *et al.* (1953) who maintain that unless the social milieu in which the patient functions is understood and given adequate consideration, significant errors in psychiatric management and prognostic factors will occur.

- ○ *Psychotherapies:* Patients from ethnic minorities are frequently not offered counselling or psychotherapy on the premise that such individuals are not psychologically sophisticated or psychologically minded. Therein lies another fallacy, because psychological concepts practised and taught in the West are very culture-bound and the indigenous psychologies and psychological interventions are ignored. There is plenty of clinical evidence to suggest that in spite of language barriers, group therapy works in ethnic minorities and with appropriate modifications family therapy can be undertaken successfully (Bhugra and Bhui 1998).

The clinical management of ethnic minorities' healthcare needs is in the context of social, economic, political and healthcare systems and the trends that lead to application of the standard psychiatric criteria for diagnosis, treatment and prognosis. We have not discussed problems associated with psychological testing and the decisive influence of cultural and environmental factors in determining test results and their interpretation. The concepts of underlying personality also vary across cultures, and personality itself is not a static phenomenon and needs to be assessed accordingly.

Research and racism

There is often evidence in research publications of the underlying streak of racism. The individual researchers do not often set out to be racist but owing to naivety and ignorance, the findings can be misinterpreted.

- *Findings*: One of the commonest errors is the interpretation of findings which are often seen as a result of academic research with little thought paid to the consequences of the findings – how the community would respond to these – e.g. if schizophrenia is found to be high in one group, the media and other groups may see it as a pathology and highlight it. On the other hand, the community may well see it as a result of poor social conditions. In an ideal world, both these interpretations need to find a place in any report.

- *Interpretations*: As mentioned earlier, interpretation of the data is one of the problems but it is not only simple reading of the data, it is also essential that the implications of the data are discussed before proceeding with publication. These need to be discussed with the community, community leaders, researchers from the same ethnic background and other interested parties. Second, the interpretations may need to be put into context – many papers presented earlier in this century were in the social context (and prejudices) of that time but nowhere was it suggested that this was the case.

- *Service implications*: Any kind of clinical research has to be linked very closely with provision of service. If, after repeated studies, the results are ignored by health authorities, trusts and primary care providers, the community's perceptions of the racist establishment are confirmed, and not only could they withdraw their support and resent researchers and clinicians, they are also less likely to cooperate with the researchers simply because there are no tangible observable changes at the end of it. Certainly, for clinical research with ethnic minorities, the clinician must be absolutely certain of the service implications of the research, which must be incorporated in the research planning.

Practical implications of racism

...for the society

Here the focus may well be on relationships between different groups of people and on social categorisation and the cognitive processes, which affect social categorisation and the cognitive consequences of group divisions. As noted earlier, stereotyping of individuals confirms for the observer a lazy way of not dealing with diversity and individual differences. Such a process of simple and basic pigeon-holing also allows individuals to ignore racism at an individual level and racism therefore becomes a part of the limitations of rational mental organisation and ignores emotional, motivational and ideological factors altogether. Thus, in a way, individual observers get away from their responsibility and thereby consolidate institutional racism. Stereotypes incorporate physical or behavioural traits that are attributed to the unfamiliar social group. Those who don't fit the stereotype are exceptions and are even more threatening. Society finds ways of dealing with the threat or making it less immediate.

...for the patient

If the patients are buried heavily with the load of society's perceptions and behaviour on racist lines then not only are their significant others being affected but also their ideas, beliefs, and values on the one side and materials and objects on the other.

These interconnecting features are affected by various social, establishment and political systems, and both the individual and social cognitions contribute to this interaction. The impact of racism is not static. Although it is recurrent, patients may forget it and may develop features of post-traumatic stress disorder. The patients' sets of assumptions, strategies and questions about behaviours meted out to them are crucial in making any interaction – therapeutic or other – possible (see figure 9.2).

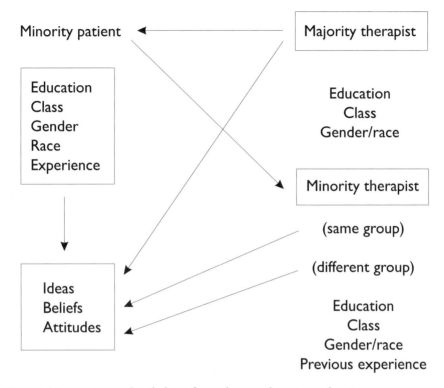

Figure 9.2 Interactions and underlying factors between therapists and patients

…for the clinician

As noted earlier, the clinician's experiences and specialist interest will affect racism and vice versa. The dimensions of institutional racism do produce an impact on the clinician and the clinical practice. There are both implicit and explicit aspects of institutionalised racism. The implicit aspects may be absorbed in the medical school or specialist training and explicit aspects reflect the structural aspects. When confronted with crises in black–white relations most white psychiatrists tend to focus on the helping role that they can play in resolving these conflicts for other organisations rather than looking closely at the ways that psychiatry has perpetuated myths of black inferiority (Sabshin, Diesenhaus and Wilkerson 1970). Under these circumstances the clinician may not have realistic concerns. Black patients have been stereotyped. Institutional racism has been linked with individual clinicians' blind spots, stereotype images and reactive guilt as well as unconscious prejudice. For a long time, a lack of clinical data was seen as a reflection of the institutionalised racism, but the relationship of inappropriate research and inadequate interpretation continues to confirm these processes (of institutionalised racism). A lack of appropriate services affects the patient and the clinician alike. The pathways into care for ethnic minorities may thus be blocked. As Sabshin *et al.* (1970, p.787) observed, 'unfortunately, greater attention has been paid by white psychiatrists to extending mythical definitions of black psychopathology than to providing psychiatric services for actual black patients'. Psychiatrisation or medicalisation of social issues for ethnic minorities does contribute to clinicians' behaviour, which may be inappropriate.

Models of management

The first step in attempting to deal with racism is to recognise its existence and then develop models of organisational management, which will include ways and means of dealing with individual stereotypes and encourage community and clinicians to work together. Some of the recommendations are listed in the box below. The underlying desire to scapegoat individuals must be addressed.

Lock (1993) suggests that race be seen as a politically motivated category which allows for an inherent racial difference and thereby reinforces a continuing ghettoisation of ethnic groups. Individual biology needs to be correlated with population biology. Useful generalisations are possible, some of which may well assist in clinical practice (e.g. in remembering that pharmacodynamics and pharmacokinetics may well differ across ethnic groups). Quantitative biological differences need to be linked with qualitative, culturally constructed categories of race (Lock 1993). On the other hand, recognition of an ongoing dialectic between culture and biology in which both are recognised as fluid entities will contribute to dealing with individual as well as institutionalised racism. Wade (1993) argues that once racism is embedded within the structures of society, the prejudice of individuals is no longer the main problem.

Recommendations for change

1. Organisations take the lead

2. Understand social and individual racism

3. Set up local groups to deal with research and clinical services

4. Suggest means of eliminating stereotypes

5. Encourage equal opportunities

6. Clinicians must provide leadership

7. Clinicians report successes and failures of their services

8. Researchers report successes and failures of their projects and interpret data in discussion with the community

9. Clinicians made aware if their everyday practices perpetuate institutional racism

10. Clinicians to sanction and support efforts to provide culturally appropriate services.

Three psychological approaches – individual, inter-personal and inter-group – need to be understood and developed in order to deal with racism. There is obviously a likelihood that on an individual level personality differences (such as an authoritarian personality) may contribute to individualised racism. The inter-personal approach will deal with what goes on within social groupings and an individual's links with other members is related to the in-group identity. Such an approach attempts to discover the extent to which people conform to the dominant values of a particular social situation. Such a management model therefore can deal with intra-group and individual as well as inter-group situations (where relationships between social groups play an important role).

Thus, social psychological explanations of prejudice and conflict sensitise clinicians and patients alike to the evils of racism and to a certain extent ignore the social context such as culture, social and economic factors and the historical background. Therefore, a clinician planning to set up management of clinical situations in ethnic minorities also has the influence, but he or she has to put all the above-mentioned factors into an appropriate context.

Conclusions

Institutional and individual racism are a result of three levels or approaches – individual, intra-group and inter-group. The experiences that a patient brings along to the clinical encounter have to be seen in a historical and macro-economic as well as social context. Training for clinicians has to consider aspects of both institutional and individual racism so that clinicians are able to recognise the impact of such phenomena and deal with them appropriately. The emphasis on biological race needs to be shifted on to qualitative aspects of individual's functioning and the therapeutic encounter must take broader factors into account.

Chapter 10

Please Don't Let Me Be Misunderstood

Importance of Acknowledging Racial and Cultural Differences

Xavier Coll

In this chapter Dr Coll gives some vivid and moving accounts of misidentifications and their impact on vulnerable children and adults. The tenacity with which such complexity is unravelled is engaging, but the effect of humankind's imperfect ways of relating through race becomes very clear.

> Long before Horrett Campbell was arrested, long before his description or picture was circulated, I guessed he would be black… Campbell set about a group of toddlers with a 2 ft. machete because he thought they were 'little devils'. He heard their voices taunting him calling him 'nigger'. (Victor 1996)

The objectives of this chapter are:

1.   to clarify the concepts of culture and race

2.   to explore some of the dynamics of cultural differences and racism in clinical work

3.   to illustrate (using vignettes and clinical narratives) that race and culture often play a significant role in any psychotherapeutic relationship.

The word 'ethnology' refers us back to the science of race, and traditionally the description of the superficial physical characteristics, the ways of
life, and modes of thought, of the distinctive types of man (New Caxton
Encyclopaedia 1977). The original idea of a 'race' was nearer to that of a
nation than to a biological unit or complex (Coll 1998). Culture, defined
as a system of beliefs, values and behavioural patterns, plays an important
role in psychotherapy. Culture, a concept established by Edward Tylor,
who took the term from German social thinkers in his famous definition
'Culture (or civilisation)...is that complex whole which includes knowledge, belief, art, custom, and other capabilities and habits acquired by man
as a member of society', was developed mainly by anthropologists and
ethnologists, but used and experienced by all of us (The New Caxton
Encyclopaedia 1977).

Racism can be understood as an inability to accept and acknowledge
differences of race. It might involve the treatment of some people as
inferior because they belong to a particular race, and it is usually used to
demonstrate disapproval. Where racism is present, there is an attempt to
control and dominate the object that is felt to be different and separate.

Definitions of racism tend to centre around three elements: social
attention to 'racial' (phenotypic and observable) differences among individuals as members of distinct groups; belief systems concerning characteristic inferiority or superiority associated with group membership; and
patterns of behaviour that differentially affect the esteem, social opportunities and life chances of members of racial groups as a function of those
belief systems (Jones 1997; van den Berghe 1967). Jones (1997) has discussed racism on individual, institutional and cultural levels, reflecting
many ways in which racism is perpetrated, transmitted and maintained.
Whereas racism connotes a disturbance in human relationships that leads
to differentially negative outcomes for its victims (and ultimately for its
perpetrators), mental health is concerned with appropriate and effective
adjustment to social reality (Rollock and Gordon 2000).

Racism can be overt or covert, intentional or unintentional (Ridley
1995), and is often intertwined with other processes such as
class/economic disparity, sexism and heterosexism. Racism can engender
in its victims a number of powerful physical and emotional consequences,

of which mental health practitioners must become intimately aware and which they must be comfortable in addressing with their patients (Ring, 2000).

On writing about violence and trying to make sense of it as a public health problem one might be misled into thinking that England probably has more violent, drunken and racist hooligans than other countries because English society celebrates violence, indulges drunkenness, and is racist (see for example BMJ Editor 2000). However, these hooligans are probably not a totally alien or different population, but are more likely to represent the tail end of a normal distribution. It is harder to accept this than to locate their hatred under a deviancy label, separating them from the rest of society.

Racism can traumatise, hurt, humiliate, enrage and confuse, and ultimately prevent optimal growth and functioning of individuals and communities. Despite progress on various indices of equality, racism-related occurrences continue. These include racially motivated hate crimes; political activities suggestive of anti-immigrant sentiments; backlash related to racial equity efforts; and the free expression of racial intolerance, hostility and violence on our streets and the Internet. All of this suggests that racism is 'alive and sick' in our neighbourhoods, institutions and consciousness (Harrell 2000).

Over the past half-century, a great deal of research has been conducted to help explain the personality and attitudinal structures of people who practise racist behaviour. It is safe to say that if members of non-dominant groups could do so, they would choose not to experience the social and psychological manifestations of racism. Thus, racism may be characterised as unsolicited and unwarranted violence, whether physical or mental; covert or overt; transpiring within individuals, institutions, or cultural transactions (Dobbins and Skillings 2000). Social scientists have tended to view racism as an artefact of social forces and structures, and clinicians have generally circumvented diagnostic consideration of overt racism expressions, in much the same way that they might work around a client's political views or religious affiliations (i.e. as relevant only if it is the explicit focus of investigation).

It is the thesis of Dobbins and Skillings that racism is maintained in members of the dominant culture as a result of their becoming addicted to the exercise of power, i.e. having relatively unrestricted access to 'doing it our way' (Dobbins and Skillings 2000). At the same time, projection of blame helps to maintain a system of denial. Another type of defence used to maintain denial in racism is rationalisation. To rationalise is to ascribe (one's acts, opinions, etc.) to causes that superficially seem reasonable and valid but that actually are unrelated to the true reasons. Grandiosity, another defence that serves denial, tends to go hand in hand with a sense of entitlement. Finally, a fourth way that denial can be maintained is through selective comparison.

Ideas of white supremacy form part of the fabric of many societies, and play a part in the way that white people relate to non-white people. The working through of issues of racism seems to be relatively unimportant for trainees in the different mental health disciplines. I believe it has proved difficult for them to deal with this issue, perhaps because trainees and supervisors alike have little awareness of the significance of race and racism in the therapeutic process.

Psychotherapy is about human relationships, having also a component of foreignness, where both patients and therapists bring with them their own prejudices from their respective cultures. Foreigners, in particular, have to negotiate themselves through the maze of covert and even overt prejudices and discriminations. The experience of these prejudices, which may be real or imagined (via projection or projective identification), leads to a difficulty in assessing the situation realistically. The ability to contain and make sense of these feelings is therefore essential to rational functioning. Unlike the external world, the prejudices of patients have to be explored as they might be the very defences that prevent them from benefiting from treatment.

The persistence and virulence of racism in our society has recently encouraged health professionals and public commentators alike to suggest that it be identified as a clinical disorder, a pathological syndrome that is, like other diseases, diagnosable and treatable (Pouissant 1999; Dobbins and Skillings 2000). The conception of racism as disease is based on four assumptions. First of all, racism is assumed to be a matter of misperception.

Second, since racism is constructed as ideological activity, it is assumed to be a hold-over from slavery. The third assumption is that, since racism is an anomaly, it is not normal. That is, a deviant and abnormal state. Thus, it meets the specifications of any medical-dictionary definition of illness. The fourth assumption is that this particular disease takes the form of an addiction to believing that the standard and style of living that is enjoyed by 'successful' people is due exclusively to their individual efforts. The problem with these assumptions is that they are not supported by empirical evidence (Wellman 2000).

Unfortunately, there are few data to support the proposition that racism is deviant. There is much to suggest that racist beliefs are normal, routine and acceptable in our developed society, that racist practices are culturally sanctioned, as well as economically and politically profitable (Morrison 1992).

Managing complicated transactions

Ms A was a 35-year-old single woman with a long history of anorexia nervosa, who attended an outpatient clinic to see a young non-British-born psychiatric trainee. Initially, things were going well, good therapeutic alliance, good rapport, and good attendance. 'You are doing well,' the supervisor said. After five months of seeing the trainee on a two-weekly basis, the frequency of the meetings was spread out. The foreign trainee began to hear a rumour that Ms A no longer wanted to see him. Interestingly enough, the pathways that this information follows can be rather variable. It might travel from the receptionist to the consultant, via a letter (often written by the client and signed by a submissive boyfriend, mother, or father), a caring occupational therapist, a colluding secretary, or even a multi-functional domestic. Sure enough, two weeks later, the consultant informed the trainee that Ms A no longer wanted to see him because she could not understand him. By then, the trainee was probably feeling rather vulnerable, beginning to doubt his abilities, with the situation being both distressing for him and detrimental to his other patients. It is therefore important to understand what happened. Clearly, there was more than one possible reading. First, the more concrete interpretation:

'She does not understand the trainee because his English is not good enough to be a psychiatrist in England.' While possible, this is highly unlikely as he had already been working with this client for several months, and is understood by other patients and colleagues. Why, in these situations, do only the complaints seem to count? Second, a more likely hypothesis is that this complaint is an expression of the client feeling confused and misunderstood. The foreign therapist becomes the perfect recipient of anger, so that 'I don't want to know' and 'it is painful', are easily translated into 'I cannot understand him.' The part of the patient that does not feel understood can easily be projected onto the therapist. In this instance, the consultant responded appropriately by offering a place and a time to talk. Both the trainee and Ms A benefited from this. Once she was aware that she was making the foreign doctor a scapegoat, it was possible to work through these feelings, and Ms A managed to move on, while the trainee felt understood and supported.

Racial transference amongst non-racists

A middle-aged white civil servant who prided himself on being racially aware and whose work brings him in constant contact with members of the African-Caribbean community, was referred to an Asian therapist for treatment. Mr B felt that the therapist was just as racially aware and open-minded as he was, and that the obvious racial difference between them was not an issue. He was having difficulties in his relationship with his girlfriend, as well as feeling low, tense and anxious. Coming to the foreign and non-white therapist for treatment gave him a sense of validity, and reinforced his denial of any racial feelings. These created an ideal space for projections onto the therapist of the unwanted parts of himself. After three months of fortnightly sessions, Mr B complained of being stuck in both his work and his therapy. He felt frustrated with his work because he was made to feel helpless and useless by his clients, because of their lack of understanding of the English language and way of life. He was contemplating terminating therapy as 'it was not doing him any good'. The therapist's counter-transference feelings matched those of the client. He too was feeling extremely frustrated, and felt unable to understand what Mr B was trying to communicate. Mr B was, at a deeper level, aware of the differences with the therapist, which he could not face. This awareness, once made conscious, gave him the opportunity to acknowledge the therapist as being in possession of some goodness, in having the ability to contain his fantasies without being hurt. This credibility in the therapist and the therapy is a central factor in psychological healing. This is, of course, a cultural factor. Credibility of psychotherapeutic rationales depends to a large extent on the acquaintance of the general public with the set of ideas used in therapy. For instance, 'talking helps', 'behaviour is mostly learned and can be changed by relearning', and 'emotions that are not expressed cause sickness' are all beliefs, typical of the Western middle class. They are not shared by, and probably also not true for, people outside this particular culture or subculture. Talking about one's emotions, for example, which is encouraged in most Western therapies, is considered harmful to mental health in many non-Western cultures (Kleinman and Good 1985).

Racism and cultural differences for children

Islam was nine years old when he was referred for individual therapy by his school doctor. The school was concerned about his lack of progress, his inability to make friends, and his tendency to 'opt out'. His parents had been living in England for several years, but spoke no English, and lived and worked among their close knit community. They were very concerned about their son and felt lost as to how to help him. Islam was very curious about the therapist's origins. He looked at him and said 'you are not Egyptian but you are not English' and demanded to know where the therapist came from. Islam looked at the therapist seriously and then said that at school sometimes they called him 'Paki'. He looked at his dark hands and shouted 'I am not a Paki, those boys are nasty to Pakis'. This boy was unusually open and he verbalised his anxieties about the therapist, who represented someone alien to him, arousing his own feelings of being an outsider, and his confusion at being an Egyptian child brought up in England. Islam had never been to an English household. He said that 'he didn't want to anyway, because English mums feed their children junk food, and then throw them out'. Difference in cultures can be a good vehicle into which our bad and good feelings are projected. Parents, to safeguard their idealised own culture, also use this. The more frightened and threatened a minority culture feels by the majority culture, the more protective and enclosed it becomes, keeping the 'bad' influence (English in the case of Islam), outside. Unless children are helped to understand both their native culture and the culture in which they are living, they might face unnecessary conflicts with their therapist's values, and the values of the society where they live (Kareem and Littlewood 1992).

Problems with administrative staff

She was, sometimes, an efficient secretary, also showing remarkable skills in diverting work to other people, and being superficially helpful when she needed to be. To her, things were not good enough if they were not 'British made'. Dr X was neither born nor bred in the UK, although she had proved that she was up to British standards, after several years of training and passing her exams in England. After a year of Dr X working in the department, and while Dr X was on holiday, the secretary said to the consultant that she was editing Dr X's letters, to make them understandable. On her return Dr X sensed a 'strange atmosphere' and brought up the subject at the next supervision session. The supervisor arranged a meeting with the secretary, consultant and Dr X present. The secretary was very reluctant (even though it would not represent extra work), but finally agreed to print both the letter that she called 'laughable' and the amended one. Over the next three months, only one draft was received, in which two words were changed for a synonym. Dr X was encouraged to think that this had not been a personal vendetta by a racist secretary, but, deep inside, she knew that her successor, who was also a foreign trainee, could also have her work, efforts and hopes undermined.

One must recognise the fundamentally narcissistic issue of unspoken cultural, ethnic and racial prejudices in order to comprehend the difficulties and pain that Dr X encountered. Microaggressions (Franklin and Boyd-Franklin 2000) are subtle acts or attitudes that are experienced as hostile, and that fit a history and pattern of personal racial slights and disregard. They act as status reminders by their implicit suggestion of unworthiness, and have a levelling effect on the recipient (i.e. 'Stay in your place!'). They promote 'defensive thinking', a mode in which thoughts are reactive, mixed with inner deliberations about what one desires to do and what one shouldn't or can't do.

Conclusions

> Am I being too sensitive, are these things really happening? Where does awareness end and paranoia begin? Without the privileges I enjoy, would I even now be in a secure mental home? Or would I be heading for a local school, clutching a machete, like Horrett Campbell? (Victor 1996)

The clinical narratives in this chapter demonstrate that racial differences are important in psychotherapeutic relationships. Cultural schemas can be defined as those schemas that are characteristic of a particular cultural group, but not shared by other groups. An obvious objective of the clinician is to resolve any schema incongruences, so that the clinician becomes more congruent with the client. For as long as there are schema incongruences between clinicians and clients, clinicians are bound to misinterpret clients, and the potential benefits of therapy will not be fully realised. Unfortunately, many clinicians conduct therapy as though they hold schemas identical to their clients. Ridley, Chih and Olivera (2000) argue that cultural schema is a useful construct for helping clinicians identify, organise, interpret and integrate cultural data into clinical practice. Further, they propose that training in the use of cultural schemas will also serve to reduce the prevalence of unintentional racism in the mental health field. As a psychiatrist, it is vital to see behind provocative or difficult behaviour, establishing a good therapeutic alliance with the patient. Not using one's mother tongue to communicate with our patients can be like participating in a pilot study of feedback all the time, having subtle effects on the behaviour of doctors during consultations. It leads them to be even more aware of the need to ensure that patients properly understood what they were saying.

There is now some consensus that, like any cultural product, racism is transmitted across generations by reciprocal interactions between individuals and the social institutions they create, and to which they are subject.

Rather than being a prescription for social change, the medicalisation of racism can be a model of social control. Designating certain beliefs and behaviours as diseases supports dominant social interests and institutions; it does not change them (Wellman 2000). The disease model perpetuates racism, as it removes it from the public realm. Defining racism as illness absolves the citizenry of responsibility for its behaviour. What are needed are policies that hold people accountable for their actions. Medicalising racism makes accountability impossible because it removes the matter from the social, political and economic context that produced it.

This chapter has attempted to show the importance of highlighting our differences. By being aware of these differences, we can spare ourselves a painful struggle and avoid undermining our therapeutic efficacy (Holmes 1992). A way in which we could reverse the cycle of racism in mental health practice could be by replacing therapist cultural encapsulation with cultural competence. This could be achieved by implementing multi-cultural diversity, and anti-racism training into our organisations.

Chapter 11

London's Ethnic Minorities and the Provision of Mental Health Services

Kamaldeep Bhui

A shortened version of this chapter appeared in a King's Fund report on mental health service provision for London. This chapter fleshes out the sociological, psychological and psychoanalytic analyses with facts and figures that help further analysis of mental health services and the way ethnic groups experience them.

The current position

The last two decades have seen little change in the effective delivery of mental health care to Britain's black communities. Epidemiological data indicate an excess of schizophrenia amongst African-Caribbeans and possibly amongst all minorities, an excessive use of the Mental Health Act and medication, an excess of suicides amongst Asian women and possibly young black men (Merril and Owens 1990; Bhugra 1996a, b, c; Raleigh *et al.* 1990). The Mental Health Act in the UK is under review. The legislation from the European Convention on Human Rights promises a radical reappraisal of all aspects of British and European law where this addresses mental disorder and its treatment. Patients continue to voice intense dissatisfaction with psychiatric services and the people involved in the provision of care. Suspicions of racism and oppressive practices have resulted in increased funding of research into the amount of mental illness amongst ethnic minorities. In the UK the voluntary sector has emerged as a provider in response to the inflexibility of statutory services and has been charged with the responsibility to develop better services, but usually on a short-term funding basis, and in the meantime the statutory sector remains not only unattractive but aversive to black users. Research continues to confirm inequity of service provision.

Attention to injustices within existing practice is focused by tragedies such as the death of Jonathan Zito by the actions of Christopher Clunis, a black man with schizophrenia. Christopher Clunis's pattern of contact with services was described as a catalogue of missed opportunities, poor communication and disastrous care provision in terms of service structures, individual professional practice and the manner in which British society (people) alienates the mentally ill as well as black and ethnic minorities. The pattern of care received by Clunis has been identified as typical of care received by black communities in Britain.

So decades of persuasive research findings, tragedies, working parties, committees, enquiries, political 'first aid' and health service restructuring, all designed to deliver effective care to all people, have failed black people. What is the solution? More research? More voluntary sector project funding? More guidelines? Another health service revolution? More black people in responsible positions? More conferences? The Department of Health, The King's Fund, The Mental Health Foundation, The Institute of Psychiatry, The Transcultural Psychiatry Society, The Ethnic Health Unit and many university departments as well as provider units have all hosted consultation meetings and conferences to seek a solution. Each of these events has reaffirmed that the facts are well known, the barriers to progress diverse, institutionalised and manifest through contradictory ideologies and theoretical frameworks for conceptualising a solution.

Cries of racism within the very fabric of health service public institutions have not been limited to mental health care; what is surprising is that a specialism which demands effective, contextualised communications and seeks to understand extremes of behaviour had failed to deal effectively with the greatest 'breakdown' of all: that is, communication with black communities who mistrust the mental health care system (Wilson 1993; NHS Task Force 1994). This breach is not monopolised by black communities (Rogers, Pilgrim and Lacey 1993). It seems a history of oppressive experiences including continued racial persecution compounded by the emerging data on the excess of mental disorders amongst certain black groups has, despite a justified apoplectic rage amongst black communities, led to no substantial and widespread change in practice. The degree of mistrust engendered can only reflect the inertia of statutory sectors to engage actively, in spirit as well as on paper, the necessary issues which can so readily be relegated in favour of more immediate 'merry-go-round' priorities in a rapidly evolving mental health care system which appears to replicate the policy errors of the USA (Hadley *et al.* 1996).

In order to illustrate the outcome of the process discussed so far, in this chapter I set out the evidence for inequity of service provision to black communities in London. Responsible factors are identified where these are significant barriers; some solutions are proposed in the next chapter. I present misgivings about the suitability of the existing services to deal with our (society's and the profession's) notions of mental distress and its remedies. Nowhere is this latter disparity greater than where the cultures, histories, religions and languages of the patient and healer (or consumer and provider) differ; this is so in the provision of mental health care targeting ethnic minorities in this country. Data about social inequality, special problems amongst London's ethnic minorities, and special limitations of London's mental health services will be presented. There is then a summary of the research evidence for each level of service provision (hospital care, primary care, community and voluntary sectors). Barriers to change are discussed with a broad focus on service-based issues and the ethos of mental health care including professional attitudes, research ideology, competing priorities and the politics of racism and anti-racism in mental health care.

Injustice is the responsibility of society as a whole and all members of that society have valuable contributions to a resolution. By drawing attention to what for black people is a daily source of distress and concern, a normally very private experience, I hope to share something personal to black people, of black people's perspective on why the existing services are inadequate and what of their experience is denied by an institutionally determined approach to mental health care delivery. The intention is to truly involve people of all backgrounds in a task which simply seeks a just system of health care; this common aim is often forgotten in the emotive exchanges when black mental health care is discussed.

First, my use of the term 'black', in this chapter, requires some thought. It is inaccurate. It is deploying the very terminology which, in other chapters, I describe as leading to misidentification. Nonetheless, it is a term that black and ethnic minorities themselves have chosen to use in order to demonstrate a communality of issues. It is a term that might be misread to indicate that all minority groups share all the experiences and world views described under the term. That is not the intention, but my aim is to identify common areas of dissatisfaction, and to not become, in this chapter, restricted by racial, cultural and ethnic boundaries imposed by people who are not the subject of the chapter.

London and Britain's black communities

The census and ethnic minorities in Britain

WHERE DO MINORITY ETHNIC PEOPLE LIVE?

Over 70 per cent of the combined UK ethnic minority population is found in the standard regions of the South East (56% of minorities) and the West Midlands (14% of minorities), which together contain only 40 per cent of the total UK population. A quarter of the population of Great Britain live in Greater London, Greater Manchester and the metropolitan areas of the West Midlands and West Yorkshire. Yet 83 per cent of black Africans, 79 per cent of black Caribbeans, 75 per cent of Bangladeshis and nearly two-thirds of black other (1991 census category), Indians and Pakistanis do so. Only the Chinese are less concentrated than the other ethnic groups, although in these regions they represent over 50 per cent of the total Chinese community in Great Britain. Examining the whole country, just under 60 per cent of the African-Caribbean population live in Inner London; a third of the Bangladeshi population are in Inner London; almost a third of the Indian community live in Outer London. Of the Pakistani community, 6 per cent live in Inner London and over a third of the Chinese people live in London, but they show no particular concentration.

PROBLEMS OF MEASURING THE POPULATION SIZE AND DISTRIBUTION

Census data have become a means for estimating the distribution and needs of the population. In a mental health care system with an increasingly community-based focus, such data are utilised for planning purposes. In the 1991 census black and Asian ethnic groups were relatively poorly enumerated in the country because of their demographic concentration within low coverage areas of Britain (Simpson 1993). The effect is greatest for the black African and black other groups. Under-enumeration is operative in estimates of population size, population distribution, sex ratio and dependency ratios. This differentially affects each specific ethnic group. Minorities comprise more young men and children but the distributions of age, sex, fertility and mortality vary between ethnic groupings, generations and by place of birth (UK or not) even within one census-defined ethnic group (Bulmer 1996; Peach 1996). Specific groups arrived in the UK at different times and during a diverse range of economic and political climates (Figure 11.1). Thus to speak of black people and ethnic minorities is insufficiently specific when considering needs, but such terminology is employed in this chapter in order to explore policy.

MAKING SENSE OF THE 'OTHER': HIDDEN MORBIDITY?

The 1991 census does not contain a category for people of mixed ethnic origin, who are instead included in one of the three 'other' groups (though 3800 people of mixed white ethnic origin are included in the white group; Owen 1996). In the census, 12 per cent (309,000) of ethnic minorities in Britain were estimated to be of mixed origin; over three-quarters are UK-born and a half under the age of 15 (Berrington 1994). The 'other' category contained 290,000 people in total. This outnumbers the black African, Bangladeshi and Chinese ethnic groups put together, but 'other' groups appear not to have their own cultural needs assessed. Greater London accounts for 5.2 per cent of the 'other' category nationally, 57.1 per cent of the 'other–Asian' and 41.7 per cent of the 'other–other' group. Who comprises otherness? Owen (1996) cites that North-Africans, Arabs and Iranians cannot be distinguished within the other–other group, of which they collectively form 22.5 per cent. So the existing ethnic categorisation overlooks a significant proportion of people who would require specialist services.

Population

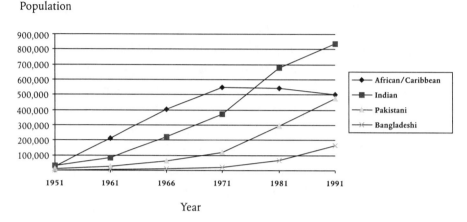

Figure 11. Growing ethnic minority population in Great Britain
Using figures from Peach (1996; Source: OPCS)

London's mental health services

Psychiatric morbidity in London

The OPCS (1995) national UK survey indicates variation of morbidity according to urban or rural locality. The prevalence of generalised anxiety disorder, depressive episodes, phobias, psychosis, alcohol and drug dependence was approximately twice as high overall in urban areas in comparison with rural areas. The prevalence of drug dependence for women was 18 and 12 per 1000 in urban and semi-rural areas compared to 2 per 1000 in rural areas. Living in an urban rather than a semi-rural area increased the odds of having fatigue, irritability, worry, depression, depressive ideas, somatic symptoms, phobias, worry about physical health and panic by around 10–40 per cent; for panic symptoms urban dwellers were 1.72 times as likely to suffer with them as rural and semi-rural dwellers. Furthermore, the at-risk population comprises not only those who live within Greater London but also those who travel into London throughout their working lives. Indeed, London teaching hospitals have traditionally been the site of healthcare access for residents and all those who work in the capital and those who require specialist care available only in teaching centres. The Association of London Government estimates (from Department of Environment figures) that in Inner London 993,330 people enter the capital during the daytime (ALG 1995). London's homeless or temporary accommodation households account for 69 per cent of England's total. London is second only to Merseyside in terms of notified drug addict numbers who also will require specialist services (ALG 1995).

Services in London
HIGH-RISK SERVICES

Traditionally there has been no mechanism for monitoring the state of London's mental illness services or for gauging the effect that the various initiatives have upon it (Milimis Project Group 1995). There are high hospital admission thresholds and few beds concentrate severely ill people on acute units, creating a culture of violence and sexual harassment. Such living conditions are intolerable and not surprisingly many patients will not accept them. 'Those who are not safe in the community have to be compulsorily detained to keep them in hospital' (Lelliot *et al.* 1995). The Milmis Project Group (1995) reported last year that secure beds in London were under-resourced and that the actual bed occupancy when waiting lists are taken account of was 162 per cent; 16 additional general psychiatric beds were required per 100,000 of the resident population; 23 per 100,000 crisis assessments were carried out in a week. CPN caseloads were of the order of 37. Hence, with severe under-resourcing of beds in London, 'there will be times when suicidal or dangerous patients abscond while waiting for admission' (Lelliot *et al.* 1995). A recent enquiry has demonstrated that those detained patients who commit suicide after absconding do so usually within a few days (Banerjee *et al.* 1994). London's services are therefore high-risk services to encounter; they are services that a disproportionate number of ethnic minorities will encounter. Is this racism or just badly organised health care? It disadvantages black and ethnic minorities more than other groups. It is an inherited form of service that has never really considered accessibility to black and ethnic minority groups from inception. Some inferences can be drawn from Sheehan *et al.* (1995), who examined inpatients in Guy's Hospital in London (48 beds; catchment 94,000) with those in Maidstone, (35 beds;

catchment area 105,000) for differences in admission rates and violent incidents as a function of ethnicity. There were 849 admissions in London compared to 292 in Maidstone, again reflecting a greater workload in accord with social deprivation indices. In the inner cities violence was associated with ethnicity (excess amongst African-Caribbean). This might be explained by readmissions being more likely in the inner-city areas, where community care effectiveness is compromised by poor social conditions, stretched resources and multiple problems (for example dual diagnoses or multiple diagnoses); unfamiliarity with culture issues and greater social adversity make it more likely that black people will 'fall out of care' and present in crisis to the criminal justice system (Bhui *et al.* 1998). Ethnic minorities historically have been given consideration only as an afterthought in terms of the new NHS structures (Bhui *et al.* 1995a; Ahmad and Atkin 1996). It is likely that community care changes will continue to be implemented as part of unevaluated policy fuelled by a new political ideology (Hadley *et al.* 1996).

HAS COMMUNITY CARE POLICY WORKED?

Doyle (1995) and Doyle *et al.* (1994) examined the use of carers across diagnostic groups. The amount of care received by disabled, low income people was extremely variable and much of the resources were devoted to providing care for a small percentage of those eligible and in need of care. The most disabled appeared to obtain care through informal carers. Over half of this group received no formal care at home. Already lagging in terms of equitable service provision in a resource-hungry healthcare system, it is likely that unless ethnic minorities' mental health needs are given consistent and ongoing consideration from the inception of any new ideology, they will continue to receive a crisis-only service at the behest of legal powers designed to maintain public order and safety. Indeed there are few evaluations of the equity of care distributions across diagnostic and ethnic groups. There are no studies that examine the implications of new community care policy and new service models amongst mentally ill ethnic minorities in London, prior to the introduction of a new service.

Social adversity: a double jeopardy

Unemployment and housing

Ethnic minorities living in London are exposed to the social problems of living in inner cites as well as to services which are themselves in crisis. Black people experience a disproportionate amount of social morbidity. Unemployment affects under 10 per cent of the white group, yet over 30 per cent of the Bangladeshi and Pakistani group, over 20 per cent of the black other and black African group, and between 10 and 15 per cent of the Irish, Indian and other Asians and nearly 20 per cent of the other–other and black Caribbean group (Peach 1996; Figure 11.2). Of those employed, the rates of self-employment vary markedly between ethnic groupings. The use of local authority housing, the quality of housing, marital status and household constitution also vary by ethnic group, with minorities consistently faring badly, with the black African, Bangladeshi, Chinese, Pakistani and black other groups always having the worst experience (Peach 1996). Unemployment and housing have independently been associated with psychiatric morbidity (Craig and Timms 1992; OPCS 1995) and the disproportionate excess of minorities living in inner cities, in poor quality housing, with an over-representation amongst the unemployed all require attention as part of any overall plan to address mental health needs on a community and population basis (Health Advisory Service 1994).

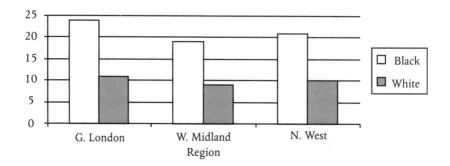

Figure 11.2 Unemployment amoungst black people in inner cities
Source: 'Black and Betrayed: A TUC report of black workers experience of unemployment and low pay in 1994–95.' Data based on Labour Force Survey (TUC 1995a).

Community care and social adversity
SOURCES OF CONFLICT

Atri *et al.* (1996) confirmed that, amongst GP-registered patients in Tower Hamlets, ethnic minorities were five times more likely to be living in over-crowded conditions, were less likely to own their own homes (11% vs. 36%), twice as likely to be in social classes 4 or 5 and were less likely to be employed (46% vs. 20%). Furnham and Shiekh (1993) interviewed 100 Asian immigrants resident in Greater London. Women immigrants were more liable to suffer psychological distress. Morbidity correlated signifi-cantly with employment, children living at home, association or club membership and experience of racial abuse/prejudice; parents living in Britain was a protective factor. There are few systematic studies of the Chinese population in London. Inferences can be drawn from Furnham and Li (1993) who examined how values, social support and expectations across generations influenced mental health in a Chinese community sample of 70 drawn from Manchester, Edinburgh and the West Midlands. They found that 44.2 per cent of first generation and 22.2 per cent of second generation had significant morbidity and reported psychological symptoms; 32 per cent of the first generation also scored as being mildly depressed on the Beck Depression Inventory and 9.3 per cent as highly depressed; 18.5 per cent and 3.7 per cent of the second generation respectively had mild and severe states of depression. Amongst the second generation, the less proficient an individual was in English the more likely it was for him or her to report psychological symptoms. There is also little data on London's Vietnamese communities, though a recent study in Nottingham (Nguyen-Van-Tam *et al.* 1996) supports the impression in London (Tang and Cuninghame 1994) that there is considerable difficulty in using English as a second language to secure effective healthcare. There was low uptake of preventive programmes, and high levels of disadvantage including traumatic experiences. Racial prejudice was confirmed by Pilgrim *et al.* (1993) in Bristol to be a major stressor.

SOCIAL MEASURES AS TREATMENT

Social adversity has been associated not only with causal explanations for greater morbidity but also as an impediment to recovery and rehabilitation; indeed targeted mental health care has been demonstrated not to improve patient outcomes in isolation from critical social interventions (Conway, Melzer and Hale 1994). Community care policy is therefore always likely to be less efficacious amongst ethnic minorities; no account has been taken of this by policy makers or providers.

Refugees and asylum seekers
London's refugees and psychiatric disorders
HOW MANY REFUGEES ARE THERE IN LONDON?

The United Nations High Commission for Refugees estimates that there are 20 million refugees worldwide yet less than 5 per cent of them come to Europe (Medical Foundation for the Care of Victims of Torture 1994). The Home Office figures suggest that in 1994, 32,800 asylum seekers entered the UK and made applications; this was 10,000 greater than in 1993 (Home Office Statistical Bulletin 15/95). London is the favoured destination for refugees arriving in the UK and most will live in inner-city areas;

estimates from studies in North London indicate that 116,000 refugees live in London (Karmi 1992a, b).

PSYCHIATRIC DISORDERS AMONGST REFUGEES

Refugees are especially vulnerable to psychiatric disorders including depression, suicidality and post-traumatic stress disorder (Ramsay, Gorst-Unsworth and Turner 1993; Medical Foundation for the Care of Victims of Torture 1994; Gorst-Unsworth 1992). Indeed mental health is the single most important problem facing refugees (Gammell *et al.* 1993). Gammel *et al.* demonstrated that one-third of refugees in Newham were depressed. Depression was associated with having spent little time in the UK (36% of recent arrivals), with not speaking English (37% of those with no English compared with 25% of those who could speak some English); 62 per cent reported constant worrying and about a half reported other symptoms consistent with a diagnosis of post-traumatic stress disorder. Their needs for health care are therefore significant. King *et al.* (1994), when measuring the incidence of psychosis amongst ethnic groups in North London, found that 11 per cent of their hospital or community contact patients were refugees compared with only 5 per cent of the population of the catchment area, further supporting the evidence that refugees are over-represented amongst psychiatric populations.

Children either as victims or passive observers of violence are often neglected as a necessary focus of therapeutic attention, yet such neglect can result in post-traumatic stress disorders, depressive reactions, somatic symptoms and what Richman (1993) refers to as the existential dilemma of distrust in others and facing an uncertain future.

London's refugees and neglect by health, social and legal agencies
ACCESS TO SERVICES

Of Newham's depressed refugees (Gammel *et al.* 1993) 70 per cent wished to talk to a counsellor or professional in their own language. Less than a quarter of this sample were in full-time, part-time or occasional work. Most refugees were registered but often had difficulty registering with GPs, who in some instances were not sympathetic and did not wish to have refugees on their list. Over a third of the refugees who were depressed felt they needed to talk to someone in their own language compared with 10 per cent of those who were not depressed.

The *Refugee Arrivals Project Annual Report* (1994) gives graphic examples of how housing and basic needs are met only with great difficulty, with statutory organisations not recognising the special needs of this population. This is compounded by the black and ethnic minority population's difficulties in utilisation of social benefits agencies, the rules and regulations of which disproportionately deprive ethnic minorities of the benefits they are due (TUC 1995b). Any multi-agency service addressing the mental health needs of ethnic minorities must consider access to basic social provisions and the negotiation of institutional barriers to social and health care (Atkin and Rollings 1993). Indeed the tragic case of Christopher Clunis, said by some to be typical of the care received by the black population (Francis 1994), was characterised by residential instability, which made the task of delivering essential care more difficult; Clunis had been resident in eight hospitals, two prisons, four hostels, four bed-and-breakfast settings and one self-contained flat (Lambeth, Southwark and Lewisham Health Commission 1994). It was clear that whatever the strategy adopted, it was flawed or compromised by a system of care that did not accommodate a man who faced multiple problems. Those responsible for providing care continued to be defeated by institutionalised barriers as well as their individual oversights.

AN IMBALANCE OF PRIORITIES

Traumatic experience needs to be conceptualised in terms of a dynamic, two-way interaction between the victimised individual and the surrounding society, evolving over time, and not only as a relatively static, circumscribed entity to be located and addressed within the individual psychology of those affected (Summerfield 1995). In relation to refugees' experience of the legal system, lawyers too often see a decision at a particular point in time as a legal process or as an isolated matter, as something logically separable from what surrounds it in the processing of cases, and thereby end up doing violence to the inherent complexity of decision (Juss 1993). Healthcare professionals are similarly focused on their limited brief of treating disorders without attending to the wider picture, which is increasingly an essential approach throughout psychiatric practice. The specific traumatic experiences of refugees are too little addressed, yet the undermining effects of insecurity over deportation, extreme poverty, poor housing, and racism are underestimated and should be distinguished from what is generally meant by the stresses of acculturation (Summerfield 1995). Such populations would be rarely included in any ethnic monitoring exercise, precluding any attempt to plan for their potential needs.

Black people and medical and psychiatric services

Cultural competencies of the professionals

WORKING PRACTICES

In all statutory services time constraints determine the level of attention and degree to which a professional really comes to know the characteristics of any single patient. Where a patient presents their distress in a manner which is unfamiliar to the healthcare professional, more time and attention to detail are required if the level of knowing that patient is to be comparable to that in a patient who shares (with the professional) the same language, social class, culture and world view about health, illness and help-seeking (Bhugra 1996). Not only is such time not usually available but professionals are often unaware of the limitations of their own assessments. They may make no effort to address adequately the shortfalls in a psychiatric assessment having raised the assessment and diagnostic process to a level of objectivity that can be safely adopted in other branches of medicine. This is especially a problem in emergency situations, where decisions are often made in a hurry, within the constraints of legal and professional group precedents. Thus, although psychiatric nosology and the needs-based and diagnosis-based approach serves health professionals well in the majority of their encounters with patients, there are times when such models of distress expression and amelioration are inadequate (Bhugra 1996). A more detailed account of service adaptations, including the use of interpreters, is dealt with elsewhere (Bhui *et al.* 1995a; Westermeyer 1990), but culture-specific assessment and treatment practices should be developed in alliance with patients and their relatives.

SOMATISATION

Much has been written on somatisation of depression, especially amongst non-Western communities (Bal 1984; Burke 1986; Leff 1988), although somatisation is common among white British patients also and can occur in people at any age, from any social class and intellectual level (Helman 1990). The absence of shared meanings, lexicon, concept of self and world view contributes to the emphasis on physical symptoms, which are more directly amenable to undistorted translation (Mumford 1992). Somatisation as a term is often applied when, owing to premature closure of assessments or of 'cultural distance', there is a poor shared understanding of the therapeutic encounter (Bhui 1994). Such a scenario has more recently been demonstrated to be associated with non-recognition of psychiatric disorder in primary care (Jacob *et al.* 1996). GPs attend to physical symptoms, which are less liable to communicative distortions where there is not a shared language and world view of ill health. Wilson and MacCarthy (1994) demonstrated that even when patients presented with psychiatric complaints, Asians were more likely to be diagnosed as suffering from physical illness; where physical complaints were presented, more of the white group were identified as having psychiatric problems than the Asian group. Jacob *et al.* (1996) confirmed that a sample of West London GPs correctly diagnosed less than a fifth of those Asians identified by a questionnaire as being mentally ill. Thus, existing models of treatment need adaptation; more assessment sessions are necessary to explore the cultural context in which symptoms arise and in which treatment is to be given.

Hidden morbidity and factors determining the delivery of effective interventions
EXPLANATORY MODELS

Cultural conflict, hopelessness in the face of social adversity, employment disadvantage and racism have all been put forward as explanations for the different rates of disorder and different degrees of service utilisation. Unique explanations of patients' misfortune, including illness, linked with characteristic help-seeking behaviours, have been termed by Kleinman (1980) as an explanatory model. This model has been suggested to influence help-seeking and hence the nature of treatment received. High levels of morbidity may go undetected if an individual's appraisal of their symptoms involves an explanatory model (private explanations of their state along with a help-seeking map) that is out of keeping with that expected by GPs and psychiatrists. Thus, Beliappa (1991) reported an inter-personal social interpretation of depression by Bangladeshi people in East London. Krause *et al.* (1991), in an ethnographic study, demonstrated that Punjabis in Bedford could communicate their distress by the use of idioms of a sinking heart (literally translated). MacCarthy and Craisatti (1989) interviewed Bangladeshis in East London and confirmed significant degrees of hidden morbidity and that the impact of life events could not readily be translated across cultures. The GP was seen as a village elder and was often approached for a multitude of difficulties and so detecting illness was just one of many issues presented to GPs.

In some instances explanatory models and patterns of help-seeking encourage other sources of help, for example prayer or increased attendance at a temple. The specific sources of help will be unique to each culture and are likely to involve traditional healers and complementary medicine practitioners (Bhopal 1986; Wilson and MacCarthy 1994) as well as GPs. For example, Balabil and Dolan (1992) report that British-Asian attendees of two London GP surgeries had lower expectations of counselling and that this may explain their hesitancy in seeking this form of intervention. Yet Littlewood and Cross (1980) illustrate that it is not just the patient who determines what help is offered. Black psychiatric outpatients in this study received more physical treatments (major tranquillisers and ECT) than white patients. Black and white immigrants received intra-muscular injections more often than non-immigrants and their pattern of outpatient attendance was characterised by self-referrals, missed appointments and being booked in to see the most junior member of the team. The expectations of health professionals therefore appear to be as important as those of the patients.

PATHWAYS INTO CARE

Goldberg and Huxley (1980) describe the filters and stages which must be negotiated in order to receive help. Most psychiatric morbidity in the UK presents to the GP and as such the GP has become the focus of delivering community-based healthcare. Goldberg (1999), using WHO data, has demonstrated that the help-seeking process and the care giver sought vary in different countries; this is likely to be a function not only of the local political and structural basis of healthcare in these countries but also of health beliefs pertaining to health-related culturally sanctioned healing processes (Kleinman 1980) and lay epidemiology (Frankel *et al.* 1991). Ethnic minorities appear to present to their GPs often. Some groups have very high consultation rates in comparison with the indigenous popula-tion, yet psychiatric morbidity is less often identified (see section on primary care, pp.161–4). This contrasts sharply with the findings that black people are over-represented in psychiatric hospitals and forensic units and are more often identified to be in need of psychiatric help through crisis services and by the use of the Mental Health Act (see sections on general psychiatric inpatient and forensic services, pp.158–61). For example, Davies *et al.* (1996) found that section 2, 3 and 136 of the Mental Health Act were more often used amongst blacks. Bhugra *et al.* (1996c), in a study examining the incidence and outcome of schizophrenia, found that only 1 of 36 African-Caribbean patients with schizophrenia presented through their GPs. Bhui, Strathdee and Sufraz (1993) demonstrated that despite 54 per cent of Asian psychiatric hospital admissions having an Asian GP, only 24 per cent were admitted at the behest of their GP. Healthcare systems do not fit the preferred pathways to ensure early intervention for black patients and may do so to a lesser extent than envisaged for all patients. The dilemma remains that either GPs can and should receive better training so as to improve their detection rates, or patients need more information and health education on the fundamental nature of services. Persistent states of distress in the absence of timely inter-vention may encourage presentation in crisis with more severe disorders. Recovery times will then be longer and a greater intensity of input will be necessary in view of the greater degree of impairment.

ALTERNATIVE SERVICES AND SOURCES OF HELP

Black people who were born in other countries have also to negotiate unanticipated generational changes of attitude to success, work and family commitments; sources of dignity and pride will be under threat. Traditional sources of support may disappear and the statutory sector, unless sensitive to culturally sanctioned sources of support, may undermine them and attempt to replace them with health and social service-funded alternatives, which are likely to be unreliable (short-term funding) and less culture-specific. Traditional remedies and culturally consistent healing strategies may not be within the realms of accepted medical practice, especially when there is such a focus on evidence-based medicine. Even black people can internalise racism and dismiss traditional remedies as third world mumbo-jumbo, but choice is rarely available to those who do wish to use different approaches to distress (see Huka 1995). The popularity of these approaches bears witness to the failure of statutory services to manage effectively the totality of an individual's distress. The statutory sector needs to change the configuration of their services and the roles that they are expected to fulfil. Working in closer liaison with alternative practitioners and changing the style of service delivery (e.g. use of homecare) would also prevent patients from 'falling between stools'.

Special medical problems
ALCOHOL USE

McKeigue and Karmi (1993) reviewed the data on alcohol consumption amongst ethnic minorities from published and unpublished sources. Alcohol consumption was found to be lower in African-Caribbean men and women than in British men and women, as indicated by hospital admission data. Among South Asians, average alcohol consumption is also lower than native British but within certain sub-populations alcohol-related morbidity rates are higher. Amongst Sikhs, heavy spirit drinking is especially high. They have higher rates of morbidity compared with Hindu and Muslim men and the alcohol-related admission rates are increasing amongst South Asians. Although Cochrane *et al.* (1999) indicate that the second generation have moderated their drinking patterns significantly there was a tendency to drink amongst the Sikhs and Hindus so as to forget their problems. It may be that the low rate of service use, presumed to reflect less morbidity amongst Asians in the UK, is a manifestation not only of low detection but also of self-medication and use of alternative approaches (including alcohol) to deal with distress.

SUICIDE

Using routine mortality statistics, suicide amongst ethnic minorities has been reported to be on the increase, especially amongst Asians and specifically Indian women from India and East Africa; they have recently been reported to have between two and two and a half times the all-England and Wales rate respectively (Mental Health Foundation 1995b). Bhugra *et al.* (1996a) recently reported on findings in West London: South Asian women showed crude rates of attempted suicides that were 1.6 times that of white and black women and 2.3 times that of South Asian men. Age-specific rates confirm that amongst the 16–24 age group, South Asian women have rates that are 2.6 times that of white women and 7.5 times that of South Asian men in the same age band; Asian men under 30 have half the rate of Asian women under 30. Balarajan (1996) reports that rates are elevated amongst Indians, Irish and Africans; the rate amongst Caribbeans is reported to be the same as that of the British population; Pakistani and Bangladeshi rates are lower than those of the British population.

Methods of suicide vary according to locally available methods and ascertainment may be a problem, hence an assessment of open verdicts is also essential for a full evaluation; for example, self-immolation has been shown to be the chosen method amongst many Indian women but was not found in West London (Bhugra *et al.* 1996a). Precipitating factors include inter-personal difficulties within families or intimate relationships. Alcohol use and financial worries also have been invoked as potential explanations (Bhugra *et al.* 1996b). Issues of low self-esteem, early marriage, expectations of marriage and unresolved conflicts as factors are especially pertinent to British Asians. Those who were in inter-racial marriages, had resisted arranged marriages, or had changed religions were more likely to have attempted suicide, hence social support plays an important role in the development of pyschosocial distress.

Utilisation of London's Services: Summaries of main findings

General psychiatric inpatient services

- African-Caribbeans have 3–13 times the admission rates of white patients. This is for schizophrenia and affective psychoses (Bebbington *et al.* 1981; King *et al.* 1994; Moodley and Perkins 1991; van Os *et al.* 1996).

- Formal admission rates are higher for African-Caribbeans than for comparable samples of white and other ethnic groups (Wessley 1991; Bebbington *et al.* 1981; Moodley and Perkins 1991; Bagley 1971; King *et al.* 1994; Davies *et al.* 1996; Callan 1996).

- The magnitude of the excess varies in different parts of London and is likely to be a function of not only the population but also the configuration of the local service (Bebbington *et al.* 1981).

- Fewer black inpatients are diagnosed as having depression or a neurotic illness (Lloyd and Moodley 1992; Bebbington *et al.* 1981; Cochrane *et al.* 1977; Cochrane *et al.* 1989; Dean *et al.* 1981).

- Diagnostic (schizophrenia) excess and challenging behaviour amongst black patients has been cited as the cause of this finding (Sheehan *et al.* 1995; Lloyd and Moodley 1992).

- Once admitted, young Caribbean men were more likely to be readmitted. Young men (under 30) were more likely to have a first admission (Glover 1989).

- A cohort effect was hypothesised amongst young men (Burke 1974; Glover 1989) suggesting that there had been an epidemic.

- Using self-reported utilisation of acute inpatient and outpatient services using the General Household Survey data aggregated over 1983–87, a higher rate of utilisation amongst young males of all ethnic groups was found with a decline with increasing age and an increase in the older age groups (Balarajan, Raleigh and Yuen 1991).

- Asians have lower admission rates than white patients and fewer readmissions, and spend less time in hospital than a comparable sample of white patients (Gupta 1991).

- Black patients more often receive depot medication (Lloyd and Moodley 1992).

- Littlewood and Cross (1980) demonstrated that black outpatients received more physical treatments and along with white immigrants received a poor service as outpatients.

- Perera *et al.* (1991) showed that Asians appeared to be exposed for longer and African-Caribbeans for shorter periods of time (than a control group) to anti-cholinergics. Asians also had more discrete treatment episodes (including for benzodiazepines).

- Black patients have also been identified to be involved in more violent incidents as inpatients (Moodley and Perkins 1991; Sheehan *et al.* 1995; Bebbington *et al.* 1994).

- Callan (1996) reported that African-Caribbeans had shorter readmissions than a British-born white control group; a milder course was hypothesised to exist among African-Caribbeans.

Forensic services

- Among patients admitted to secure units in England and Wales, 20 per cent were African-Caribbean in origin (Jones and Berry 1986).

- On a medium secure unit serving parts of South London, it is usual for the majority of the patients to be of African-Caribbean origin (Maden 1999).

- Among sentenced prisoners, the prevalence of mental illness amongst African-Caribbeans is 6 per cent compared with a prevalence of 2 per cent amongst the white population (Maden 1995).

- Amongst remanded prisoners referred to the prison medical officer, 68.2 per cent described themselves as white, 10.8 per cent were black Caribbean, 6.1 per cent were black African, 4.3 per cent were black British (BB) and 3.6 per cent Asian; 4.7 per cent regarded themselves as belonging to another group (Bhui *et al.* 1998).

- Amongst a sample of remanded mentally disordered offenders diagnosed as having schizophrenia, 17.6 per cent were white, 68.8 per cent were black Caribbean, 43.8 per cent were black African, 58.3 per cent were black British and 42.1 per cent fell within another non-white ethnic group (Bhui *et al.* 1998).

- Banerjee *et al.* (1995) reported a higher prevalence of schizophrenia amongst black remanded men who were transferred to hospitals.

- In certain areas black men are more likely to receive a custodial sentence than their white counterparts (NACRO 1989).

- A survey examining decision making for remanded people regarding psychiatric reports demonstrated that 37 per cent of white defendants were granted bail and only 13 per cent of the black group (NACRO 1990).

- Black defendants received a smaller range of potential disposals after court appearance and three-quarters have had previous contact with psychiatric services whereas half of the white groups have had previous contact with a psychiatric service (NACRO 1990).

- Black people comprised 47 per cent of those appearing before courts and in need of psychiatric assessment whereas they represented only 24 per cent of those detained within police stations indicating again that there is a failure to divert black mentally disordered offenders effectively (Robertson *et al.* 1996).

A and E studies

- Tyrer *et al.* (1994) in a study of A and E presenters concluded that 63 per cent of caucasians were regarded as having personality disorder compared with only 25 per cent of non-caucasians who were mainly African.

- Turner *et al.* (1992) report on section 136 referrals (112 patients) by the police to City and Hackney Health District over a period of 24 months. Of 39 repeat admissions 26 were due to 11 African-Caribbean men. The African-Caribbean men were mainly under 30 years of age. Fifteen of all thirty-two men with a prison record were African-Caribbeans. Half of the repeaters had been in prison before compared with less than a quarter of the non-repeaters. Forty-seven per cent of section 136s were of African-Caribbean origin although they represented only twenty per cent of local population. Just under 40 per cent of male African-Caribbean referrals were due to 4 individuals while nearly a third of the white female population presentations were due to 2 females.

- There is little data available on numbers of mentally ill people presenting to A and E and little evaluation of hidden morbidity at this level or of patients' experience of services.

Primary care

Consultation rates

- In Tower Hamlets', general practices, there was equity of recording of preventive activity for major causes of death between black, white and Bangladeshi populations. But amongst the Vietnamese and Chinese community there were lower levels of activity recorded for a mammography and cervical smears; unfortunately mental health episodes were not examined (Atri *et al.* 1996).

- Carr Hill *et al.* (1996) demonstrated that in 60 volunteer general practices those fully employed consulted the least and those who lost their jobs in the last year consulted the most. In the crude analysis, patients of Indian, Pakistani and Bangladeshi origin consulted the most, but after adjustment for confounders this finding held for women only. The GP was consulted more often where there was geographical proximity. But there was no measure of diagnostic groups by ethnicity and hence the mental health burden of consultation is undefined.

- Gillam *et al.* (1989) studied the patterns of consultation in seven general practices in the London Borough of Brent. Male Asians had substantially higher standardised patient consultation ratios. Consultations for anxiety and depression were reduced in all immigrant groups (72%–76% of white group rate). British patients more often left the surgery with a repeat appointment, prescription or certificate.

- Kiev (1965) reported a higher overall consultation rate amongst Black (Jamaican) primary care attendees in Brixton. The rate of psychiatric disorder was also higher than amongst the British population. West Indians were more likely than British patients to seek help from alternative and traditional sources.

- Twenty-one GPs were selected from a sample of one hundred and two in Tower Hamlets (Li *et al.* 1994). There was an over-representation of white and black Caribbean patients and an under-representation of Bangladeshis, Chinese, black Africans, and black other. Of all attendees 13.3 per cent had a mental health problem and 0.6 per cent were referred to a specialist.

Detecting psychiatric morbidity

- Lloyd and St Louis (1999) interviewed a sample of black women primary care attendees and compared them with a matched sample of white British attendees. On the

General Health Questionnaire (GHQ) responses there were no differences between black and white women. Within the black group however, black African women had higher scores. There were differences between scores on the clinical interview schedule: GPs noted psychiatric problems in 26 per cent of black patients and 34 per cent of white women, all of whom had scored as 'cases' on the GHQ.

- Jacob *et al.* (1996) examined Asian primary care attendees in West London and found that 42.4 per cent of them presented with non-specific complaints; 38 per cent reported specific medical illness and only 6 per cent reported psychological problems. GPs recognised only a fifth of those identified as cases on the GHQ. In this study vignettes were also presented and although patients identified the depiction of psychiatric disorder correctly as phobia, somatisation and depression in 47 per cent, 50 per cent and 33 per cent of instances, they felt that biomedical treatment was necessary in only 24 per cent, 29 per cent and 14 per cent of instances respectively. Notably least so for depression. Individuals with psychiatric morbidity had higher consultations rates for the previous year, more often had unemployed relatives and were more often of Asian origin. Not telling the GP about their complaints was associated with psychiatric morbidity as was dissatisfaction with the GP's treatment and contact with an alternative practitioner.

- Wilson and McCarthy (1994) explored the causes of low utilisation of mental health services by interviewing Asian attendees of five general practices in NW London. There were equivalent rates of true non-psychotic morbidity in the white and Asian sample with no difference in the way in which their symptoms were reported. Those Asians who had a psychiatric illness were more likely to report physical complaints (65% compared with 46% amongst whites); GPs were more likely to identify 'physical and/or other' as psychiatric morbidity amongst white (46%) rather than Asian (19%) patients. Of patients with a high psychiatric score on a screening instrument, whites were more often identified by GPs as having a psychiatric disorder compared with Asians. If patients presented with a physical complaint GPs were more likely to agree that their complaint was a physical one if they were Asian (61% of them compared with 28% of white patients). For those patients who came and reported a mental health problem, GPs agreed with 15 per cent of the white group and with 3 per cent of the Asian groups.

- Li *et al.* (1994) report that in Tower Hamlets, 2.2 per cent of all attendees had needs that could not be met within the district services. Detection of morbidity for the Vietnamese was almost a quarter of that for the white population. Black African and Bangladeshi patients had nearly a half the detection rates of conspicuous morbidity.

- Although there is greater emphasis on the detection of depression in primary care GPs are unlikely to offer treatment to the elderly patients from ethnic minority groups. In London in particular 30 per cent of GPs (especially Asian GPs) were likely to see elderly who could not speak English (Pharoah 1992). Inaccurate translation and embarrassment were the main problems expressed by both Asian and white GPs (Pharoah 1992). Over 60 per cent of London GPs said it would be helpful to have more staff to provide education and information services. The high consultation rates amongst the elderly from ethnic minorities was not attributed to illness by the GPs but to health beliefs, expectations, anxiety and misunderstandings.

Access to primary care

- Cole *et al.* (1995) demonstrated that for first episode psychosis in Haringey compulsory admission, admission after a section 136, first contact with a services other than health and no GP involvement were all associated with being single. Not having a help-seeker was associated with compulsory admission, admission after a section 136 and police rather than GP involvement. Compulsory admission was also associated with the family of origin living outside of London and the absence of GP involvement.

- Nguyen-Van-Tam *et al.* (1996) and Nguyen-Van-Tam and Madeley (1996a and 1996b) cite evidence from Nottingham that greater than a half of their sample of Vietnamese had *not* gone to their doctor because of language problems and that there was a popular misconception that Vietnamese people have adapted to life in UK and therefore require little attention just because they are not conspicuous.

- Lloyd and St Louis (1999) reported that black women less often knew what they wanted from their GP (25% of white rate) and they were less likely to make multiple requests of their GP (23% of white rate). During the follow-up year none of the white patients self-referred to A and E but 5 per cent of the black patients did so. Black African women consulted less often than other women. Black patients were less satisfied than white patents and this was especially so for black African women, who also were the most distressed and attended the least often.

- Amongst Vietnamese in London and Nottingham, there were difficulties in consultations with GPs. Although the majority of respondents were registered with a GP, 20 per cent often needed an adult relative to interpret and 35 per cent reported using children to interpret (Nguyen-Van-Tam *et al.* 1996; Tang and Cuninghame 1994).

- Of those attending the Brixton refugee health project, nearly 50 per cent had not sought help for psychological problems since arrival in this country, although just under 30 per cent had consulted their GPs (Grant and Deane 1995).

Community Studies

- Few local or health authorities consider making any systematic attempt to consider race in service delivery. It is not only provision of services (quantities) but how they are provided (quality) that is important (Atkin and Rollings 1993).

- Doyle (1995) examined disability and the use of an 'independent living' fund in South East London and users' views about the system of cash versus care provision amongst 198 patients registered as potentially subject to the scheme. Despite mental health not explicitly being excluded, there were no psychiatric diagnoses seen but general inferences about disability and care preferences can be made. Ninety-eight per cent of ethnic minorities opted to take cash for care; this must reflect a dislike of existing provisions and preference for self-directed alternatives; yet eighty-three per cent of ethnic minorities saw being an employer of care providers themselves as a difficult role and most who had money paid relatives or friends.

- Doyle *et al.* (1994) explored the views of 65 young adults with physical disabilities; 43.1 per cent were from various ethnic backgrounds in London. It appeared that those with greater need were not necessarily supported more; indeed people were actually losing contact with agencies, especially social services. Access to respite and social events was very limited and this was especially the case amongst those with complex disabilities. Ethnic minorities were less optimistic about their future and feared that poverty, disability and their ethnic origin would isolate them from them. Indeed there was poor interagency co-operation and a resistance to changed practice. Most coped with the aid of family, and mothers were the main carers.

- Pharoah (1992) demonstrated a difference in the perception of white and Asian GPs regarding the low uptake of community services amongst the ethnic minority elderly. Asian GPs cited a lack of service-based patient knowledge, language barriers and poor service response while white GPs emphasised the existence of family support; the latter as an explanation has attracted much criticism as a mechanism for ignoring large populations with need on the basis of a stereotype (Ahmad 1996).

- Davies *et al.* (1996) scrutinised the record of all prevalent cases of psychosis from hospital and community contact data and concluded that 70 per cent of the black Caribbean group, 69 per cent of the black African group and 50 per cent of the white group had previously been detained under the provisions of the Mental Health Act.

- King *et al.* (1994) examined all cases of hospital and community presentations of psychosis in North London and found the annual incidence of schizophrenia to be 2.2 (per 1000) for the whole sample and 3.6 (per 1000) for the non-white groups aggregated. Although there were some major limitations in terms of the conclusions drawn on the basis of small numbers of cases, this study suggested that the rates of psychosis may be elevated for all immigrant groups.

- The NHS Taskforce (1994) reported that of the Chinese community in the Oxford region, nearly half did not know how to obtain a doctor in an emergency. Language and lack of familiarity were cited as the responsible barriers. Furthermore, 43 per cent of those surveyed reported that they preferred Western medicine and 50 per cent a combination of Western and Chinese medicine. Long and unsociable hours in the catering trade also made it difficult to secure healthcare.

The voluntary sector

There are a large number of voluntary organisations delivering social and health care; at least a half of those listed by SHARE (database at The King's Fund Centre, London) to be providers of mental health care were in London. The full potential of their role in healthcare provision remains undefined and part of this is due to a lack of information about client groups, caseloads, effectiveness of models of care employed and basic demographic and health-related information about users; all these data have now become more important to the provision of health and social care but it seems there is no overall co-ordinating strategy for the voluntary sector or routes for the scrutiny and dissemination of information. If this sector is to become a major provider then an overall strategy is urgently required to ensure that provision of specific services meets the care needs of local populations in a systematic way.

WHAT DO VOLUNTARY ORGANISATIONS DO ABOUT MENTAL HEALTH?

Webb-Johnson (1993) gives an account of 32 Asian voluntary sector organisations' activities and their users' views on sources of health and preferred health education strategies. It seemed that the organisation met the social, religious and cultural needs of users. The disabled, the elderly housebound and those who were lonely or mentally ill were identified as neglected groups, although mental health was covered by only 14 organisations in the two years before the survey. Six of the organisations said they would prioritise mental health in their organisation if they had resources. Eleven organisations reported that mental health was a priority. The use of videos, speakers and discussion groups seemed to be the preferred media for communicating health-related matters by these organisations. Users (n=95) seemed to prefer leaflets (50), videos (46), group discussion (43) and Asian radio (42) as popular media. Speakers and posters were identified by only 30 and 23 people respectively. Only six groups had a health-related post. Two-thirds of the organisations had links with GPs and a half with their district health authority. The voluntary organisations had most contact with health promotion units. GPs and health authorities were regarded as beneficial contacts by only five and two organisations respectively. Two-thirds preferred health information to be communicated in Asian languages. Of 105 users, only 4 reported mental health as a main concern. The Confederation of Indian Organisations in one year received over 400 enquires in relation to mental health, 331 on health information in general and 161 on disability, out of a total of 1100 written and 4300 telephone enquiries (CIO 1994).

Kumar (1991) described an Asian mental health project (not in London) that was creative and innovative in building and refining its own expertise and in making a continual upgradation to policy. This project also demonstrated the tentative nature of funding such a project with several funding bids being enacted as the project proceeded. Referral sources were GPs (5%), psychiatrists (10%), social workers (20%), inter-preting services (22%), self- referrals (13%) and other sources (30%). The diagnoses presenting were depression (23%), anxiety (15%), stress (15%), relationship problems (13.5%), schizophrenia (8%) and personality disorders (10%). Of those presenting, 35 per cent had previously had treatment with medication, 65 per cent had no previous treatment, 37 per cent were chronically ill and 40 per cent had not sought help before because of a lack of faith in confidentiality. Sixty-five per cent of problems were related to depression, anxiety or stress associated with isolation, language problems, cultural barriers (housewives), uncertainty about employment and climactic factors.

THE VOLUNTARY SECTOR AS ADVOCATES

Jamdagni (1996) examined special projects and highlighted many areas of improved quality in comparison with mainstream services but identified some problems: these include consultation fatigue and the suggestion that regular consultees should be paid for giving up their time. Race-specific standards were also incorporated into the patients' charter by some providers but others preferred separate sections added to the charter, again reflecting an uncertain debate about how black mental health service provision should be orientated in relation to mainstream services. In Camden (Jamdagni 1996) nearly half of the community workers had come across people who chose not to use the service, suggesting that services were not acceptable in their current form. Interesting insights into black carers' views about the system of service provision were also gleaned.

Twenty-eight per cent of carers in Camden did not want to be put in touch with social services or a mainstream voluntary organisation because of previous bad experiences and language barriers. English was not the first language in almost two-thirds of carers and 80 per cent of users, and 62 per cent of carers had not had a break in the last year.

Yee (1996) advocates that support for black carers should be a mainstream service issue, raised at senior management level, and that this could be one criterion of service quality for purchasers to adhere to. Carers and families have received little systematic attention where priority care is often directed to the index patient. Yee (1996) outlines the position in relation to black families and dispels three major myths: that black families look after their own; that a colour-blind approach is inherently racist as carers' (and patients') needs are dismissed as not fitting the recognised needs and that black carers continue to be seen as immigrants rendering their whole claim to better care as an unreasonable demand from a generous state. Yee (1996) concludes that support for black carers should be a mainstream issue and that the commissioning process should ensure this; all agencies should consider the needs of black carers and it should not just be the remit of the black agencies; short-term projects for black carers should cease as a sustained service is necessary.

Some examples of good practice

- The Brixton Circle Project provides to the black community what the community care act suggests should be provided to all patients. Attention is given to accommodation, education, counselling and employment, and even involves the users after a period of stability and training in service provision (Brixton Circle Project 1992). Is it not possible that the necessary client-centred approach may serve as a model for the future standard services (Greenwood 1993)?

- The Chinese Mental Health Association is one of the few Chinese organisations providing alternative models of engagement and therapeutic work for those of the Chinese community who are distressed. They specifically avoid the label 'mental illness' as this is heavily stigmatised and people would be unlikely to attend. Counselling, advocacy, befriending and support are provided, but yet again funding is an ongoing issue. The organisation actively works with the statutory sector from which it received over a third of its referrals last year. Of note is that self-referral and voluntary sector referrals each account for about another third. Referrals are received from all over London and in a third of cases their role is partially that of giving advice and consultation. A quarter of referrals have depression and a fifth have schizophrenia. In over 40 per cent of cases further services are offered and accepted (Chinese Mental Health Association 1995).

- The African-Caribbean Mental Health Association Brixton was founded in 1982. It epitomises the response of the black community to poor statutory sector services and created an alternative to hospital-based care whilst using a multi-disciplinary approach. Housing, counselling and legal advice as well as therapeutic alternatives were all available.

- Nafsiyat in North London is a well-established source of inter-cultural therapy; the founders of the organisation and those who work in an inter-cultural context have been successful at providing counselling in a friendly and culture-sensitive manner even when the models of therapy had to be adapted (Acharyya *et al.* 1989). For example, an especially empowering adaptation is the right of clients to express an opinion on the ethnic origin of their future therapist; not all want an ethnically matched therapist. Furthermore, clients can bring a friend, relative or confidant with them during therapy sessions, which allays much anxiety about communication and trust. Robins (1992) reports that 90 per cent of patients reported a 'good outcome'. Referrals included rape and sexual abuse amongst women (25%), psychoses (15%), 46 per cent had depressive syndromes and only 12 of 52 had pre-treatment GHQ scores that were less than 12 and 38 had post-treatment scores of less than 12.

- The Manchester Action Committee for Action on Health Care for Ethnic Minorities appears to be the first city-wide, independent multi-ethnic umbrella body dedicated to health and community care. Thus, direct access to decision makers is made possible for all black groups. This scheme is in the process of being replicated in Camden and Islington (Camden Health and Race Group *et al.* 1992).

- Wilson (1995) compiled a conference report describing the sanctuary model as an alternative to hospital admissions and statutory service care. An assessment service in a safe and a calm area (also the designated place of safety), a 10-bedded crisis service, family respite beds, 24-hour advocacy/advice, counselling, outreach and community education are components. Outcome data (although sought for this report) were not available but these projects approximate best to the requirements expressed by African-Caribbean people.

National organisations, surveys and reports

National data on the prevalence of morbidity using more refined methodologies continue to suggest that there remain differences in morbidity between ethnic groups. Pilgrim *et al.* (1993) and OPCS (1995) data indicate that ethnic minorities report poorer health than white groups. What is clear is that different ethnic groups remain dissatisfied with their GP (Health Education Authority 1994). Longer waiting times than white patients, greater distance from the surgery, the absence of same-sex GPs, GPs less often calling in black patients for health checks and information not being available in the patient's own language all contribute. Loneliness, racist attacks and financial difficulties are also factors which add to morbidity (Pilgrim *et al.* 1993). FHSAs, providers and purchasers still do not all have active and operational policies; in the ethnic health unit survey, equal opportunity policy had been adopted by 54 per cent of purchasers, 35 per cent of FHSAs and 42 per cent of providers. A regular review of the content and effectiveness of this policy was held by 62 per cent of purchasers, 69 per cent of FHSAs and 88 per cent of providers. Forty-eight per cent of purchasers, 46 per cent of FHSAs and 73 per cent of providers made provision for regular training on anti-discriminatory policy and cultural awareness. (Task force, Institute of Psychiatry, Mental Health Foundation and Department of Health reports are summarised at the end of this chapter.)

Barriers to progress
Health service research
CONFLICTING RESEARCH METHODOLOGY AND IDEOLOGY

The debate about epidemiological data and the public perception of health-related behaviour and risks is of course not limited to cross-cultural psychiatry, yet in this realm the damage caused to a working relationship between the academics from different disciplines and between academics/clinicians and advocates of the black communities is counterproductive. The communities are suspicious of the intentions of all research and see it as a further pathologisation of being black. The unique position of psychiatry as a discipline of judgement yet entertaining extensive legal powers generates a 'very potent brew of racial suspicion and distrust' (Cochrane and Sashidharan 1996). Health service research as a discipline is itself evolving. An accepted publication bias was attended to by Donnan (1996), who advocates a need for new broader-based but rigorous techniques to test hypotheses and that such an approach should be the foundation of progressive health service research rather than just descriptive studies. Yet here is the paradox: much of the work that is cited by the minority communities themselves as coming closer to their experience of mental health services is indeed qualitative and takes account of context rather more than diagnosis (Littlewood 1990; Fernando 1988). The methodologies for these approaches have developed largely from the discipline of anthropology. Yet anthropology and epidemiology as approaches have always had an uncomfortable relationship (Inhorn 1995; Janes, Stall and Gifford 1986) but one that must now be harmonised in order for high quality cross-cultural health service research to develop (Smaje 1996). Anthropology as a discipline has challenged many psychiatric conceptualisations of distress (Kleinman 1980; Littlewood 1990; Good and Good 1981) and although it has been involved in rapid ethnographic work in acute life-threatening conditions such as diarrhoea in developing countries to improve the implementation of public policy (Scrimshaw and Gleason 1992; Bentley *et al.* 1988; Bennet 1995) such an application has not been seen on a substantial and pragmatic basis in the realm of health services research and public health policy development for the mentally ill in the UK. For example in the realms of compliance, much in the medical literature fails to take account of compliance as a medical ideology far removed from the realities of a patient's life and his or her perception of risk (Trostle 1988; Bhui 1996a). Such inattention to culturally consistent therapeutic practice could explain the persistent use of traditional healers (Kleinman and Sung 1979).

Sociology as a discipline also laments at the lack of attention to qualitative methods as part of a health services research strategy which delivers experience-near data (Pope and Mays 1993).

> Widely used medical sociology texts have edited out race and racism as legitimate areas of scholarship or at best provide patronising cultural reductionist, stereotyped accounts of Asian and African-Caribbean patients. (Ahmad 1993)

> Publication and dissemination of the results of qualitative research have often been difficult partly because different formats were required…the assessment of proposals for qualitative research and of papers submitted for publication is likely to have been hampered by a lack of agreement on criteria for assessment, although providing clear guidance on to reviewers on this point is made possible. (Jones 1995)

Epidemiology, although suited as a methodology in many medical specialities, encounters, in the realms of mental health, major limitations in terms of assumptions and inferential validity. The shortfalls will not be discussed but are extensively considered by Cochrane and Sashidharan (1996); suffice it to say that there is a diversity of opinion even within academic circles such that a consistent, cogent view has not emerged about the appropriate and valid methodology; but worse than that, this fragmented approach manifests itself in a paralysis of service and policy development maintained by the belief in a purist method, yet if such focused attention were directed to the practicalities of service delivery many pragmatic changes could be adopted within services at no additional cost (Bhui *et al.* 1995b). Additional cost-implicative but essential alterations of service structures could at least be timetabled in accord with potential future resource availability. There needs to be a social research agenda concentrating on black people's perceptions and perspectives on healthcare delivery that are not concerned with fundamental biological and aetiological truths but with making the system fit the needs of the population (Ahmad 1993). Notable exceptions to this absence of culturised research using integrative methods on mental health are the studies of Abas *et al.* (1996) and Lloyd *et al.* (1996) in London and Patel *et al.* (1995) in Harare.

RACISM AND THE ANTI-RACIST MOVEMENT IN MENTAL HEALTH

Fernando (1992) criticises the historical foundation and contemporary practices within psychiatric establishments as racist and specifically draws attention to the perpetuation of this state by racist ideology in research. Such a notion is supported by the racist categories of violent Caribbean male youths and hysterical South Asian girls as a focus of research (Black health workers and patients group 1983) and by the clearly documented historical accounts of social sanctions and research that we today would consider blatantly racist (Fernando 1988; Littlewood and Lipsedge 1989). Stuart (1996) proposes that there are limits on what ethnic minorities can blame on the inequities of white supremacy; he argues that the term 'institutional racism' (p.89) has been used in a reductive manner to imply that racist processes are the only primary cause of all the unequal outcomes and exclusions that black people experience: '...there are two sides to the black experience of subordination, that which is inflicted from without and the response to this from within'. Yet ethnic minorities seek no more than equal opportunity of access in health and social care provision, and not to the detriment of other players in the 'bazaar' of healthcare. One must beware that although crude racist conclusions are no longer apparent in transcultural psychiatry research, implicit or subtle racism still pervades the discipline (Cochrane and Sashidharan 1996). Perhaps what Stuart (1996) alludes to is an unacceptable inertia in the national debate about how to prioritise, a debate that is beset with powerful emotions transmitted through generations of oppressive experiences which, although vividly remembered, seem redundant in contemporary service developments if they serve only to generate mistrust between British people as citizens, patients, carers and providers. This 'game of chess' of course affects clinical service developments, the research agenda and, ultimately, patient care.

An epidemic of schizophrenia among African-Caribbeans in London was suggested. The difficulty is that findings are too readily interpreted in the context of favoured aetiological hypotheses and drawing conclusions that the data do not support. This intellectual leap to causal attribution becomes reified. The Flu Hypothesis, one example of this process, was advanced to explain the epidemic among men born in the 1950s and early 1960s. Yet at no point is there any consideration of whether these hypotheses are likely to be welcomed and considered by the black community as being of public health interest or of direct therapeutic relevance. Consequently what in scientific circles can be considered as a tentative hypothesis worthy of exploration is to the community a far-fetched attempt to further exoticise black mental health with little attempt to explain or interpret the findings to those whom the findings should most affect, that is patients.

An interesting hypothesis based on routine data and with potentially unresolvable residual confounding and biases in the data collation is identified by the black media as further evidence of at least disrespectful regard if not an insidious form of racism. Nonetheless, it was these hypotheses that led to much perplexed disbelief amongst the black communities where conference speakers were heard to say 'so not only do we have more schizophrenia but they now want us to believe that we get it because our mothers caught the flu'.

While the evidence for this suggestion (flu hypothesis) is not strong it would, if correct, have important implications for how services would need to respond to the phenomenon both in terms of the cost effectiveness of adapting services to what may be a transitory phenomenon and in terms of prevention of epidemics of schizophrenia. (Cochrane and Sashidharan 1996)

This is an example of how inferences of public health importance based on a lore of rational scientific principles can neglect the actual impact of this revered scientific rationality on public perceptions. The implementation of public health measures and the pursuit of quality research in this field requires a much greater collaboration at the planning stage, taking account of ethical considerations, interpretation and presentation of the findings. Representation on ethics committees could be one useful yet limited approach. Yet ethical committees themselves have been demonstrated to draw inconsistent and questionable conclusions (Alberti 1995; Hotopf *et al.* 1995); such a flaw in the realm of health service research related to race and ethnicity would further compound accusations of racism. Greater collaboration or seeking consultation with existing voluntary agencies or a sample of the public or perhaps even the study populations would lead to more creative and fruitful solutions, even though establishing such a process would require much mutual effort especially around issues of ownership and disagreements between parties. Inevitably this would introduce another component to what is often an already complicated process.

There are specific gaps in our knowledge about minority ethnic communities: for example the Chinese and Vietnamese communities have received far less funding or research than some other communities. Refugees have received relatively little attention despite their growing number and their burden of morbidity (Mental Health Foundation 1995b). Research is therefore necessary if we (as a society) are to maintain an advantage in the prevention of mental ill health and in order to plan services effectively with ever-restricted health budgets. It becomes of increasing importance then to ensure that all research carried out in this field is properly considered and that the evaluation of new health services research projects (including voluntary sectors) is properly co-ordinated from inception. Any sustained effort must be based on reliable data so as to ensure that resources are best spent; however, in view of the dynamic nature of population demographics as well as culture, it appears that whichever model of delivery is adopted it must retain the capacity to change the profile and quantity of interventions provided as well as retain expertise within teams and not rely on single individuals to become representatives of whole cultures. A closer connection with communities on social as well as health-related (medical-model based) issues seems to be essential.

Many commentators suspicious of the 'schizophrenia epidemic' suggest that the findings summarised above reflect the racism or ethnocentrism of British psychiatry (Smaje 1995). The word 'racism', however, is imprecise and can do violence to the distinctions between injustice based on ignorance or omission and injustice that arises from a vindictive prejudicial attitude. The consequences of course of either of these scenarios may be identical, and if one defines racism by the outcome of action rather than the intentions of individuals and organisations then such blunt application is valid, but such a process is not likely to encourage dialogue and invariably will jeopardise collaborative public health efforts. Future research needs to be relevant to practice and a means of improving it.

Voluntary sector and partnerships
EMERGENCE OF THE VOLUNTARY SECTOR

Griffiths outlined how the voluntary sector could provide several different types of care of which information resource, public educator and constructive critic of service providers are but a few (La Grenade and Bhugra 1999). Gray (1999) outlines how there has been little progress over the last decade in the provision of services appropriate to black communities and concludes that psychiatry as a discipline chooses not to hear the tenacious demand for a radical change in service delivery; psychiatric racism is again invoked as an explanation without attending to other operational factors; hence voluntary black organisations are identified as the only source of culturally sensitive practice. Gray (1999) goes on to suggest that such black-led services cannot be matched by mainstream psychiatric services, which lack the black perspective, and that as voluntary sector services arise from the community they are able to adopt creative and innovative strategies. Their freedom from institutional legislation and a professional body of esoteric knowledge to which practitioners conform in accord with the requirements of professional status is their strength; such procedures, although essential as a safeguard, do bureaucratise any effort to change existing patterns of service provision. The black mental health-dedicated voluntary sector has then become the guardian of good practice and the convenient solution for the colour- and culture-blind approach of the statutory sector. The voluntary sector cannot be seen to represent their communities, but they are advocates for the needs of the communities and a convenience for service planners to explore the needs of black people; yet such a position is fragile; the casualties of a failure of this policy will be of course the groups of patients for whom such services are essential.

JOINT WORKING: IS IT HAPPENING?

A recent survey of voluntary organisations indicated that 53 per cent had past contact with mental health services (La Grenade and Bhugra 1999). Only one organisation recalled positive experiences from the statutory sector; 26 per cent admitted negative perceptions and 47 per cent acknowledged negative experiences. These included eurocentric practice, slow response to crisis, lack of preventive measures, lack of respite services, racist treatment, bureaucracy, poor support, lack of cultural and religious sensitivities and an inflexible approach. Fifty-two per cent of agencies said that they did network; thirty-three per cent wanted more information from the statutory sector on mental illness and on local services. Information available on a 24-hour basis was deemed essential; training of voluntary organisation workers and joint working was regarded as important, perhaps again reflecting that the statutory sector may not be receptive.

A study in the North West Thames region (NW Thames RHA 1994) demonstrated that both the voluntary and statutory sectors lacked an understanding of each other's sector; specifically there was a low level of mutual knowledge between commissioners and voluntary providers about the structure, policies, planning, ethos and management processes of each other's sector. There were few examples of commissioning from the voluntary sector and an absence of named commissioners carrying responsibility for the commissioning process from voluntary agencies. One specific recommendation was that the voluntary sector infrastructure needed improvement and that information standards that yield comparable voluntary sector cost and performance data should be developed. Yet who decides these standards and to what extent a purchaser will address the cost of evaluations of innovative projects is unclear. Indeed, it is essential that the evaluative criteria are agreed by the voluntary provider, the purchasers and those responsible for the evaluation such that the end of a project is not met with uncertainty about the effectiveness of the project, the measure of effectiveness to be adopted and the cost implications. Yee (1996) warns that the danger of asking service efficacy questions is that too much time is spent in feasibility work and too little in actually providing the service; as the competing pressures on the contracting cycle do not make changes in health and race easier to achieve, race work has to be a long-term priority for purchasers (Jamdagni 1996). No public-funded service can or should escape rigorous evaluation; it is the resourcing and the criteria which deserve greater attention such that the providers are not constantly undermined by a perpetual search for funds to keep afloat and those responsible for providing the service are not constantly distracted by an evaluation which they do not own and indeed an evaluation that may ultimately not be accepted as sufficiently rigorous to secure longer-term funding. Specifically, the voluntary sector arose from the need to address the social ills faced by minority populations, and hence the transition to a provider of mental health services requires a clear delineation of the target population (severely mentally ill, in need of counselling, social adversity, poverty, unemployment) and the 'model for working' such that their role is not misconceived by purchasers or users.

Jamdagni (1996) scrutinised the barriers and opportunities for improving service delivery to black populations as a consequence of the purchasing and commissioning process, but this analysis was not restricted to mental health care provision. The work highlighted three instrumental factors: the political will of the purchaser, access to and relationship with local black communities, and a relationship between purchaser and provider that is based on a shared understanding and a degree of trust. An outreach approach and partnership with a community health council (CHC) are described as mechanisms to improve communication and generate better working relationships between the various players. Use of the CHCs in this manner could fill an essential gap where channels of communication, decision-making processes and political know-how are essential to ensure that services offer all patients (including black patients) an ongoing and optimal service. The CHCs themselves recognise this potential role but also the need to properly co-ordinate efforts between purchasers, providers, voluntary organisations, social services and NHS facilities (Hendessi 1994).

The voluntary sector has now had its level of responsibility raised to resolve the difficulties faced by the statutory sector in providing services with limited funding on a short-term 'project basis' (Jamdagni 1996). These groups often face severe marginalisation as a result of their campaigning role or race focus, which can set them at odds with conventional services. A lack of information and of a supportive infrastructure and under-resourcing further limit their impact (Jennings 1996). Such organisations are set the double task of providing services and evaluating their services in terms that would fulfil and satisfy both the statutory services who work alongside them and the purchasers, all within the budget designed to provide a service (Ahmad and Atkin 1996). It is conspicuous that data often sought regarding effectiveness of voluntary organisations is absent, yet such organisations clearly bridge a gap in service provision and provide high quality care in terms of cultural sensitivity. Even when monitoring and evaluation data are provided they receive scant attention from service providers and purchasers (Watters 1996).

WHAT RESPONSIBILITIES SHOULD THE STATUTORY SECTOR RETAIN?

Having established that the voluntary sector providers can deliver quality care effectively, where does this leave the responsibilities of the statutory sector, who are charged by their professional bodies with clinical and ethical responsibilities and by the public through the law with civil and potentially criminal responsibilities to provide care and to protect the public and the patient? Can hospitals and consultants divest themselves of responsibilities in all these arenas? Indeed, is the voluntary sector prepared to adopt a professional code of ethics and to take legal responsibilities that any government of the day would not readily welcome? All of these dilemmas arise if one conceptualises the two sectors as separate in ideology, geography and funding. Separatist services fiercely retain their autonomy and have an important advocacy role to play for those who are most dissatisfied with and alienated from health services (Mental Health Foundation 1995a, b). Indeed, their success arose out of their difference in approach from traditional health services enshrined within a medical structural context and invested with powers to limit the freedom of an individual. Yet if the psychiatric professions did not adopt changes in their practice and delegated all responsibility to other specialist teams or services, this would betray their responsibility to care for all of the community and not just those with whom they can more readily identify and those who respect the workings of the medical establishments and piously adapt to the ideology of free NHS care at the cost of personal choice. Joint working between statutory and voluntary sectors with an equal share of clinical and legal responsibilities working harmoniously in the best interests of the patient is a 'vision' which could be achieved. In some instances smaller independent providers would fear a loss of autonomy or an anticipated but unwelcome alteration of their service ideology and working practice so as to be consistent with that of the statutory partner (Atkin 1996). Where there are high-risk decisions the parties and individuals regarding themselves as having legal and ethical responsibility will try to override the opinions and suggestions of other team members. So even if black organisations were to become accepted as team members, the scope for their work to be compromised is significant. Psychiatrists like those in all other professions are members of a political system that has ideologies and institutional structures which shape the conditions of knowledge applied to such work (Kleinman 1988). If the voluntary sector were also to 'professionalise' in this way would they be in a position to retain the experience-near black perspective?

Psychiatric service models

There appears not to be a consistent view about the best mainstream model of delivering mental health care to ethnic minorities. There are those who advocate a separate statutory service for black people as a speciality. Indeed, such a service may be necessary where the statutory sector and the influential local personalities as well as organisations cannot prioritise and deal ethically with developing fully integrated services which are suitable for all – that is, in those areas which blatantly neglect the mental health needs of black people and cannot resolve this deficit. Thus, such developments mirror the need for a voluntary and independent sector in the first instance. Although such services have generated much expertise (for example the Lynfield Mount Unit in Bradford, the first transcultural psychiatry unit set up in the UK) the problem of collaboration is displaced to that of defining roles and responsibilities in relation to general adult psychiatric services. Furthermore, such a service is then likely to have referred all patients that the general services experience as 'beyond their expertise' and indeed they no longer have to acquire expertise if there is a specialist service. Although fully integrated multi-cultural services remain elusive, such a service has built-in funding, service-level agreements between component teams, and management strategies that require co-ordination and consultation and should therefore represent a rational long-term strategy. Expertise in cross-cultural psychiatry then has to emerge in generic psychiatric services, services in which users and carers are satisfied that they receive the best treatment. There are no British published evaluations comparing patient satisfaction for these two styles of service; while this debate has remained unresolved, in reality black patients continue to receive care from existing statutory services when in crisis. What happens in between crises and whether community interventions are effective across cultural and ethnic groups is untested. This issue is unresolved but the crisis of mental health services generally has distracted all from the plight of black patients, as if their interests were subsidiary. It was hoped that the home treatment movement would be a more humane and satisfactory solution (Sashidharan 1994) but again such service models have not been evaluated across cultures and also appear to be costly. It may be that a lack of resources, lack of managerial skills, the weight of institutional inertia and the external imposition of other priorities frustrate attempts to create better and more responsive services (Cochrane and Sashidharan 1996).

Training and education

HEALTH SECTOR PROFESSIONALS

There have been numerous publications, books and an annual calendar of conferences on cross-cultural psychiatry, the ineffectiveness of existing services and the need to develop new models of working. In all of these arenas the need for further training of health and social care providers has been emphasised. The aim of this training includes sharpening their ability to better define states of distress across cultures so as to know which states can be broadly defined within existing psychiatric nosology, as well as redefining the task of providing mental health care located in a community setting. The institutions that supervise the main professional groups in mental health care do not appear to be addressing the issue of race and culture to a significant extent, possible because they are inherently conservative bodies (Fernando 1996). Furthermore, in view of the recent critical changes in the provision of healthcare, the list of professionals requiring additional training has lengthened: managers, purchasers, tribunal representatives, police officers and indeed anyone that may come into contact with the mentally ill. This is often tactically presented as part of continuing education or a way of exhibiting anti-racist measures. Yet therein lies the dilemma. The whole process is not seen as an essential part of core professional training. Although psychologists and social workers do now have some race and culture training modules, psychiatrists have been slow to take up the challenge.

Continuing medical education is one vehicle of intervention, but for a subject which requires the use of perceptual judgements, is this enough and is it too little too late? The undergraduate medical curriculum, although now grasping communication and interview styles as being of importance, has not delved into race awareness training; although inequalities in health are raised in terms of indices of deprivation. Ethnic minorities remain an index of deprivation in inner cities rather than acquiring attention as a group with specific needs and therefore requiring modification of the skills, competencies and knowledge components of medical education.

The BMA survey of multi-cultural education demonstrated that 44 per cent of undergraduates, 25 per cent of postgraduates and 59 per cent of

GPs reported the inclusion of health and culture in medical education programmes (BMA 1995). Only 9 per cent of house officers reported that health and culture in relation to the local population was included in their induction. For those institutions without courses 58 per cent of undergraduates, 42 per cent of postgraduates and 50 per cent of GPs expressed that there was no need for such a course. Although this refers to all medical specialities the psychiatric postgraduate curriculum is similarly unimpressive and clearly has a number of already disparate specialities, but with a recognition of a complex interplay in the presentation, detection and treatment of distress. However, a consideration of the limitations of existing psychiatric concepts in relation to black people appears under 'Social Sciences' in the Basic Sciences and Clinical Curricula for the Royal College of Psychiatrists' Membership examination (MRCPsych). Thus 'prejudice and stigma', 'ethnic minorities and mental health' and 'social anthropological' methodology is on the curriculum but is not an essential or necessarily examined part of the examination.

The report of the working party to review psychiatric practice and training in a multi-ethnic society suggests rather non-specifically that convenors of approval visits might determine whether transcultural psychiatry is incorporated into MRCPsych courses, whilst acknowledging that it should be included in CPD workshops (Royal College of Psychiatrists 2001). There is no mention in the ethical or legal section of the MRCPsych curricula about black minorities' mental health. Such a position is untenable in light of the significant mistrust between the black communities and the profession. The argument that most psychiatrists will work in rural areas where there are few black people and therefore a just component of the training curriculum cannot be devoted to black and ethnic issues is flawed. It first assumes that black people can only expect an equitable service if they live in an area with a high proportion of black people. Second, it assumes that white people in the UK are the same all over the country – either devoid of culture or with a culture that does not warrant attention in mental health settings. The latter can be understood to be a sentiment that presumes a significant amount of cultural knowledge is shared between doctor and patient; however, with an increase in migration across the globe and most specifically from Europe, this remains a rather arrogant presumption.

On the basis of the rapidity with which the user movement is gaining momentum in Britain, perhaps psychiatrists have miscalculated. There has been concern that ant-racist training, or even training in cross-cultural psychiatry, was somehow a political activity not befitting those who have undergone an arduous and clearly ethical, scientific and hence honourable career choice. Yet in every country, psychiatry as a profession is enshrined in a social and political system, and a recognition of that is essential in all branches of psychiatry (Kleinman 1988).

VOLUNTARY AND INDEPENDENT SECTOR PROFESSIONALS

The training received by voluntary and independent sectors is often similar to that of the statutory sector in that former fully qualified NHS and social service employees may transfer to this way of working, seeing it to be more effective and less oppressive for black people. People usually avail themselves of courses and conference attendance but there are no studies indicating the levels of expertise or indeed the deficits. Sections of the voluntary and independent sector have indicated a need for mental health training and more liaison with psychiatric services. The training requirements and support with supervision is usually built into the provider function, but again these needs remain ill-defined other than where there are examples of projects not being able to function (see Jamdagni 1996). The expertise within the independent sector to provide black services is certainly not recognised within mainstream providers as a resource. A mutual exchange of expertise could be fruitful, but the task of providing and focusing on training with limited budgets and little desire within psychiatric service provider units to develop joint training has compounded a breach in joint working.

PATIENTS AND CARERS

Another avenue of training considered and in the early stages of evaluation is a training package for users to make more effective use of services and staff. Education packages for the severely mentally ill have been advocated as a solution to problems of 'compliance', but such packages have not had a cross-cultural evaluation. Education per se does not necessarily improve clinical outcome (Kemp and David 1995), but regularly giving clear information to long-term service users may be valuable. Bhugra *et al.* (1996d), in a small study involving 21 Asian GP attenders, illustrated that education leaflets in appropriate languages can make a difference to the amount of information people can report about depression and indeed to their perceived role of doctors and health professionals. The information given persuaded some individuals that depression was like any other medical condition for which help could be sought from the GP.

Chapter 12

The Primary Functions of Racial Prejudice are Psychological and Cultural. The Primary Functions of Racism are Economic and Political

Kamaldeep Bhui

This chapter proposes a number of foci for remedial attention, if service provision to ethnic groups is to improve. It draws on a number of detailed service reports, which all attempt to remedy the paralysis in mental health service development.

The title of this chapter is a direct quote from Lago and Thompson's (1996) book on racism and psychology. Any solutions must fully accommodate a broader perspective located in social institutions and symbols of social justice and morality. However, in this chapter I explore some potential practical solutions that might remedy many of the problems facing mental health services.

Progress will be achieved not just through formal contracting processes but also through key staff in purchaser and provider organisations caring about the outcomes (Chandra 1996). For many of the problems discussed there are no obvious immediate solutions. Indeed the pattern of immediate short-term solutions to allay political pressures is counterproductive. Short-term solutions only reflect uncertainty about options and hence procrastination about the commitment of resources. Each of the problem areas mentioned below could in themselves be the focus of working parties, committees, literature reviews, special projects and more searching. Yet what is required for each is an ongoing commitment to the issue, an annual plan of action, ongoing generation of expertise, co-ordination and evaluation as well as financial investments. Britain's multi-cultural society is not a temporary state and requires a flexible, consistent and evolving mental health service strategy that incorporates the interests of black people.

Mental health services: can't change or won't change?

Hospital and community-based services all need to recognise that patients or users of services are dissatisfied not only with personal interactions with staff but also with the locations, hotelling aspects, decor and information about services. Inpatient wards in particular can be very disturbing places to be and this has become increasingly so since many wards took on a 'psychosis-only' function in view of bed shortages. London has been especially hard hit by bed closure. Specific changes that might be adopted include: bilingual workers who understand the cultural context of a patient's biographical experiences; female-only areas or wards; accessible places of worship; closer liaison with those offering spiritual guidance (therapists, religious leaders); and an integration with non-medical and social models of care giving. All of these serve to address distress experiences holistically and not to deny aspects of the patient that do not conveniently fit into the accepted range of recognised problems and interventions. One of the major difficulties faced by all providers' units is 'nursing time' to attend to sensitive conversation with patients, who can share their worries, and thereby gain and honour their trust. A rushed interview in order to leave enough time for paperwork and other managerial and administrative tasks is likely to immediately prevent the possibility of sharing distress. Some of the implications require more resources, for example staffing levels; yet some require only a will to implement simple local policies which ensure that health service environments become more suitable for multi-cultural populations (Bhui *et al.* 1995b). Purchasers have not exercised their purchasing power to the advantage of black populations despite an awareness of the foundations of better provision (Health Education Authority 1996).

Professions or pretenders?

Health services and especially primary care facilities have, since the introduction of the market economy, changed in many aspects but there is no convincing evidence that a more just system of mental health care for black people is even on the agenda of individual practices, provider units and commissioners. Black patients may require more time and differ in their styles of communicating distress, and indeed English may be their second language. None of this is reflected in any systematic way either in vocational training or in the undergraduate curriculum (Huby *et al.* 1989). And why should it appear in primary care when psychiatry, as the profession claiming expertise in the assessment and treatment of mental illness, fails at this basic task? Of course, other service development priorities can always be cited as more immediate. Black patients continue to be relegated in the dominant agenda of service development. As long as services for black people are not integral to local community service plans, black service issues have to be addressed separately. Yet it seems service planners believe that the provision of services involves planning and implementing what they deem to be important at their pace and in their preferred order of priority. Rationalisations for complacency can be identified in the majority of commissioning and provider documents. The black communities (and many of the white) recognise this 'collective repression' as a further manifestation of racism; the consequences are clear, regardless of the sophistication of the reasoning offered. Not in any other arena of medical practice would such a professional 'limitation of competence' cause any difficulty for clinicians to appreciate the ethical dimensions; expertise and information would be sought. Race, culture and mental health issues appear to frighten, threaten and confuse our ethical sensitivities. I suggest this is because it remains for many a taboo subject, the handling of which is left to the individual's and the profession's delicate sense of self-esteem rather than being determined by what is ethical or just and preferred by patients.

Generating and retaining expertise

All provider units within the statutory and voluntary sectors are familiar with situations in which special expertise is required. Yet there continues to be little attempt to integrate the expertise of the voluntary and statutory providers. Indeed, there is no evidence that providers agree a process of how staff may seek advice or help where cultural issues influence the ethical, legal and treatment-related decision making for any one individual. Although databases are now more accessible through SHARE and the Department of Health, these pertain mainly to published studies. Unpublished data may be just as valuable and indeed expertise reflects more than an awareness of the research evidence; expertise should also be available in the form of advice regarding the legal and ethical position of treatment decisions as well as alternative approaches. Again the resource implications are largely of time away from busy posts and funding the process of establishing credible and balanced local panels of expertise. It is essential that legal advisors be involved in this process, as too often decision making is left to judgement, without consideration of the legal standing of decisions and least of all to individual rights. Expertise in the implementation of policy at a pragmatic level is also an essential component.

Community psychiatry and the voluntary sector

A diversity of models of dealing with suffering exist. There has been much difficulty within the statutory and voluntary sectors regarding joint working. There is no critical evaluation of potential models of joint working or in which circumstances they should be adopted. Who decides whether a treatment is effective? Who has a final word on treatment plans if a disagreement arises between parties? In recognition of the immense difficulties that the voluntary sector faces in negotiating with a more powerful provider, Jennings (1996) has outlined some of the key dynamics that can prevent necessary partnerships. Yet such difficulties are not unique to mental health services working across cultures; issues of power dynamics, a rapidly evolving health service and competing priorities all within finite budgets have been attended to in the health service management literature (Richards 1996; Bhui et al. 1995b). Yet competing priorities always serve to marginalise disabled people (Doyle *et al.* 1994) and the statutory sector must explore and redefine its relationship with voluntary agencies if patients are not to suffer as a result of administrative and political debates. The statutory sector also needs guidance on this.

The Mental Health Act

The Mental Health Act needs evaluation in the context of community and in the context of potential prejudicial interpretations, especially where judgement is required.

> Law does not exist in a vacuum. The interpretation and application of the law will vary in accordance with those in influential positions. Successful health promotion requires legal equality…not all of our actions are governed by law but many are governed by tradition, convention or even informal agreement. (Bhopal and White 1993)

The Mental Health Act is already under close scrutiny by the public, Government and the Royal College of Psychiatrists. Not only is community care bringing new clinical situations requiring greater clarity and/or amendments to the legislation but there is also a developing view that the existing legislation, although effective, is unjust and does not adequately protect civil liberties (Bradley, Marchall and Gath 1995; Pelosi *et al.*1995). The act is disproportionately enacted where black people's mental health is being questioned. These accepted flaws in our Mental Health Act, coupled with the fact that there are alternative practices in other countries, demand serious ethical appraisal. Yet there appears to be a lack of any data examining the decision-making process when black people are detained, and there has been no serious consideration of potential amendments to the act to ensure that essentials of a cross-cultural assessment are attended to. Furthermore, patients may benefit from earlier contact with lawyers who can help them (and the psychiatrist) make more meaningful decisions at a time of great distress when they are possibly under the influence of psychotropic medication.

> Laws exist for people. People do not exist for the law. Laws should make exceptions for people. People should not have to make exceptions for the

law. Law must protect human rights as its fundamental purpose. If it does not do that it will become oppressive. (Juss 1995)

The Mental Health Act is currently under review, as it is now recognised to be outdated for a modern community-based service. Its relevance in helping overcome the over-representation of ethnic minorities among detained populations (Thornicroft, Davies and Leese 1999) is yet to be seen.

Academic departments

Responsible research in conjunction with black communities is essential. Patients and relatives want research on better ways to live with their ill health, and some will declare that clinical trials based on a narrow medical model of disease have neglected their prime concerns (Fox 1996). The training of undergraduates and postgraduates and the provision of professional courses has for too long been a haphazard process. There is not even the opportunity, in the UK, to experience other styles of service delivery for those intending to specialise in multi-cultural work. It remains an unofficial activity. This is an area in which the voluntary sector could contribute substantially.

Service provision: choices and alternatives

Service provision, clinical care and communicating dissatisfaction as well as generating solutions to problems in the true spirit of a culture of diversity has progressed at a haphazard pace and in a poorly co-ordinated way. Although this diversity of solutions is heralded as the pinnacle of providing local solutions to local problems, undoubtedly there is a learning curve; there are inevitably some solutions which are counter-productive; short-term funding for projects followed by no proper evaluation is a waste of money and ideas, and serves only to defer a proper long-term solution. Similarly some potential interventions that black communities are asking for have not been evaluated and are denied in view of this, without recourse to exploration of their potential benefits and mechanism of action or to the basis upon which judgements of efficacy are made. The solution to these debates has to arise from the funding bodies that are in a position to commission quality research using the appropriate methodology sensitive to the outcome being investigated. For example, there is not a cogent view regarding the legal and ethical stance of delivering alternative treatments instead of or as an adjunct to accepted medical treatments, let alone whether public moneys should be spent on them. Sashidharan (1994) describes the need to develop a service divested of all potential sources of institutional biases and describes home treatment as culturally more acceptable. Huka (1995) concludes that even black people have become too gentrified to look at these alternatives, but as beds close down, alternatives have to be identified. Fernando (1991) describes these technologies for mental health: alternative treatments that are preferred by black people but not by evidence-based clinicians.

National reports, surveys and conference proceedings

The OPCS national morbidity survey

North East Thames was one of two national regions where a high proportion of women (26%) were identified as 'cases' by the Clinical Interview Schedule (CIS) scores. Using CIS scores depression and compulsions appeared to be twice as prevalent amongst West Indian and African women than white people in the UK. Asian and Oriental women were three times as likely to worry about their physical health. Adjusting for other socio-demographic factors (multiple logistic regression) Asian and Oriental adults were almost twice as likely to worry about their physical health (OR=1.94; 1.21–3.1). West Indians and Africans were almost 70 per cent more likely than whites to have depression (OR=1.67; 1.1–2.51). When diagnostic categories were used for a similar analysis, however, only alcohol dependence was found to be significantly associated with ethnicity, reflecting perhaps how diagnostic categories are not a good way to establish needs amongst distressed individuals, and especially so across cultures.

Policy Studies Institute

The Policy Studies Institute is currently examining the data of the fourth national morbidity survey. They have interviewed large numbers of each of the main black groups in the UK using language and ethnically matched interviewers. Physical and mental health are explored as well as social and demographic correlates. They are due to report later this year.

Bristol Study

Pilgrim *et al.* (1993) recently reported a similar study in Bristol where 574 black and ethnic minority patients were interviewed about their health using sex, language and ethnically matched interviewers. Fifty per cent of ethnic minorities report 'fair to poor' health, higher than amongst general population surveys (usually 16–37%). There was a higher prevalence of isolation and loneliness particularly amongst South Asians. People's accounts suggest that racial discrimination, racial abuse and attacks compounded their isolation (one in five had experienced abuse and one in nine had experienced attacks in the twelve months preceding the survey). Of 574 women 20 per cent had experienced racist attacks while taking their children to school, 25 per cent while shopping on their own and 18 per cent while going to parks. The commonest reason for poor sleep was worry; the commonest reason for feeling lonely was missing family who lived too far away; children and money were the commonest reasons given for worrying, work and money were cited as causing so much pressure that their health was affected. The majority expressed gratitude to their GPs; older patients tended to have been with the same GP for many years. It is unclear whether this reflects actual satisfaction with care, loyalty and reverence for the medical profession during a chronic state of ill health in the face of little knowledge about what to expect from health services. For example, one in eight South Asian women did not know about cervical smears, even after an explanation, perhaps explaining their low uptake of smears.

Health Education Authority

The HEA carried out a survey of ethnic minority residents in 12 different health areas in Britain. They report that amongst women more African-Caribbean (8%), Indian (12%), Pakistani (16%) and Bangladeshi (18%) patients report difficulties of accessing their GP compared with the total sample of whom only 7 per cent report this problem. Amongst men the percentages are not as high except for the Bangladeshi men (AC 7%, Indian 7%, Pakistani 7%, Bangladeshi 15% and UK total sample 4%). When asked for reasons for dissatisfaction, 53 per cent of African-Caribbeans, 65 per cent of Indians, 67 per cent of Pakistanis, 74 per cent of Bangladeshis and 51 per cent of the UK population reported that the surgery was too far away. Some minorities also have less access to a car (Atri *et al.* 1996) and are likely to rely on public transport regardless of the cost. Of Indians 16 per cent said that the surgery hours were inconvenient compared with 9 per cent of the UK sample. Poor public transport was a reason for 40 per cent of the African-Caribbeans, 25 per cent of the total sample, 11 per cent of Indians and 16 per cent Bangladeshis. Fewer of the ethnic minorities made an appointment, relying on just turning up more often than did the white group. But fewer of the ethnic minorities were asked to attend by their GP than the white group (latter probably not significantly different). It seems that all ethnic groups wait longer than the UK group, although this may reflect practice policy in those areas in which minorities live; yet this in itself warrants closer scrutiny. Even within the ethnic groups the variability between them for waiting 30 minutes or more was 19–50 per cent. Also, 40–58 per cent felt that they had waited too long. Although patient/GP ethnic matching does not confer less use of crisis services (Bhui *et al.* 1993), over 80 per cent of the Indian, Pakistani and Bangladeshi population had an Asian GP; African-Caribbeans were equally split between white, Asian and African-Caribbean GPs. Pakistani and Bangladeshi people more often indicated a preference for information to be presented in their own language as well as consultations to be conducted in their own language. More Indians (15%) and Bangladeshis wanted the same sex GP than the African-Caribbean (6%) and UK (5%) group. The majority were satisfied with their GP with a very high registration rate regardless of ethnic group.

Ethnic Health Unit

No single health authority in the UK has an insignificant population of ethnic minorities. In 1995 NAHAT distributed questionnaires to all existing district health authorities (NAHAT 1996). Three key policy issues were addressed and responses examined regarding implementation of policy. Equal opportunity policy had been adopted by 54 per cent of purchasers, 35 per cent of FHSAs and 42 per cent of providers. A regular review of the content and effectiveness of this policy was held by 62 per cent of purchasers, 69 per cent of FHSAs and 88 per cent of providers. In addition, 48 per cent of purchasers, 46 per cent of FHSAs and 73 per cent of providers made provision for regular training on anti-discriminatory policy and cultural awareness. Of 39 purchasers, 25 specified in their contracts that evidence of training, respect for culture and spiritual beliefs and translation or interpreting services should be provided. No breakdown was available by London boroughs but it is likely in view of the already stretched resources in London that other community care priorities have distracted from as complete an implementation as in less needy but better resourced areas. The study examining inner-city GP practices demonstrated that during focus group discussions patients reported poor communication to be a problem; no trained bilingual interpreters or advocates on the primary care teams were noted (NAHAT 1996).

Mental Health Task Force Reports

The mental health task force (NHS Task Force 1994), as part of the regional race programme, consulted black communities in seven major cities in the UK. Examples of good practice were sought as well as problems encountered in the implementation of policy. The conclusions reached were that much of what was reported was well known and had been said again and again apart from the findings pertaining to the Chinese communities (see community care section) and that what was needed was not research but an appropriate service response. Black patients wanted to be heard concerning provision of services and black service providers felt disadvantaged in securing funding. There was also a consensus on a need for: 24 7-day a week crisis services; greater use of the independent sector for advocacy; employment of users as advocates and advisers; support for those complaining about the quality of services they have received; respite for refugees; women-only services; child-care facilities; accessible services for the elderly disabled; appropriate stable accommodation; counselling in different languages and more and better interpreting services or bilingual services. There was throughout this report an emphasis on alternatives to medication and the need to discover alternative approaches.

Mental Health Foundation

The Foundation held a national seminar in London in order to identify the priorities as seen by a broad group of professionals from the independent and health care sector (Mental Health Foundation 1995a). Although many of the conclusions were similar to those of the other major bodies debating the issues, there were some which deserve special emphasis and some which were original and likely to play a pivotal role in the future.

It was recommended that all national organisations should integrate into their ongoing work the concerns raised by black organisations, users and carers. Networking between the national mental health charities was proposed as an essential yet so far elusive circumstance which would help. There was again expressed a need for a route to disseminate information from and to all black groups. Alternative models of mental health care should be explored and the Foundation had already undertaken a review of the use of alternative therapies in mental health. Purchaser, provider, health professional communication and training were seen as essential components. There was also a separate point that all those groups on whom there was little information needed further work to identify needs (Chinese and Vietnamese communities).

DoH and Institute of Psychiatry

The Department of Health in conjunction with the Institute of Psychiatry held a conference on service provision in order to better develop a shared vision of what was required (proceedings in press). It was clear however that service development was but one aspect of a whole range of research projects into cross-cultural mental health care delivery and only the conclusions regarding service provision are attended to here. The bad press received by the clinical and academic sections of the psychiatric community in this country requires that complacency amongst mental health professionals regarding training and changes in practice be abandoned. Training must begin at undergraduate level for it to be effective, and voluntary organisations, social scientists and users should be involved. Furthermore, in view of the increased emphasis on community care as a solution to the dilemmas facing a health service in crisis, the measures to ensure cultural sensitivity must be invoked from inception. Preventive strategies have received insufficient attention and a more widespread educative intermingling with local communities should be on the service plan of all community-based providers. Any future research strategies must have the communities' confidence and indeed enrol their expertise in helping researchers pose relevant and pertinent questions and avoid making inferences from the data that serve only to disadvantage black communities further. The role of purchasers and providers in the discussion of research and its processes must be clear from the outset. This also requires that funding agencies take greater care in evaluating the ethical dimension and involvement of the community in the planning of research and the implementation of research findings.

Chapter 13

Contemporary Dilemmas

Kamaldeep Bhui

This chapter brings home the everyday nature of racism, and experiences of racism in professional–patient encounters. It looks at human relationships and their tendency to develop along racialised narratives whilst subtly introducing imbalances of power. In this chapter I consider what it means to call someone a racist and to be called a racist. It concludes with an analysis of what qualities of humans and human relationships will allow some resolution of racial conflicts and inter-group hatreds across cultural boundaries. Some recommendations for practitioners and service providers follow.

You're a racist: malevolent practitioners or malevolent organisations?

The data demonstrate inequalities of access and treatment across ethnic groups. There are few data on cultural or national groups that take account of place of birth, subjective identity, and recent ethnic/cultural groupings. Most data talk simply of racial categories or ethnic categories in which the colour of skin seems to be given undue prominence. How does one explain the findings? It is tempting and relatively easy to attribute the findings to yet another manifestation of racism. The word 'racism' does not really explain how or why these findings emerge. Its use does, however, organise the general sense of dissatisfaction experienced by people in positions of disempowerment, where they consider their racial and cultural origins to be significant impediments to full acceptance and equality of opportunity. I have outlined how racism as an outcome can have many precursors with attitudinal, emotional/affective and organisational components. There-fore, research findings might emerge if the assessment and diagnosis of distress among ethnic minorities is less accurate (Bhugra and Bhui 1997a), or the routine assessment and diagnostic practices applied to Euro-American populations are less valid for ethnic minority groups (Littlewood 1990). For example, the majority of clinical trials are not con-ducted on representative samples, that is, people who are representative of the populations likely to use the medication.

One imbalance between the subjects of medical research and the recip-ients of medical interventions, especially in the field of pharmacological management, is that captured in the categories of race, culture, ethnicity and religion. Widely accepted clinical management and treatment practice might be unhelpful for ethnic minorities, and so sustain and compound disability among them (Bhugra and Bhui 1997b). For example, adverse effects, when complained about by ethnic minorities, could reflect a higher dose of medication used where the professional and patient are unable to develop psychotherapeutic opportunities to address the patient's distress. Professionals automatically fall back on the interventions which, appar-ently, least require them to change and develop their skill mix. Thus, their practice goes unchallenged. However, the complaints of adverse effects may reflect a dissatisfaction with medication-based interventions that are devoid of adequate explanation and support. Or they may reflect the development of adverse effects at lower doses, or they may reflect an antip-athy to the use of medication to deal with emotional distress. Specifically, people develop their own explanations for their distress, and wish to inter-vene in those areas of their lives. They do not automatically see distress as an illness that needs medication.

Another explanation for the data is the psychiatric organisational emblem. This may be perceived as powerful and coercive and aversive to ethnic minorities. If people hold fears about the stigma attached to mental illness, mental illness services and coercive measures of treatment that include the police, locked wards, the courts and forensic services, they are highly unlikely to be attracted to use mental health services as a first option (Sashidharan 1999; Thornicroft, Davies and Leese 1999). Even if they are able to benefit from services, if the services are known to be 'bad' for particular groups, it is inevitable that people will avoid those services. This, coupled with mental health services in the less industralised countries only working with psychoses and extreme disturbances, where mental health care does not receive much funding or priority, adds to people's fears of the treatment they might receive here in the UK. This is a general issue affecting all groups; however, if black people's experience has been particularly poor, then they are the group most likely to avoid services unless there is no alternative or they are forced to use the service.

In mental health services, the word 'racism' has been muttered by a minority of professionals who have been marginalised over decades. 'Racism' is often used in a context where prejudicial attitudes are not permissible, and its use to describe a situation of dissatisfaction and deep discontent triggers a negative response amongst professionals. One explanation is that psychiatrists, and by implication anyone working in the psychiatric system, are prejudiced, and conduct their work with prejudicial malevolent attitudes so as to dis-benefit ethnic minorities. This is usually the assumption that triggers the negative response rather than allowing professionals really to reflect on their practice and consider why it is that they are not providing as wonderful a service as they aspire to do. The faulty assumption is that racism exists as a conscious activity, so that poorer or inhuman treatment is given to people on the basis of their cultural origins. How does one distinguish ignorance about cultural taboos, appropriate treatments and culturally appropriate forms of distress from individual prejudicial attitude? The latter is the interpretation that was used in response to the MacPherson report on the murder of Stephen Lawrence by racists (MacPherson 1999). The police service felt attacked and undermined for doing what they consider their duty, and for ensuring high standards of public safety. However, the individualised interpretation is a damaging response in the face of accusations of institutionalised racism. It is simply the wrong interpretation. First, institutionalised racism says little about individuals, but speaks of procedures and processes and cultural attitudes that disadvantage some 'racial' groups. Here 'racial' is read as ethnic, cultural, religious and non-white, although the lessons apply to any group of people that are disempowered. Of course, those procedures and practices are built up of individual and collective views and values about the appropriate and clinically correct treatment strategies. This is precisely why accusations of institutionalised racism are so difficult to handle, as a good proportion of people, in whichever service, organisation or country, reject it as contradicting their rules for personal morality and professional competence. Statements of institutionalised racism reinforce the race category, using the characteristic most associated with minority status. Race may be one such characteristic, but gender, class, country of birth, language and religion are amongst other such personal characteristics that can give rise to prejudicial responses.

Prejudicial and hateful attitudes are very difficult to investigate as so few people, even if they have such attitudes, would admit to such beliefs. Furthermore, doctors, nurses, social workers, managers and psychiatrists have high levels of training, and this is always within a framework of care, equity, ethical practice and, for the nursing and medical professions, medico-legal precedent. Professional ethics, however, can reinforce organisational prejudice. This means that individual practitioners may not mean any patient harm, but the procedures by which assessment, admission, referral and treatment are evaluated and offered, inadvertently disadvantage black and ethnic minorities. Even where individuals discover they hold attitudes that are based on stereotypes, such individuals are wounded and furious if they are considered to be acting in a prejudicial way. Any other area of professional knowledge would lead to a response that redresses a knowledge gap.

It is possible to over-emphasise the intentions of the practitioners and develop a desire to explore their motivations. When misdiagnosis is promoted as a major problem, the assumption is often that of individual practitioners intentionally labelling 'black' protest as a form of madness. 'Misdiagnosis' has been popularised as a slogan for critics of the culture in which psychiatry has evolved (Fernando 1998, pp.53–56; Littlewood and Lipsedge 1981). Hickling et al. (1999), in a recently published preliminary report, offer doubts about the validity of research instruments (the Present State Examination) among African-Caribbeans. In this study British psychiatrists and a single African psychiatrist showed poor agreement on diagnosis. British psychiatrists showed even poorer agreement with the structured interview called the Present State Examination. This interview is supposed to be highly structured and therefore to offer value-free diagnostic judgements. Fulford (1999) has shown that all diagnostic judgements are value-laden, no matter how much we try to develop criteria and algorithms. The value-laden aspects arise from social identification of deviance and pathology, and this is always influenced by sanctioned norms of behaviour, thought and interaction. Although this study was rather poorly constructed methodologically (Jones and King 1999) it does illustrate some of the fundamental problems of making diagnoses across cultural and ethnic groups. Lewis *et al.* (1990) in another study used vignettes of black and white people and asked psychiatrists to comment on them. They concluded that British psychiatrists were not racist but that they did label black people in the vignettes to be more violent. Is this not racist? 'Culture has a fundamental role in the articulation of diagnostic systems, which are children of their history and circumstances' (Mezzich *et al.* 1996, p.xxii).

Contributions have recently been made to upgrade the cultural suitability of diagnostic systems in the USA (*ibid.*). Similarly the International Classification of Disease (10th edition) gives more attention to culture than previous diagnostic manuals. However, the everyday practice of clinical psychiatry appears not to have grasped the importance of contextualising assessment to the culture of patients' social world. Diagnosis is more than ticking a collection of symptoms. It requires clinicians to explore the patients' world views and the way they experience their problems, and to attach relative importance to specific phenomena identified. This requires empathy and understanding with shared reference points around which to map or locate any variations. This is the difficulty in patient–professional encounters. How do racial difference, ethnic difference and cultural distance lead to inaccurate conclusions and disadvantageous management? Probably through a fundamental failure of empathy, understanding and engagement. Therapeutics requires a two-way process, and not a one-way technical activity. If ethnic minorities do not experience an engaging encounter with clinicians, they will lack trust and confidence, and the clinician will rely on rules of thumb devoid of cultural and empathic understanding.

Clearly, communication, and its authenticity, are essential to the development of a shared understanding. Psychiatry as a subject requires careful verbalisation to describe complex phenomena; it requires an understanding of patient problems, and a capacity to show and feel empathy with subjects so as to appreciate their distress fully. Empathy acts as an organiser of potential exchanges of thought. I was once asked to see a Nigerian lady who was recovering from surgery following the removal of a tumour. The very concerned team managing her asked me to see her because they could not make sense of her minimal emotion about the matter, or indeed her reluctance to actually respond to their efforts to make her comfortable. She showed no gratitude. They wondered if she was depressed, but at the same time felt that her manner was typical of Nigerian people. This was not meant in an unkind way, but as a statement of their experiences of relationships with Nigerian people. The patient seemed dismissive of her own feelings, and seemed not to talk about herself. I met with her and concluded that she was depressed and that this was fairly marked. The unemotional countenance and distancing in white English patients might be readily attributed to depression because of the way they would talk about it. This patient's expressionless face, which in medical practice is a sign of depression, was given a racialised explanation, rather than the first explanation that might come to mind with a white English person. She spoke good English and so language was not a barrier. Depression was considered, and the team referred her for an opinion, which is exactly what to do when there is uncertainty. However, I was left feeling uncomfortable about how many people may not be referred, because depression was not thought about and a racialised explanation found instead. Indeed on this occasion there was a marked response to anti-depressants and supportive psychotherapy such that she no longer displayed the lack of facial movements, and could relate to all in a more understandable way. Here pharmacological management was very successful; there was no need for more sophisticated cultural explanations to explain her presentation. However, it was not the medication that engaged with her experience of illness and allowed her to make sense of her difficulties and make some decisions. The medication was delivered and taken within a therapeutic context in which she felt understood, and in which her views and concerns were aired, giving her a sense of mastery over the events. She was not being 'done to' but was recovering a desire to manage her life again. The difficulty was in professionals' appraisal of problems and their perceptions of the role played by race, culture and ethnicity, and in their style of engagement. Is this racist, or ignorance or professional incompetence? It's all three but which do we dare talk about and which language will lead to a change in the clinician's ways of working?

How is it that culture, ethnic and racial group origins interfere with human empathy? At a linguistic level this is a straightforward equation between language skills and communication. However, many black African and Caribbean groups speak English well. One could hypothesise that dialect determines subtle miscommunications, but this would be expected in all groups to an equal extent. The black groups (African and Caribbean groups) that are reported to have higher rates of schizophrenia speak English. Understanding is also determined by shared experiences, and a knowledge that words succeed in conveying meaning between speaker and hearer. It seems less and less likely that the research data showing excesses of psychiatric disorders among black people are simply a result of poor communication, as the excess incidence of schizophrenia is reported to be highest in second-generation African-Caribbean people. It is more tenable that symptom significance varies across cultures, and that symptoms in the UK that would lead to a schizophrenia diagnosis present more commonly in other cultures in non-schizophrenia states, and specifically in manic states (see McKenzie and Murray 1999). Is the pathway of presenting distress in any way fixed to cultural origins, ethnicity, religion and ancestry? Religion and culture are known to influence personal beliefs and explanations for distress, and therefore shape the recruitment of culturally sanctioned 'displays' of distress. Poor communication with poor conceptualisation of distress states for a particular cultural group, alongside readily available racialised interpretations, may make it easier to make sense of complicated presentations of culture and mental disorder. Patients generally do not challenge professionals, assuming their skills are adequate. Yet the skill mix of professionals is seriously lacking, as reflected in recent British mental health policy.

The colour of a patient's skin generates a whole host of expectations about an anticipated consultation. Such anticipations must exist in the mind of the patient and of the professional. This quality is termed a fantasy (Adams 1996), or a passion or a primordial quality (Fenton 1999) of racial impressions. The patient's expectations are often the subject of the assessment, but little time is spent considering the professional's value orientations. Ethnic matching has been proposed as one solution. The evidence suggests that matching patient and professional at the level of world view and value orientation is more important than ethnic matching (Ponce 1998, pp.69–87; Callan and Littlewood 1998). Thus, value judgements imposed on isolated mental phenomena can lead to incorrect interpretation of languages and displays of distress (see Lowenthal 1999; Fulford 1999). Fulford (1999) examines the value-laden aspects of disease and illness and considers the value-laden aspect of mental distress to be far greater than that with physical illness or disease. Does skin colour play a part in the in-vivo assessment of psychiatric symptoms? No study has really attempted to fully investigate this, perhaps as it is so divisive or it threatens the professions. However, the issue is not only one of black vs. white politics. The Irish in Britain also have poorer health outcomes (Leavey 1999; Bracken *et al.* 1998), but their plight has been less publicised. Social status and opportunity, distress in response to adversity, and then misunderstanding communications of distress may all contribute. African and Caribbean cultures differ, and within Africa there are multiple cultures and languages, and so there is a possibility of cultural mismatches between patient and professional at many levels, the constant one usually being one of social class.

World racism is understood as one manifestation of a worldwide oppression of the working class, and the economically deprived (Fenton 1999). White East European refugees and Gypsies are under close scrutiny from the Home Office (in the UK), immigration agencies and local authorities. Indeed the mechanisms supporting oppression might be quite different today when compared with those in post-slavery and post-colonial situations. Capitalism per se does not sufficiently explain racist outcomes (see Fenton 1999), but it seems there is a new discourse around nationalism that exists in many continents. Britain is clearly a post-colonial country, and much of the imbalance of power between national minorities and the national majority might be understood as the inheritance of power relationships and internalised representations of the 'colonial other'. This coupled with British class politics portrays racism as one manifestation of class rivalries. These collective representations might be so endemic in everyday organisational existence that services developing in a culture that is insensitive to black distress are likely to replicate this trauma (see Chandra 1999). So an explanation of the research data is that organisational pressures mould individual perceptions and the scope of decisions about care for any particular ethnic group. They not only mould but guide and gate the choices professionals can make, whilst still practising competently. Deviation from such accepted practices is likely to attract scrutiny from peers and professional bodies. For example, inpatients belonging to specific religious groups do not routinely have access to places of worship although recent government plans are beginning to address this. Women and men are often mixed on wards, and for some ethnic/cultural/religious groups this is unacceptable. When these issues were first raised they often led to amazement and concerns about budgets. However, after much discourse, such measures are now given strong emphasis in the British government' plans for mental health services.

Body language and facial expression, expressions of anger and of distress, the inter-connection of spirit, emotion and social ties are known to be communicated through subtly different body postures, verbal expressions and inter-personal tensions where culture is a variable (see Segall et al. 1990; Krause 1999). If these are not understood a more familiar label of pathology can be applied. Where there is an abundance of non-understanding, the confidence with which one can make judgements about 'risky situations' is diminished. Hence, more coercive methods are employed in the absence of clarity and certainty, which is inevitable without a full appreciation of another's culture. This might explain the over-representation of black people in mental health services and in forensic services (Coid et al. 2001), and the readiness of GPs to refer them to secondary care if they suspect an illness, rather than treat them in primary care (Commander et al. 1997). Yet variations in minority group representation between different mental health services show that the issues are not simply about different patterns of interaction between black and white, or black and brown people, but that sub-cultural groups require more consideration if we are to unravel the explanations for the data. Ethnic group categories have outlived their usefulness in this endeavour, and clinicians, researchers and policy makers must consider other 'categories of person' to make progress.

Failed empathy and accusations of racism

Empathy reflects the capacity to make sense of another's distress by sharing in some of those feelings. In psychoanalytic circles a more precise term of 'counter-transference' is used to reflect the experience of the analyst in response to the patient's total situation and world view expressed in the transference. This is a very normal process, a way of sharing meaning; however, if it fails or is too intense then there is either a block to full communication or there is disturbance. An example of the latter is what happens when people believing themselves to be moral and righteous are called racist – or, if one chooses a more contemporary theme, a policeman is called a racist, or a psychiatrist is called a racist. The truth of who is a racist becomes a mystery. The criteria by which one labels a racist are poorly defined in the absence of conscious and willing prejudicial beliefs and acts. The British police now consider that racist crimes must be investigated for racial motives, if anyone involved suspects race to be a factor. That is, racism and racist motives are defined by the existence of some injustice, some power inequality, and the recruitment of racial difference to explain misfortune. Some of these events will, of course, be directly related to actual racial hatred. But many will not. However, to deny victims the right to explore their sense of disempowerment through their preferred explanation is to compound a sense of disempowerment and victimhood.

What happens when A calls B a racist? The important function is the act of accusing, the motivation to do so and the effect this has on the recipient of this powerful projected idea, and the urgency with which such an explanation is recruited to make sense of powerlessness. The motivation is surely to do with a feeling of being treated badly, or indifferently, or as less important because of one's skin colour or other cultural signifiers. This is the context, and such experiences set the tone for all inter-personal experiences. The accusation returns the experiences of dehumanisation to the perceived 'assailant'. In some instances one might argue that there is a reality to the way the alleged 'assailant' handles inter-personal communication with the alleged 'victim', who is experienced only as an unknown 'other'. On the other hand one might argue that the 'perceived assailant' either meant no harm and actually did not treat the 'victim' any differently to other people; or that the 'assailant' meant no harm but because of his or her background and culturally limited field of perception, treated the person in a manner that was less than respectful within the victim's cultural world. Taking offence and recruiting a racialised explanation completes the failed communication. The latter proposition begs further refinement as social situations themselves are governed but culturally determined rules of engagement.

So the proposition might become that A says something or does something that violates B's cultural expectations of a cordial encounter. If B perceives the origin of this violation to be one of disrespect, or at worst a direct hatred consistent with a racial attack, then B might say 'you're a racist'. If B understands A's behaviour to be common in A's culture, and understands the meanings attached to it, then of course B may not recruit a racism label but a label of benign cultural ignorance. Is this still racism if the potential victim understands the difficulty and labels it as ignorance? In the latter situation, it is easy to forgive A or overlook the personal wound, assuming A is educable of a minor misjudgement. For example, bartering for fixed priced goods in a shop is an uncommon practice in the UK and attempts to do so in the UK high streets is likely to be met with abrupt dismissal. What if the misjudgement holds immigration, economic or legal consequences? These are then *survival exchanges*.

One might imagine the more intense statement: 'you're a racist'. If the fixity of A's judgement is backed up by a refusal to consider B's circumstances and world view with any respect or validity then B will feel attacked. A may well be simply conducting business as usual, implementing local laws: 'when in Rome do as the Romans'. If you are not a Roman, then this presumes that you are worthless; your opinion and way of seeing the world, and the laws you understand to be moral and just, are inadequate and not valued. This clearly is looking more like a transaction between powerful and powerless. Racism is, in my view, an expression of an imbalance of power in the face of 'perceived survival threats.' The instrumental and situational construction of ethnicity suggests that groups mobilise identity in order to pursue collective interests, or even that a collective identity is constructed in order to make material gains (Fenton 1999, p.174). Race, ethnicity and nationhood are all used in such ways. This means that violence and protest about violence start life as imagined events. They are then actualised as expressions of the ideas and the social forces that are mobilised by powerlessness and hunger.

Defending imagined identity and fighting reality

A passionate and emotionally volatile aspect of ethnic identity discourse is given by Young-Bruhl's (1998) concentration on 'ideologies of desire' and Benedict Arnold's concept of 'imagined communities'. Ideas are wished-for events and relationships are desired and actions move toward the realisation of these ideas. Ideas may include hopes for and dreams of experiences that offer the individual continuity of identity and security in the face of adversity, or in everyday life. Fenton (1999) gives vivid examples of the reality of such ties with a long-lost past, and the deified reverence with which ethnic, national and cultural groups worship their past. Yet the manner of expression of these inheritances is rarely a cool intellectualised recall of great achievements, but more of a passionate call to arms to protect. These views take us back to Tebbit and Hanson, and more recently Milosovic (Fenton 1999, p.214).

How does this help us with empathy and understanding across cultures? First, empathy appears far too sophisticated a subject to explore, when the breach in communication in cross-cultural encounters touches on a more fundamental and disturbing layer of the psyche. One can of course, through training and intellectualisation of a subject, suppress or repress or deny or ignore the deeper disturbance (the colour-blind approach). This is not the same as preventing it having some expression. In public services, where there is a potential to oppress the public that one serves, it is better and professional to be prepared and listen out for the unverbalised disturbing aspects of the therapeutic relationship and subject it to interrogation 'in supervision' or as part of personal development. In all other aspects of professional life a limitation of skills and understanding is acknowledged and identified as a training need. Such an acknowledgement in the arena of race, culture and mental health service provision, and open identification of training needs and limitations of understanding are long overdue. Those in public services really do not have the privilege of being wounded by such matters, but should recognise them as legitimate and acceptable aspects of professional practice that require attention.

Finding reality and fighting prejudice

None of these discussions about the micro-consultation detract from the importance of a pragmatic anti-racist and anti-discriminatory approach. Although much prejudicial thought is private, and its expression obscured by institutional procedure and practice, where public services potentially disadvantage special social groups, 'safeguards' can help support the promotion of anti-discriminatory practice. These safeguards cannot by themselves change the cultural environment of organisations but organisational theory applied to the problem of racism, and better training and retention of culturally competent workers will slowly mobilise cultural considerations to take account of minority views (Chandra 1999; Foulks, Westermeyer and Ta 1998). Society itself has a responsibility to ensure that the means for restoring distressed individuals to a full state of health are humane, and that they do not violate cultural and spiritual values whilst delivering psychiatric interventions, whether these include drug treatment or psychotherapies (see Bhui and Olajide 1999). The non-institutional care of the mentally ill will also be resisted by those who excessively fear the dangerousness of the mentally ill; add to this the mixture of racial mistrusts and perceptions of threat, and the degree of feared hostility, imagined or not, and these are sufficient to perpetuate oppressive practice that cannot flourish without a local community's receptivity (see Ramon 1999).

Protest and its oppression: you've got a chip on your shoulder

The role of ethnic identity mobilisation, or even racial and cultural solidarity, in the face of adversity has been well described. The acceptance that non-co-operation by patients may be a form of protest against coercive and restrictive revival of oppression linked to collective memories of 'slavery' is scarce (See Sashidharan 1993). African and Caribbean patients are known to dislike and be dissatisfied with statutory services. Their experience of excessive sectioning is always explored as a phenomenon that must be investigated, but these efforts are conducted remotely, without fully empathising with distress and its escalation when restrictive measures are applied unjustly, and possibly unnecessarily. This violence done to civil liberties compounded with what Fenton (1999) has called 'hot ethnicity', the mobilisation of ethnic identities by recruiting the full passions of feeling accompanied by nostalgia and shared histories, surely leads to an understandable resistance to conform to a system that fails to understand one's distress. If black and ethnic minorities feel alienated, and personal pain such as racism is denied by society's sanctioned help-givers, a final breach in trust will arise. Individuals at the height of personal distress experience being categorised inaccurately. They are misidentified, misunderstood and mis-categorised, and each of these amounts to mistreatment and repeats a trauma of non-recognition. This mis-classification does not have to amount to a mis-diagnosis, but to any aspect of a consultation where there is an insensitivity to traumas of identification. The subject, the perceived victim of racism, concludes that an important aspect of his or her dignity and pride and beloved inheritance is being denigrated, be it through subtle negation of, or lack of attention to, matters of the patient's assertion, or paying less attention to matters of importance to the patient. The professional surely has a role to play in managing uncertainty and clarifying uncertainties, especially where these propagate traumas of misidentification.

The spontaneous protest of black and ethnic minorities is often perceived as a 'chip on the shoulder', a heightened sensitivity, as if this were itself a pathology. In other spheres of trauma, an over-sensitivity to it is readily accepted. Consider sensitivity to re-exposure to threatening situations in post-traumatic stress disorders, where these are a consequence of exposure to violence, rape or torture. Sensitivity to a threatening world also occurs when I avoid busy inner-city areas late at night when such areas are known as trouble spots. These are ordinary enough precautions, and apprehension about future violence is understandable. It is a normal response. The sensitivity that persecuted groups develop to persecution is not abnormal. Yet the notion of 'he's got a chip on his shoulder' expresses sentiments in which protest is silenced. The very protest of persecution, the very reminder of a history of persecution, and the very sensitivity developed by raw experience of traumas are denied and reformulated as a pathology of the perceived victim. And so many responses to accusations of racism can be obscured by pathologising protest.

Nonetheless, care must be given not to over-indulge in accusations of racism where these, although soundly based, detract from the deeper trauma of not being understood, or of a failure in attunement. Overcoming such failures is a given in any therapeutic work. Therapists and professionals who underestimate the intensity of disturbing feelings in the patient and in themselves during a breach in trust that centres on issues of race, ethnicity or culture do so to the detriment of their patient. Policy makers and organisations do so to the detriment of the public. Only by professionals and organisations developing a capacity to hold disturbances of this kind in mind, and approaching a consultation or therapeutic encounter with neutrality and open curiosity, will patients afflicted by racialised traumas be able to begin to talk about their trauma. The same can be said of professionalised discourses about improving services, offering more training, and recruitment of more representative staff. Each is vulnerable to racialised disturbances undermining the main purpose of such tasks.

Research as oppression; research as deferred action

Similar difficulties abound when research into mental health is discussed. There is a whole literature on the difficulties of making psychiatric diagnoses when these do not reflect actual truths but more a model of distress which psychiatrists find helpful to alleviate the distress. There has been a great deal of research into schizophrenia, with little effort to interrogate the validity of the concept across cultures. The dangers that researchers neglect are the inattention to the historical origins of research methodologies, and the pursuit of research in a politically naive framework. Researchers continue to perpetuate potentially racist findings. I use 'racist', in this context, to indicate a mis-representation that either directly disadvantages black and ethnic minority groups, or which, by omission, delays the reception of appropriate treatments. Another way of seeing racism in a research context is the emphasis of particular theses which are of less interest in the pragmatic treatment and service response of those suffering with schizophrenia. But these consume resources from limited budgets. For example, schizophrenia diagnoses were justified by and used to justify the 'degeneracy' of sufferers. They were then deemed to be unsuitable for humane considerations (see Fernando 1998, pp.57–58). Schizophrenia aetiologies have usually been investigated with the expectation that biological causes would emerge and that these would lend themselves to corrective intervention. This might involve appropriate treatment, or improving the genetic pool (*ibid.*). Thus, a biological and genetic emphasis tends to allow such interpretations as explanations of the higher rates of schizophrenia identified amongst African-Caribbean peoples in the UK to flourish. Linking genes, ethnicity and disease models is the stuff of scientific racism.

An example of this pursuit of research priorities with little actual attention to addressing service needs of those afflicted was the preoccupation with the flu hypothesis of schizophrenia (Mednick *et al.* 1989; O'Callaghan 1998). This hypothesis motivated other studies which began to explore whether the aetiology of schizophrenia could be explained by studying cohorts of West Indian immigrants exposed to the flu virus. This theory was used to explain away the higher rates of schizophrenia amongst young black men in the UK (see Fernando 1998, p.53 and McKenzie and Murray 1999 for a critique), with no efforts to question the findings in a cultural context or to provide a service, if the findings were authentic, to treat the 'epidemic' of schizophrenia (Sashidharan and Cochrane 1996). Their emphasis on biological issues was automatic, without consideration of how such inferences might further perpetuate notions of racial inferiority. This unnecessary focus on a remote biological theory was at the expense of more obvious and simpler explanations such as unemployment and social adversity and discrimination (Bhugra *et al.* 1997; Leff 1999; McKenzie and Murray 1999). Genetic and biological arguments alone do not account for the findings, and once one begins to investigate sociological phenomena as a risk factor for schizophrenia, then sociological mechanisms, including racism, have to be entertained. These may have a complex interplay with pathophysiological mechanisms. For example, the concerns about hypertension and its origins among African-Americans exposed to discrimination cannot all be explained as sociological. There are currently no studies of exposure to racist events and schizophrenia.

One way of evaluating such research is to consider who benefits from it. Does it directly improve living standards, unemployment, economic stability and mental distress today? Certainly, careful and complicated studies to explore the aetiology of schizophrenia are essential for the long-term aim of prevention and early detection; however, research to date has focused almost exclusively on aetiologies mirroring the frankly racist preoccupations of the 17th-, 18th- and 19th-century academics: biology as the only explanation of essentialised differences. Oppression is easy to reinforce, but introducing a paradigm shift in the way we think about distress and the manner in which we investigate mental illness whilst trying to manage it effectively and humanely has proved more difficult. The path ahead will be no less problematic, but might benefit from some critical work around epistemology and our capacity to avoid thinking about unbearable feelings that we all must entertain.

Chapter 14

The Future of Mental Health Care
Essential Elements

Kamaldeep Bhui

This, the final chapter, summarises some of the main initiatives necessary to address racism in the healthcare system, and so address the impact of racism on mental health. Action is necessary at a societal level, but the response of health services and government departments such as the Department of Health, symbolise the responsibilities of public institutions generally. It is poignant that the very institutions and practices intended to support the mental well-being of the public are themselves afflicted with institutionalised procedures and practices. Recommendations are not cost-neutral emotionally or in economic terms. Refinements will of course be necessary depending on local implementation practices, but the general principles, or essential elements, are summarised to guide social action to improve the mental well-being of people from all cultures. However, there are some common mind traps that need to be borne in mind. In summary of much of the emotional obstacles outlined in this book, I notice several emotional positions in which debate becomes paralysed. Debators on the subject of racism are often preoccupied by specificity of terms and concepts devoid of practical implications (intellectualisation). They might take a particularly defensive yet personal position of perfection, or give the impression that perfection is the objective of all change (supermoral). Others prefer to think of racists as ill people or diseased, and if the ills could be removed (medical or social) then such thinking would disappear (illness or disease model). Some argue that racism must be stamped out and eradicated, denying that prejudice of all sorts is part of our human make-up and a product of our fundamental thinking processes, which include suspicion, hatred and aggres-

sion (eradication myth). Associated with this view is that racist people are a deviant minority, and such thinking cannot exist in all of us (deviant model). Resistance to thinking about racism also emerges in the form of comparisons with other more intolerant societies, and celebrating the success of our own local worlds, with examples of successful multi-ethnic ventures in business, entertainment and working professional lives. None of these positions allow movement to explore the confusion and impact of racist thinking and action. Each of these positions are comfortable for us to occupy but the first stage of addressing racism in public life and institutions is an awareness of how uncomfortable it will be and the tenacity necessary for benefit.

Emphasis on redefining the unit of analysis

An analysis of information on the basis of ethnic groups is clearly inadequate. National variations in criteria for ethnic group definitions, not to mention historical changes, reflect that ethnic groups are social constructions, designed to give information to policy makers and governments about the public. This unit of analysis does not help unravel the findings generated by its use in research and clinical settings. It is a simple proxy measure that reflects many components: cultural characteristics, country of origin, colour of skin and race, religious group (see Bhui and Olajide 1999; Bhui 2001). To generate findings by using ethnic groups and then explain them only in terms of ethnic groups is to analyse in a closed system that does not open up other risk factors, or explanations based on social class, language, mode of migration, unemployment and acculturation. Routine data should be collected on users of public services; however, the returns for ethnic group data are notoriously incomplete. This partially reflects a lack of recognition that such a task is important, but also highlights the perplexity which people face when trying to classify themselves or someone else. Ethnic-group belonging is not the person's self-chosen style of classifying his or her identity. We need both in research and in routine clinical services, perhaps even in census data, to include more relevant characteristics that reflect cultural identity, which changes for subsequent generations; we need to have classifications that reflect diversity within the white and black groups; we need classifications that include religion, place of birth, country of identity, age at migration and socio-demographic characteristics that have a bearing upon the meaning of ethnic group. Experiences of discrimination and their cumulative effect should also be borne in mind when interpreting information about black and other ethnic groups.

Overhaul the culture of psychiatry, mental health care, health services generally and government departments of social and health care delivery

Mental health practitioners must exercise more care in the delivery of interventions which may be scientifically advocated, may not have a sufficient body of recommendations or may simply be a product of historical and institutionalised practice. The development of culturally acceptable practices requires close and reflective scrutiny, bearing in mind what patients want, what is available and where we most focus our evaluative efforts to ensure that equitable care is a reality rather than a transitory hope, dream, or memory. MacPherson (1999, p.28) defined institutionalised racism as:

> The collective failure of an organisation to provide appropriate and professional service to people because of their skin colour, culture, or ethnic origin. It can be seen or detected in processes, attitudes and behaviour which amount to discrimination through unwitting prejudice, ignorance, thoughtlessness and racist stereotyping which disadvantages ethnic minority people.

> Racism persists because of the failure of the organisation openly and adequately to recognise and address its existence and causes by policy, example, and leadership. Without recognition and action to eliminate such racism it can prevail as part of the ethos or culture of the organisation.

The Department of Health conducted a review of its activities and in particular its intended action to address institutionalised racism (Alexander 1999). This found examples of institutionalised racism. Training and education are offered as one solution to change attitudes and knowledge. Alexander (1999) recommended changes in service delivery, workforce initiatives to offer equal opportunities and redress some of the inequalities experienced by the workforce in health and social care. Coker (2001) has reminded us that racism is present in the medical professional at all levels, from recruitment to appointment of senior staff. How are professionals to offer a service free of racism when they themselves have to survive it on a daily basis, often without opportunities to address it? They will of course come to consider discrimination as the norm, with little understanding or motivation to mobilise change.

Training and education have rightly been emphasised in the National Service Framework for Mental Health in Britsh policy that promote changes in professional accountability and improved performance within public services. The MacPherson report and the amendments to the Race Relations Act together signal the duty on public bodies and individuals to address discrimination in its widest and institutionalised sense, as well as ensuring that individual instances of prejudice and inequality in care provision that disadvantage ethnic groups are eradicated. The evidence demonstrates inequity of service provision as well as differences in mental health needs among black and minority ethnic groups. Other socially excluded groups such as the Irish, refugees and migrant populations also have special care needs that existing provision does not fully address. These needs include cultural issues in communication as well as care provision.

To date, the education and training of health and social care professionals has relied on uni-professional training programmes completed before certification to practice, with little opportunity to revisit new ways of working and delivering effective interventions. In the provision of mental health services there are special problems for professional practice which derive from the historical development of psychiatry, scientific methodologies and mental health care. In some instances scientific arguments have contributed to discriminatory outcomes by providing a body of knowledge that is used to justify prejudice on natural or scientific grounds. Fortunately, such historical and blunt examples are difficult to demonstrate in today's climate, but a more refined presence of these forces is now widely recognised, even making its way into parliamentary debate. In this volume we have reviewed the fact that colonial psychiatric practice has lent professionals in their home countries around the globe the same models of mental disorder and treatments that problematise, largely in a medical or illness paradigm, the distress of people and populations. Thus, highly qualified and well-trained professionals are also professionals trained in a particular style of working that is ethnocentric, and includes elements of 'professional knowledge' that are potentially discriminatory, to the disadvantage of black and minority groups. This means that it is not only differences in skin colour and language between professional and patient that lead to potential discriminatory practice, but also the professional training itself, and the organisational procedures that organise the professional practice. Thus, discriminatory practice is not just poor practice. Good practice may be discriminatory practice working to disadvantage particular ethnic groups. Deficiencies in the current mental health care services are of sufficient importance to service users and minority groups in general, but people from black and minority ethnic groups have had particularly detrimental experiences of mental health services, most notably of compulsory inpatient care, with excessive representation in forensic services and fewer opportunities to engage with different service styles.

Organisational Interventions

Changing practice requires a great deal of concerted effort that addresses individual skill deficits and learning needs whilst promoting individual level innovations in practice, and ensuring organisational constraints on innovation and improved practice are also lifted. Therefore any agenda for training and education has to address organisational issues in practice (see Table 14.1).

Table 14.1: Organisations and service provision and discriminatory outcomes

Service	Organisational Constraints	
	Discriminatory	Achieve equity
Current statutory sector	-	-
Envisaged statutory sector	-	+
Voluntary sector	-	+/-
Envisaged voluntary sector	-	+

+ *good non-discriminatory practice*
- *potential discriminatory practice*

'Organisational constraints' refers to funders of services, commissioners of services, service evaluators and auditors of services, as well as professional bodies that require a particular style of practice in accord with particular professionally sanctioned approaches to the management of distress in a particular society. An alternative and non-discriminatory statutory sector can be developed with learning from the alternative voluntary and traditional sectors. These might work with and complement the corporate existing statutory sectors, assuming their organisational constraints are addressed and good practice is promoted. This sets the tone for improved individual practice (see Table 14.2).

Table 14.2: Individual practice and discriminatory outcomes

Mental health care	Organisational constraints	
	Discriminatory	Achieve equity
Poor practice	-	-
Good practice	-	+

+ *good non-discriminatory practice*
- *potential discriminatory practice*

Of course we wish to have good practice at an individual level and this requires careful preparation in undergraduate and basic level training, as well as ongoing professional development work. However, discriminatory practice cannot be explained away as poor practice. Where poor practice contributes to discriminatory outcomes it should, of course, be addressed. Can discrimination arise as a result of good practice? This is the very issue which tends to wound practitioners when their practice is subject to scrutiny and identified to be potentially discriminatory. Such wounding and protest were witnessed in the police service when the MacPherson report was published. Nonetheless, because of the value base of mental health care, and its development in Euro-American societies, it is imperative to question the silence around how value judgements can pervade the practice of mental health care, where only facts are visibly given credence, as if decision making were devoid of values that are vulnerable to human subjectivity.

Individual-level training (cultural awareness or cultural competency) has not delivered a change in practice, partly because organisations can undermine innovation in practice that aims to meet cultural needs. For example, taking more time to assess someone with an interpreter, or needing to meet with families, or making contact with the voluntary sector, or indeed not making a diagnosis within accepted practice, or needing to learn about another culture and draw on the literature and expertise of another before formulating a care plan may all be considered to be too demanding of professional time. These activities take more service time that few practitioners have in under-staffed services undergoing massive reorganisation. The consequence is that individual training aims are seen as futile and of no benefit, or discordant with other policies and procedures. Hence the organisational component is essential to address alongside individual-level training.

Individual interventions

At an individual level, anti-racist training is often very challenging for participants who find it unbearable to have their integrity questioned. It touches on something very deep in terms of individual identity as people discover the stereotypes they apply. Yet the focus on race alone is too simplistic. Cultural awareness training has arisen that assumes discriminatory practice is inevitable, and that if people are more aware of other cultures and their mores, then stereotypical interpretations of distress and human behaviour will be apprehended by practitioners themselves in their practice so they can prevent it. More recently cultural competency has emerged as a concept. The absence of skills can be considered as something that should prevent certification to practice, or as a 'limits of competency' issue of which practitioners should be aware so they can practice ethically, and seek assistance if necessary. Although the latter is not ideal – that is that all practitioners should have core competencies to perform their duties and work with difference – in reality not all practitioners will be able to meet the demands of such self-reflection and self-appraisal. They will find it a challenge to become aware of their limitations in practice and this is especially likely amongst the most senior and confident, who have much-valued service experience. Thus, it is also essential to emphasise capabilities. Practitioners have to develop their capability to perform certain roles and not just consider themselves competent or not.

Methods to teach and train on the subject of race, ethnicity and culture

As a society and as organisations we lack the capacity to talk about race and culture and the meaning of this in our everyday lives. Some would prefer a colour-blind approach: we treat everyone the same. However, the capacity to talk about this subject and 'think' about it is crucial. The process needs to be legitimised without undue over- or under-emphasis. In such a context the workforce can explore the implications of their experience of and attitudes to patients, but also to their colleagues. Some evidence from the King's Fund Institute and from a number of high-profile publications show how discrimination is operative in medical training and practice, where the victims are other doctors (Coker 2001; Bhopal 1998, 2001). If the workforce find themselves dealing with a subject that is wounding but taboo within the profession, of course, this also works against open dialogue and a removal of the glass ceiling among minority workers.

Indeed, workers from minority groups are an asset to the development of cultural practices; however, that is not to say that their cultural competencies can be assumed. They will for example have been trained in a similar manner, and perhaps are even more conservative, in order to preserve what status they have achieved in a system in which they must work harder than colleagues to succeed and be rewarded.

Service models and style of engagement

Mental health care offers a complex series of interventions delivered through a number of agencies. Such services may develop out of historical precedents or in response to new policy, but they are rarely properly evaluated for all members of the public. Therefore, such innovations tend to work least well on the more marginalised groups in society, and for groups with more complex and less represented needs. Where African-Caribbean people are over-represented in locked institutions of mental health care, one can either explore and dismiss or affirm racist intentions or procedure, or stand back and consider why care cannot be delivered to this group by similar channels to other groups. Why are the forensic and secure mental health facilities seeing so many black people? This is where courage is needed to expose injustice and explore alternative ways of providing care (see Bhui and Olajide 1999; Bhui, Bhugra and McKenzie 2000; Bhugra and Bhui 2001).

Active dialogue with representative public bodies and groups

The modification of existing practice must depend on active and open dialogue with the public and alternative systems of delivering care to the mentally ill. It may be sensible to restrict the interventions offered by mental health services to those for psychosis only, or severe mental disorders, whilst allowing primary care to manage commoner states of distress in partnership with the public. Voluntary organisations are free of professional and managerial restrictions where their remit is to engage those that will not engage with statutory services. Something of the skills necessary for this success might be transferred, but it needs continuing open dialogue and a more rapid feedback loop to modify service specifications than is currently permitted, given the policy and practice priorities that restrict innovation and focus all resources on one or two priorities. The alternative is to develop specialist services for each cultural group – yet these also cannot perform if funding is limited, and they effectively undermine the task for all practitioners, that is to develop better practice suited to all cultural groups (Bhui, Bhugra and McKenzie 2000).

Race equality policy linked to equity of access and utility of services

Each organisation must have a grievance procedure and a race equality policy which informs staff of the issues, and how to deal with difficulties. These must be supported by open dialogue and a review of the returns. The accessibility of services also warrants close and regular review. Access here means an awareness of specific services, a desire to use those services, geographical and economic feasibility to use services, and then the availability of interventions delivered in a culturally acceptable manner. The latter requires additional skills. If these skills are absent in the workforce, medication becomes the main intervention on the assumption that it does not need a cultural assessment. Yet we know that pharmaco-kinetic and pharmaco-dynamic processes vary across cultures as a result of changes in environment, diet and metabolic enzymes (Bhugra and Bhui 2001). So, how often are race equality policies used to improve practice? Is there a senior manager responsible for reports of institutionalised procedures that function to the detriment of individual patient care?

Research agenda

This has been briefly discussed in an earlier chapter. Researchers need to be much more aware, and be able to debate, the potential racist impact of their research findings. We propose that ethical committees and funders of research take proper action to ensure research is culturally accountable and competent. The general issue of researching issues of relevance to the public is increasingly being tackled with an emphasis on consumer involvement in the research process. Research is not objective, but subject to all the value-laden activities of human activity. Research will not lead to a total understanding of the connection between racism and mental ill health, but it does help us unravel the link, and there are now several studies underway looking at perceived racism and its impact on health outcomes. The perception of racism emerges in the face of repeated micro-oppressions where race seems to be the only explanation for events which otherwise seem unbelievable. This aspect of human relationships and therapeutic relationships requires some urgent attention. But raising societal awareness of the issues requires gifted communicators who are sensitive to the languages people use, and their styles of receiving information in a way that allows thought, rather than convictions to emerge from a vacuum. There is not a vacuum. There are people and their conscious and unconscious thoughts, and there are groups and conscious and unconscious processes. Whatever language of research and research method we adopt, this is the subject matter for future work. Racism is often contested on the basis of a lack of evidence. Racism is not invoked lightly as an explanation, but its use can become over-exercised if care is not applied. Perceived racism is not the first explanation that leaps to offer itself in the understanding of oppression, but where repeated, and often individually minor, but cumulatively major, events build up to sustain poor care in the context of an imbalance of power, the terms 'discrimination' or 'racism' might offer a coherent explanation, where this imbalance of power and oppression is experienced between racial, ethnic, cultural or religious groups. The future research agenda must address the impact of perceived discrimination on health outcomes, and on well-being and citizenship. However, there is also an issue of where research resources currently go. Do they get used to improve care for minorities, or are the minorities relegated to less financial resource, or to a mainstreaming agenda, in which their interests are not represented? Alexander (1999) concluded the latter to be operative. Scientific racism appears to survive, and the responsibility of all researchers and funding organisations must be to stamp it out.

We aimed in this book to stimulate debate and dialogue, and to provide some of the thinking tools to promote the mental well-being of people with rich and diverse cultures. Some readers might find the contents disagreeable. Our measure of success for this book is that it makes an impact on readers' thinking about the subject; that after reading it, readers will be stimulated to disagree, agree, write and think and debate the contents. Only in such an atmosphere of open debate will sustained change emerge.

References

Abas, M. *et al.* (1996) 'Depression and anxiety among older Caribbean people in the UK: Screening unmet need and the provision of appropriate services.' *International Journal of Geriatric Psychiatry 11*, 377–382.

Acharyya, S. *et al.* (1989) 'Nafsiyat: A psychotherapy centre for ethnic minorities.' *Psychiatric Bulletin 13*, 7, 358–360.

Adams, M.V. (1996) *The Multicultural Imagination: Race, Colour And The Unconscious.* London: Routledge.

Adorno, T. *et al.* (1950) *The Authoritarian Personality.* New York: Harper and Row.

Ahmad, W. (1993) 'Making black people sick: Race ideology and health research.' In W. Ahmed (ed) *Race and Health in Contemporary Britain.* Buckingham: Open University Press.

Ahmad, W. (1996) 'Family obligations and social change amongst the Asian community.' In W. Ahmad and K. Atkin (eds) *Race and Community Care.* Buckingham: Open University Press.

Ahmad, W. and Atkin, K. (eds) (1996) *Race and Community Care.* Buckingham: Open University Press.

Alberti, K. (1995) 'Local research ethics committees.' *BMJ 311*, 639–640.

Alexander, Z. (1999) *Study of Black, Asian and Ethnic Minority Issues.* London: Department of Health.

ALG (1995) *The cost of care: Is London getting its fair share of NHS resources?* Association of London Government.

Allport, G.W. (1958) *The Nature of Prejudice.* Reading, MA: Addison Wesley.

American Medical Association Council on Ethnical and Judicial Affairs (1990) 'Black–white disparities in health care.' *JAMA 263*, 17, 2344–2346.

Anonymous, (1999) 'Unanswered questions.' In K. Bhui and D. Olajide (eds) *Mental Health Service Provision for a Multiethnic Society.* London: Saunders.

Arnold, B. (1999) *Imagined Communities.* London: Arnold.

Atkin, K. (1996) 'An opportunity for change: Voluntary sector provision in a mixed economy of care.' In W. Ahmed and K. Atkin (eds) *Race and Community Care.* Buckingham: Open University Press.

Atkin, K. and Rollings, J. (1993) *Community Care in Multi-Racial Britain. A critical review of the literature.* London: HMSO.

Atri, J. *et al.* (1996) 'Fair shares in health care? Ethnic and socio-economic influences on recording of preventive care in selected inner London general practices.' *BMJ 312,* 614–617.

Bagley, C. (1971) 'The social aetiology of schizophrenia in immigrant groups.' *International Journal of Social Psychiatry 17,* 292–304.

Bagley, C. and Verma, G.K. (1979) *Racial Prejudice, the Individual and Society.* Farnborough: Saxon House.

Bal, V. (1984) 'The symptomatology of mental illness amongst asians in the West Midlands.' BA Dissertation. Dept of Economics and Social Sciences, Wolverhampton Polytechnic.

Balabil, S. and Dolan, B. (1992) 'A cross cultural evaluation of expectations about psychological counselling.' *British Journal of Medical Psychology 65,* 305–308.

Balarajan, R. (1996) 'Health trends ethnicity and variations in the nation's health.' *Health Trends 27,* 4, 114–119.

Balarajan, R., Raleigh, V. and Yuen, P. (1991) 'Hospital care among ethnic minorities in Britain.' *Health Trends 23,* 3, 237–239.

Banerjee, S. *et al.* (1994) *Deaths of detained patients: A review of reports to the Mental Health Act Commission.* London: Mental Health Foundation.

Banerjee, S. *et al.* (1995) 'The Belmarsh Scheme: A prospective study of the transfer of mentally disordered remand prisoners from prisons to psychiatric units.' *British Journal of Psychiatry 166,* 802–805.

Bebbington, P. *et al.* (1981) 'Psychiatric disorders in selected immigrant groups in Camberwell.' *Social Psychiatry 16,* 43–51.

Bebbington, P. *et al.* (1994) 'Inner London collaborative audit of admissions in two health districts. II: Ethnicity and the use of the mental health act.' *British Journal of Psychiatry 165,* 743–749.

Beliappa, J. (1991) *Illness of distress. Alternative models of mental health.* London: Confederation of Indian Organisations.

Bell, D. (1998) *Ngarrindjeri Warruwarrin: A World that Is, Was and Will Be.* Melbourne: Spinifex Press Ltd.

Bennet, F.J. (1995) 'Qualitative and quantitative methods: In depth or rapid assessment?' *Social Science and Medicine 40,* 12, 1589–1590.

Bentall, R.P., Kinderman, P. and Kaney, S. (1994) 'The self, attributional processes and abnormal beliefs: towards a model of persecutory delusions.' *Behaviour Research and Therapy 32,* 331–341.

Bentley *et al.* (1988) 'Rapid ethnographic assessment: Applications in diarrhoea management program.' *Social Science and Medicine 27,* 1, 107–116.

Berrington, A. (1994) 'Marriage and family formation among white and ethnic minority populations in Britain.' *Ethnic and Racial Studies 17,* 3, 517–546.

Bhopal, R. (1986) 'The Inter-relationship of Folk, Traditional and Western Medicine within an Asian Community in Britain.' *Social Science and Medicine 22,* 1, 99–105.

Bhopal, R. (1998) 'Spectre of racism in health and health care: Lessons from history and the United States.' *BMJ 316,* 1970–1973.

Bhopal, R. (2001) 'Racism in medicine.' *BMJ 322*, 1503–1504.

Bhopal, R. and White, M. (1993) 'Health promotion for ethnic minorities: Past, present and future.' In W. Ahmed (ed) *Race and Health in Contemporary Britain*. Buckingham: Open University Press.

Bhugra D. (1996) 'Depression across cultures.' *Primary Care Psychiatry 2*, 155–165.

Bhugra, D. and Bhui, K. (1997a) 'Cross cultural psychiatric assessment.' *Advances in Psychiatric Treatment 3*, 103–110.

Bhugra, D. and Bhui, K. (1997b) 'Clinical management of patients across cultures.' *Advances in Psychiatric Treatment 3*, 233–239.

Bhugra, D. And Bhui, K. (2001) *Cross Cultural Psychiatry. A Practical Guide*. London: Arnold.

Bhugra, D. *et al.* (1996a) 'Attempted suicide in West London I: Rates across ethnic groups.' *Psychological Medicine 29*, 5, 1125–1130.

Bhugra, D. *et al.* (1996b) 'Attempted suicide in West London: a case control study of South Asian women.' *Psychological Medicine 29*, 5, 1131–1139..

Bhugra, D *et al.* (1996c) 'Setting up psychiatric services: Cross cultural issues.' *International Journal of Social Psychiatry 43*, 1, 16–28.

Bhugra, D. *et al.* (1996d) 'A pilot study of the impact of patient fact sheets and guided discussion of knowledge and attitudes regarding depression.' Manuscript submitted.

Bhugra, D. *et al.* (1999) 'Pathways into care for ethnic minorities.' In D. Bhugra and V. Bahl (eds) *Ethnicity: An agenda for mental health*. London: Gaskell.

Bhugra, D., Leff, J., Mallett, R. *et al.* (1997) 'Incidence and outcome of schizophrenia in Whites, African Caribbean and Asians in London.' *Psychological Medicine 27*, 791–798.

Bhui, K. (1994) 'Somatic symptoms in Asian patients.' MSc Thesis. UMDS. University of London.

Bhui, K. (1996a) 'The language of compliance: Health policy for the severely mentally ill.' *International Journal of Social Psychiatry 43*, 3, 157–163.

Bhui, K. (1996b) 'Checklist: Addressing the needs of minority ethnic groups.' In *Effectively managing mental health service development*. London: The Sainsbury Centre for Mental Health.

Bhui, K. (2001) 'Transcultural psychiatry: Some social and epidemiological issues.' In Bhugra, D. And Cochrane, R. (Eds) *Psychiatry in Multicultural Britain*. London: Gaskell.

Bhui, K. Bhugra, D. And McKenzie, K. (2000) *Specialist Services for Minority Ethnic Groups: Maudsley Discussion Documents*. Institute of Psychiatry, King's College.

Bhui, K. *et al.* (1995a) 'Essential elements of culturally sensitive psychiatric services.' *International Journal of Social Psychiatry 41*, 4, 242–256.

Bhui, K. *et al.* (1995b) Developing culturally sensitive community psychiatric services. *British Journal of Health Care Management 1*,16, 817–822.

Bhui, K. *et al.* (1998) 'African Caribbean men remanded to Brixton Prison Psychiatric and forensic characteristics and outcome of final court appearance. *British Journal of Psychiatry 172*, 337–366.

Bhui, K. and Olajide, D. (1999) 'Transformations and New Beginnings.' In K. Bhui and D. Olajide *Mental Health Service Provision For A Multi-Cultural Society.* London: Saunders.

Bhui, K., Strathdee, G. and Sufraz, R. (1993) 'Asian inpatients in a district psychiatric unit: An examination of presenting features and routes into care.' *International Journal of Social Psychiatry 39*, 208–220.

Black health workers and patients group (1983) 'Psychiatry and the corporate state.' *Race and Class 25*, 49–64.

Bleandonu, G. (1994) *Wilfrid Bion: His Life and Works. 1897–1979.* London: Free Association Books.

BMA (1995) *Multicultural Health Care: Current Practice and Future Policy in Medical Education.* London: British Medical Association.

BMJ Editor (2000). 'Editor's choice.' *eBMJ*, 30 June.

Bogdan, R.J. (1986) *Belief, Form, Content and Function.* Oxford: OUP.

Bracken, P.J. *et al.* (1998) 'Mental Health and Ethnicity: An Irish Dimension.' *British Journal of Psychiatry 172*, 103–105.

Bradley, C., Marchall, M. and Gath, D. (1995) 'Why do so few patients appeal against detention under section 2 of the mental health act?' *BMJ 310*, 364–367.

Brah, A. (1996) *Cartographies of Diaspora: Contesting Identities.* London: Routledge.

Brixton Circle Project (1992) *Annual Report of the Brixton Circle Project.* London: Brixton Circle Project.

Brown, B., Nolan, P., Crawford, P. and Lewis, A. (1996) 'Interaction, language and the "narrative turn" in psychotherapy and psychiatry.' *Social Science and Medicine 43*, 11, 1569–1578.

Brown, D.G. (1998) 'Foulkes's Basic Law of Group Dynamics 50 years on : Abnormality, injustice and the renewal of ethics.' *Group Analysis 31, 391-419.*

Bullock, A. (1962) *Hitler: A Study in Tyranny.* Harmondsworth: Penguin Books.

Bulmer, M. (1996) 'The ethnic question in the 1991 Census of population.' In D. Coleman and J. Salt (eds) *Ethnicity in the 1991 Census Vol 1: Demographic characteristics of the ethnic minority populations.* OPCS. London: HMSO.

Burke, A, (1974) 'First admissions and planning in Jamaica.' *Social Psychiatry 9*, 39–45.

Burke, A. (1986) 'Racism, Prejudice and Mental Illness'. In J.L. Cox (ed) *Transcultural Psychiatry.* London: Croom Helm.

Burrow, J.W. (1968) Editor's Introduction to T*he Origin of the Species* by Charles Darwin. London: Penguin Books.

Callan, A. (1996) 'Schizophrenia in African-Caribbean immigrants.' *Journal of the Royal Society of Medicine 89*, 253–256.

Callan, A. and Littlewood, R. (1998) 'Patient Satisfaction: Ethnic origin or explanatory model.' *International Journal of Social Psychiatry 44*, 1, 1–11.

Camden Health and Race Group *et al.* (1992) 'Changing health services in Camden and Islington to meet the needs of Black and other minority communities.' Report on a conference held on 8 October. Bloomsbury and Islington Health Authority and Commission for Racial Equality.

Carothers, J.C. (1953) *The African Mind in Health and Disease: A Study in Ethnopsychiatry.* Geneva: WHO Monograph No 17.

Carr Hill, R.A. *et al.* (1996) 'Socio-economic determinants of rates of consultation in general practice.' *BMJ 312,* 1008–1013.

Cartwright, S.A. (1851) 'Report on the diseases and physical peculiarities of the Negro race.' New Orleans Medical and Surgical Journal May, 681–715. Reproduced in A.C. Caplan, H.T. Englehardt and J.J. McCartney (1981) (eds) *Concepts of Health and Disease.* Reading, MA: Addison Wesley.

Cashmore, E. (1988) *Dictionary of Race and Ethnic Relations.* London: Routledge.

Castles, S. and Kosack, G. (1973) *Immigrant Workers and Class Structure in Western Europe.* Oxford: OUP.

Chandra, J. (1996) 'Role and models of purchasing health for black and minority ethnic populations.' In *Locating the goalposts: Health promotion and purchasing for black and minority ethnic health.* London: Health Education Authority.

Chandra, J. (1999) 'Managing for cultural competence.' In K. Bhui and D. Olajide (eds) *Mental Health Service Provision For A Multi-Cultural Society.* London: Saunders.

Chase, A. (1977) *The Legacy Of Thomas Malthus: The Social Costs Of New Scientific Racism.* New York: Alfred A. Knopf.

Chess, S., Clark, K. and Thomas, A. (1953) 'The importance of culture evaluation in psychiatric diagnosis and treatment.' *Psychiatry Quarterly 27,* 102–114.

Chinese Mental Health Association (1995) *Annual report for the year 1994/5.* London: Chinese Mental Health Association.

CIO (1994) *Annual report of the Confederation of Indian Organisations.* London: Confederation of Indian Organisations.

Clare, A. (1973) *Psychiatry in Dissent.* London: Tavistock.

Cochrane, R. *et al.* (1977) 'Mental illness in immigrant groups to England and Wales: an analysis of mental hospital admissions, 1971.' *Social Psychiatry 22,* 181–191.

Cochrane, R. *et al.* (1989) 'Mental hospital admission rates of immigrants to England: a comparison of the 1971 and 1981 data.' *Social Psychiatry and Psychiatric Epidemiology 24,* 2–11.

Cochrane, R. *et al.* (1999) 'Ethnicity and patterns of alcohol consumption.' In D. Bhugra and Bahl (eds) *Ethnicity: An agenda for mental health.* London: Gaskell.

Cochrane, R. and Sashidharan, S.P. (1996) 'Mental health and ethnic minorities: A review of the literature and service implications.' In *Ethnicity and Health: Reviews of literature and guidance for purchasers in the areas of cardiovascular disease, mental health and haemoglobinopathies.* CRD Report 5. NHS Centre for reviews and dissemination social policy research unit. University of York.

Coid, J., Kahtan, N., Gault, S. And Jarman, B. (2001) 'Ethnic differences in admissions to secure forensic psychiatry services.' *British Journal of Psychiatry 177,* 241–247.

Coker, N. (2001) 'Understanding race and racism.' In Coker, N. (Ed) *Racism in Medicine.* London: King's Fund.

Cole, E. *et al.* (1995) 'Pathways to care for patients with a first episode of psychosis: A comparison of ethnic groups.' *British Journal of Psychiatry 167,* 770–776.

Coll, X. (1998) 'Importance of acknowledging racial and cultural differences.' *Psychiatric Bulletin 22,* 370–372.

Collins Thesaurus (1986) *The Collins Paperback Thesaurus.* London and Glasgow: Collins.

Commander, M.J., Sashidharan, S.P., Odell, S.M. And Surtees, P.G. (1997) 'Access to mental health care in an inner city health district. 1. Pathways into and within specialist psychiatric services.' *British Journal of Psychiatry 170*, 4, 312–316.

Conway, A.S., Melzer, D. and Hale, A.S. (1994) 'The outcome of targeting community mental health services: Evidence from West Lambeth schizophrenia cohort.' *BMJ 308*, 627–630.

Craig, T. and Timms, P. (1992) 'Out of the wards and onto the streets: Deinstitutionalisation and homelessness in Britain.' *Journal of Mental Health 1*, 3, 265–275.

Crawford, P., Nolan, P. and Brown, A. (1995) 'Linguistic entrapment: Medico-nursing biography as fiction.' *Journal of Advanced Nursing 22*, 1141–1148.

Cross, W.E. (1978) 'The Thomas and Cross models on psychological nigrescence: A literature review.' *Journal of Black Psychology 4*, 13–31.

Cross W.E. (1991) *Studies of Black: Diversity in African-American Identity.* Philadelphia: Temple University Press.

Dalal, F. (1988a) 'The Racism of Jung.' *Race and Class 29*, 3, 1–22.

Dalal, F. (1988b) 'Jung: A Racist.' *British Journal of Psychotherapy 4*, 3, 263–279.

Davies, D. (1999) 'Welsh Psyche.' *International Review of Psychiatry 11*, 2/3, 197–211.

Davies, S. *et al.* (1996) 'Ethnic differences in risk of compulsory psychiatric admission among representative cases of psychosis in London.' *BMJ 312*, 533–7.

Dean, G. *et al.* (1981) 'First admissions of native born and immigrants to psychiatric hospitals in South East England, 1976.' *British Journal of Psychiatry 139*, 596–612.

Dennett, D.C. (1989) *The Intentional Stance.* Cambridge, MA: The MIT Press.

Dobbins, J.E. and Skillings, J.H. (2000) 'Racism as a clinical syndrome.' *American Journal of Orthopsychiatry 70*, 1, 14–27.

Dolan, B., Polley, K., Allen, R. and Norton, K. (1991) 'Addressing racism in psychiatry.' *International Journal of Social Psychiatry 37*, 71–79.

Donnan, S. (1996) 'Epidemiology and health services research in 1996.' *Journal of Epidemiology and Community Health 30*, 113.

Doyle, Y. (1995) 'Disability use of independent living fund in SE London and users' views about the system of cash for care.' *Journal of Epidemiology and Community Health 49*, 1, 43–47.

Doyle, Y. *et al.* (1994) 'Coping with disabilities: the perspective of young adults from different ethnic backgrounds in Inner London.' *Social Science and Medicine 38*, 11, 1491–1498.

Edwards, J. (1994) *Multilingualism.* London: Penguin.

Elkin, A.P. (1994) *Aboriginal Men of High Degree: Initiation and Sorcery in the World's Oldest Tradition.* Rochester, Vermont: Inner Traditions International.

Erikson, T.H. (1993) *Ethnicity and Nationalism: Anthropological Perspectives.* London: Pluto Press.

Esmail, A. (2001) 'Racial Discrimination in Medical Schools.' In Coker, N. (ed) *Racism in Medicine.* London: King's Fund.

Eysenck, H.J. (1975) *The Inequality of Man.* Glasgow: Fontana/Collins.

Fanon, F. (1986) *Black Skin, White Masks.* London: Pluto Press.

Feagin, J. and Sikes, M. (1994) *Living with Racism: The Black Middle Class Experience.* Boston MA: Beacon Press.

Fenichel, H. and Rapaport, D. (eds) (1955) *The Collected Papers of Otto Fenichel.* London: Routledge and Kegan Paul.

Fenton, S. (1999) *Ethnicity: Racism, Class and Culture.* London and Basingstoke: MacMillan Press.

Fernando, S. (1988) *Race, Culture and Psychiatry.* London: Routledge.

Fernando, S (1991) *Mental Health, Race and Culture.* London: MIND Publications.

Fernando, S. (1992) 'Roots of Racism in Psychiatry'. *Open Mind 59*, 10–11.

Fernando, S. (1996) *Mental Health in Multi-ethnic Society.* London: Routledge.

Fernando, S. (1998) *Forensic Psychiatry, Race and Culture.* London: Routledge.

Foster, P. (1999) 'Dover refugees to be moved after violence.' *Electronic Telegraph,* 20 August.

Foulkes, E., Westermeyer, J. and Ta, K. (1998) 'Developing Clinical Curricula for Transcultural Mental Health.' In S.O. Okpaku (ed) *Clinical Methods in Transcultural Psychiatry.* Washington: American Psychiatric Association.

Fox, R. (1996) 'What do patients want from medical research?' *Journal of the Royal Society of Medicine 89*, 6, 301–302.

Francis, J. (1994) 'No more excuses.' *Community Care,* 16–22 June, 21–23.

Frankel, S. *et al.* (1991) 'Lay epidemiology and the rationality of responses to health education.' *British Journal of General Practice 41*, 428–430.

Franklin, A.J. and Boyd-Franklin, N. (2000) 'Invisibility Syndrome: A clinical model of the effects of racism on African-American males.' *American Journal of Orthopsychiatry 70*, 1, 33–41.

Freud, A. (1986) *The Ego and the Mechanism of Defence 1936.* London: Hogarth Press and The Institute of Psychoanalysis.

Freud, S. (1923) *The Ego and the Id SE XIX* (1923–25) London: Vintage (2001).

Freud, S. (1930) Civilization and its Discontents SE XXI (1927–31). London: Vintage (2001).

Fulford, K.W.M. (1999) 'From culturally sensitive to culturally competent.' In K. Bhui and D. Olajide (eds) *Mental Health Service Provision for a Multi-Cultural Society.* London: Saunders.

Furnham, A. and Li, Y. (1993) 'The psychological adjustment of the Chinese community in Britain: A study of two generations.' *British Journal of Psychiatry 162*, 09–13.

Furnham, A. and Shiekh, S. (1993) 'Gender, generation and social support correlates of mental health in Asian immigrants.' *International Journal of Social Psychiatry 39*, 22–33.

Fussell, P. (1975) *The Great War and Modern Memory.* Oxford: Oxford University Press.

Gammell, H. *et al.* (1993) 'Refugees (political asylum seekers): Service provision and access to the NHS.' A study by the college of health for Newham Health Authority and Newham Healthcare.

Garety, P.A. and Hemsley, D.R. (1994) *Delusions: Investigations into the Psychology of Delusional Reasoning.* Oxford: Oxford University Press.

Gelder, M., Gath, D. and Mayou, R. (1983) *Oxford Textbook of Psychiatry.* Oxford: Oxford University Press.

Giddens, A. (1986) *Sociology: A Brief but Critical Introduction.* London: MacMillan.

Gill, P. (2001) *General Practitioners, Ethnic Divinity and Racism.* London: King's Fund.

Gillam, S., Jarman, B., White, P. and Law, R. (1989) 'Ethnic differences in consultation rates in urban general practice.' *BMJ 299,* 953–957.

Glover, G. (1989) 'The pattern of psychiatric admissions of Caribbean born immigrants in London.' *Social Psychiatry and Psychiatric Epidemiology 24,* 49–56.

Goffman, E. (1963) *Stigma: Notes on the Management of Spoiled Identity.* pp.15–18. Harmondsworth: Penguin Books Ltd.

Goldberg, D. (1999) 'Cultural aspects of mental disorder in primary care.' In D. Bhugra and V. Bahl (eds) *Ethnicity: An Agenda for Mental Health.* London: Gaskell.

Goldberg, D. and Huxley, P. (1980) *Mental Illness in the Community.* London: Tavistock.

Good, B.J. and Good, M.D. (1981) 'The meaning of symptoms: A cultural hermeneutic model for clinical practice.' In L. Eisenberg and A. Kleinman (eds) *The relevance of social science for medicine.* Dordrecht: D. Reidal.

Gorst-Unsworth, C. (1992) 'Adaptation after torture: Some thoughts on the long term effects of surviving a repressive regime.' *Medicine and War 8,* 164–168.

Grant, C. and Deane, J. (1995) 'Brixton refugee health project: Stating the obvious.' London: Lambeth Lewisham and Southwark Health Commission.

Gray, P. (1999) 'Voluntary organisations.' In D. Bhugra and V. Bhal (eds) *Ethnicity: An Agenda for Mental Health.* London: Gaskell.

Greenwood, A. (1993) 'Ethnic minorities mental health: The case for a specialist unit.' *Ethnic minorities current awareness bulletin 4,* 2, i-iii.

Gupta, D. (1995) *The Context Of Ethnicity: Sikh Identity in a Comparative Perspective.* Dehli: Oxford University Press.

Gupta, S. (1991) 'Psychosis in migrants from the Indian sub-continent. A preliminary study on the use of psychiatric services.' *British Journal of Psychiatry 159,* 222–225.

Hadley, T. *et al.* (1996) 'Mental health policy and its problems in the UK: Deja vu.' *Current Opinions in Psychiatry 9,* 105–108.

Hamann, B. (1999) *Hitler's Vienna: A Dictator's Apprenticeship.* Oxford: Oxford University Press.

Harrell, S.P. (2000) 'A mutidimensional conceptualisation of racism-related stress: Implications for the well-being of people of colour.' *American Journal of Orthopsychiatry 70,* 1, 42–57.

Harris, E., Blue, E. and Griffith, E. (1994) 'Introduction.' In E. Harris, E. Blue and E. Griffith (eds) *Racial and Ethnic Identity.* New York: Routledge.

Health Advisory Service (1994) *Comprehensive Mental Health Services.* Sutton: NHS Health Advisory Service.

Health Education Authority (1994) *Health and Lifestyles: Black and Minority Ethnic Groups in England.* London: HEA.

Health Education Authority (1996) *Locating the goalposts: Health promotion and purchasing for black and minority ethnic health.* London: HEA.

Helman, C. (1990) *Culture, Health and Illness* (2nd Edition) London: Butterworth Heinemann.

Hendessi, M. (1994) *From Here to Equality: CHCs, Race and Ethnicity.* Greater London Association of Community Health Councils.

Herbert, I. (2000) 'Refugees flee anti-slavery capital after attacks.' *Independent,* 15 August.

Hickling, F. and Hutchinson, G. (1999) 'Roasted breadfruit psychosis: Disturbed racial identification in African Caribbeans.' *Psychiatric Bulletin 35,* 723

Hickling, F., McKenzie, K. *et al.* (1999) 'A Jamaican psychiatrist evaluates diagnoses at a London psychiatrist hospital.' *British Journal of Psychiatry 175,* 283–285.

Holmes, D.E. (1992) 'Race and transference in psychoanalysis and psychotherapy.' *International Journal of Psychoanalysis 73,* 1–11.

Home Office Statistical Bulletin 15/95. Research and Statistics Department, 50 Queen Ann's Gate, London SW1 9AT.

Hotopf, M. *et al.* (1995) 'Are ethical committees reliable?' *Journal of the Royal Society of Medicine 88,* 31–33.

Howitt, D. and Owusu-Bempah, J. (1994) *The Racism of Psychology: Time for Change.* Hemel Hempsted: Harvester Wheatsheaf.

Huby, G. *et al.* (1989) 'General medical practice in a multi-cultural and multi-racial environment: report from a multidisciplinary casework seminar.' *Health Trends 21,* 36–89.

Huka, G. (1995) 'Needs assessment and civil liberties.' In *Mental Health in Black and Minority Ethnic People: Time For Action.* London: The Mental Health Foundation.

Inhorn, M. (1995) 'Medical Anthropology and Epidemiology: Divergence and convergence.' *Social Science Medicine 40,* 3, 285–290.

Institute for Public Policy Research (1997) *IPPR Attitudes to Race Survey.* London: NOP and IPPR.

Jacob, K., Bhugra, D. and Mann, A.H. *et al.* (1996) 'The use of the general practitioner by Indian females with psychiatric morbidity: Recognition of the disorder and the role of social and cultural factors in help seeking.' Brief report of preliminary findings. Submitted for publication.

Jamdagni, L. (1996) *Purchasing for Black Populations.* London: King's Fund.

Janes, C., Stall, R. and Gifford, S. (1986) Anthropology and Epidemiology. Dordrecht: D. Reidal.

Jaspers, K. (1963) *General Psychopathology.* Manchester: Manchester University Press.

Jennings, S. (1996) 'The process of partnership.' In *Creating Solutions. Developing Alternatives in Black Mental Health.* London: King's Fund.

Jennings, S. (1996) *Creating Solutions: Developing Alternatives in Black Mental Health.* London: King's Fund.

Jones, E. (1999) 'The phenomenology of abnormal belief: A philosophical and psychiatric inquiry.' *Philosophy, Psychiatry and Psychology 6,* 1–16.

Jones, E. and Watson, J.P. (1997) 'Delusion, the overvalued idea and religious beliefs: A comparative analysis of their characteristics.' *British Journal of Psychiatry 170*, 381–386.

Jones, G. (1997) 'Hague slams Tebbit over race remarks.' *Electronic Telegraph 68*, 9 October.

Jones, G. (2000) 'Hague hits out at cost of asylum.' *www.telegraph.co.uk*, 1782, 11 April.

Jones, G. and Berry, M. (1986) 'Regional secure units: The emerging picture.' In G. Edwards (ed) *Current Issues in Clinical Psychology IV*. London: Plenum Press.

Jones, J.M. (1997) *Prejudice and Racism* (2nd edition). New York: McGraw-Hill.

Jones, P. and King, M. (1999) 'Invited commentaries: A Jamaican psychiatrist evaluates diagnoses at a London psychiatrist hospital.' *British Journal of Psychiatry 175*, 286.

Jones, R. (1995) 'Why do qualitative research?' *BMJ 311*, 2.

Jung, C.J. (1921) *Collected Works of C.J. Jung*. Princeton: Princeton University Press.

Jung, C.J. (1930) 'Your Negroid and Indian Behaviour'. *Forum 83*, 193–199.

Juss, S. (1993) *Immigration, Nationality and Citizenship*. London: Mansell.

Juss, S. (1995) 'The constitution and Sikhs in Britain.' *Brigham Young University Law Review*. No 2. J Reuben Clark Law School, Utah, USA.

Kaney, S. and Bentall, R.P. (1989) 'Persecutory delusions and attributable style.' *British Journal of Medical Psychology 62*, 191–198.

Kareem, J. and Littlewood, R. (1992) *Intercultural Therapy: Themes, Interpretations and Practice*. Oxford: Blackwell Scientific Publications.

Karmi, G. (1992a) 'Refugee Health Requires a Comprehensive Strategy.' *BMJ 305*, 25, 206–207.

Karmi, G. (1992b) *Refugees and the National Health Service*. London: NW and NE Thames Regional Health Authorities.

Kawachi, I., Kennedy, P., Lockner, K. and Prothrow-Stith, D. (1997) 'Social capital, income inequality and mortality.' *American Journal of Public Health 87*, 9, 1491–1498.

Keesing, L.M. (1981) *Cultural Anthropology: A Contemporary Perspective*. New York: Holt Reinhardt and Winston.

Kemp, R. and David, A. (1995) 'Insight and adherence to treatment in psychotic disorders.' *British Journal of Hospital Medicine 54*, 222–227.

Kennedy, B., Kawachi, I., Lochner, K., Jones, C. and Prothrow-Stith, D. (1998) (Dis)respect and black mortality. Ethnicity and disease.

Kenny, M. (1985) 'Latah: Paradox lost.' In C.C. Hughes and R. Simons (eds) *Culture-Bound Syndromes*. Dordrecht: D. Reidel.

Kiev, A. (1965) 'Psychiatric morbidity amongst West Indian immigrants in urban general practice.' *British Journal of Psychiatry 111*, 51–56.

King, M. *et al.* (1994) 'Incidence of psychotic illness in London: Comparison of ethnic groups.' *BMJ 309*, 1115–1119.

Kleinman, A. (1980) *Patients and their Healers in the Context of Culture*. Berkeley, CA: University of California Press.

Kleinman, A. (1988) *Rethinking Psychiatry*. New York: Free Press.

Kleinman, A. and Good, B. (1985) *Culture and Depression: Studies in the Anthropology and Cross-Cultural Psychiatry of Affective Disorder*. London: California Press.

Kleinman, A. and Sung, L.H. (1979) 'Why do indigenous practitioners successfully heal?' *Social Science and Medicine 13B*, 7–26.

Kohn, M. (1996) *The Race Gallery*. London: Vintage Books.

Kohut, H. (1971) *The Analysis of the Self.* New York: International Universities Press.

Kovel, J. (1988) *White Racism: A Psychohistory*. London: Free Association Books.

Krause, I.B. *et al.* (1991) 'Sinking Heart: A Punjabi communication of distress.' *Social Science and Medicine 2*, 563–575.

Krause, I.B. (1999) *Therapy across Cultures*. London: Sage Publications.

Kumar, A. (1991) 'The ethnic minorities mental health development project of Tameside and Glossop association of MIND.' An evaluation report Feb 1990 to Dec 1991. Tameside and Glossop MIND.

Lago, C. and Thompson, J. (1996) *Race, Culture and Counselling*. Buckingham: Open University Press.

La Grenade, J. and Bhugra, D. (1999) 'Community organisations' expectations of mental health statutory services: A pilot study.' In D. Bhugra and V. Bahl (eds) *Ethnicity: An Agenda for Mental Health*. London: Gaskell.

Lambeth, Southwark and Lewisham Health Commission (1994) *Local responses to the Ritchie Report of three borough based conferences held in July/August 1994*. LSL Health Commission.

Lane, C. (1999) 'The Psychoanalysis of Race: An Introduction.' In C. Lane (ed) *The Psychoanalysis of Race*. New York and Chichester: Columbia University Press.

Last, J.M. (1995) *A Dictionary of Epidemiology* (3rd edition). Oxford: Oxford University Press.

LaViest, T. (1992) 'The political empowerment and health status of African-Americans: mapping a new territory.' *American Journal of Sociology 97*, 1080–1095.

LaViest, T. (1993) *Segregation, Poverty, Empowerment, Health Consequences for African-Americans*. Milbank Memorial Fund 1. 1.

Leavey, G. (1999) 'Suicide and Irish migrants in Britain. Identity and integration.' *International Review of Psychiatry 11*, 2/3, 168–172.

Leff (1988) 'Psychiatry Around the Globe. A Transcultural view.' Gaskell Series. London: Royal College of Psychiatrists.

Leff, J. (1999) 'Epidemiologic factors in research with ethnic minorities.' In D. Bhugra and V. Bahl (eds) *Ethnicity: An Agenda for Mental Health*. London: Gaskell.

Lelliot, P. *et al.* (1995) 'Resolving London's bed crisis: There might be a way but is there the will?' *Psychiatric Bulletin 19*, 5, 273.

Lewis, A. (1965) 'Chairman's opening remarks' in A.S. De Rueck and R. Porter (eds) *Transcultural Psychiatry. Cibu Foundation Symposium*. London: Churchill.

Lewis, G. *et al.* 'Are British psychiatrists racist?' *British Journal of Psychiatry 157*, 410–415

Lewis, I.M. (1976) *Social Anthropology in Perspective: The Relevance of Social Anthropology*. Cambridge: Cambridge University Press.

Li *et al.* (1994) 'The collection of general practice data for psychiatric service contracts.' *Journal of Public Health Medicine 16*, 1, 87–92.

Lillie-Blanton, M. and LaViest, T. (1996) 'Race ethnicity, the social environment and health.' *Social Science and Medicine 43*, 1, 83–91.

Link, B. (1996) 'The role of fundamental social causes in health.' *American Journal of Public Heath 86*, 471–473.

Littlewood, R. (1990) 'From Categories to contexts: A decade of the "New cross cultural psychiatry".' *British Journal of Psychiatry 156*, 308–327.

Littlewood, R. (1993) 'Ideology, camouflage or contingency? Racism in British psychiatry.' *Transcultural Psychiatric Research Review 3*, 243–290.

Littlewood, R. and Cross, S. (1980) 'Ethnic minorities and psychiatric services.' *Sociology of Health and Illness 2*, 2, 194–201.

Littlewood, R. and Lipsedge, M. (1981) 'Some social and phenomenological characteristics of psychotic immigrants.' *Psychological Medicine 11*, 289–302.

Littlewood, R. and Lipsedge, M. (1989) *Aliens and Alienists: Ethnic Minorities and Psychiatry.* London: Unwin Hyman.

Lloyd, K. *et al.* (1996) 'The development of the short explanatory model interview and its use among primary care attenders.' Paper submitted.

Lloyd, K. and St Louis, L. (1999) 'Common mental disorders among Africans and Caribbeans.' In D. Bhugra and V. Bahl (eds) *Ethnicity: An Agenda for Mental Health.* London: Gaskell.

Lloyd, P and Moodley, P. (1992) 'Psychotropic medication and ethnicity: An inpatient survey.' *Social Psychiatry and Psychiatric Epidemiology 27*, 2, 95–101.

Lock M. (1993) 'The concept of race: An ideological construct.' *Transcultural Psychiatric Research Review 30*, 203–227.

Lowenthal, K. (1999) 'Religious issues and their psychological aspects.' In K. Bhui and D. Olajide (eds) *Mental Health Service Provision For A Multi-Cultural Society.* London: Saunders.

MacArthur, B. (1993) *The Penguin Book of Twentieth Century Speeches.* London: Penguin Books.

MacCarthy, B. and Craisatti, J. (1989) 'Ethnic differences in response to adversity.' *Social Psychiatry and Psychiatric Epidemiology 24*, 196–201.

MacPherson, W. (1999) *The Stephen Lawrence Enquiry.* London: HMSO.

Maden, A. (1999) 'Forensic Psychiatry.' In D. Bhugra and V. Bahl (eds) *Ethnicity: An Agenda for Mental Health.* London: Gaskell.

Maden, A. *et al.* (1995) 'The ethnic origin of women serving a prison sentence.' *British Journal of Criminology 32*, 218–221.

McEllroy, A.J. (1999) 'Alert as NF plot refugee protest.' *Electronic Telegraph*, 28 August.

McKeigue, P. and Karmi, G. (1993) 'Alcohol consumption and alcohol related problems in African-Caribbeans and South Asians in the United Kingdom.' *Alcohol and Alcoholism 28*, 1–10.

McKenna, P.J. (1984) 'Disorders with Overvalued Ideas.' *British Journal of Psychiatry 145*, 579–585.

McKenzie, K. and Murray, R.H. (1999) 'Risk Factors for Psychosis in the UK African-Caribbean Population.' In D. Bhugra and V. Bahl (eds) *Ethnicity: An Agenda for Mental Health.* London: Gaskell.

Medical Foundation for the Care of Victims of Torture (1994) *A Betrayal of Hope and Trust: Detention in UK Survivors of Torture.* 96–98 Grafton Road, London NW5.

Mednick, S.A. and Owens (1989) 'Adult schizophrenia following pre-natal exposure to an influenza epidemic.' *Archives of General Psychiatry 45,* 189–192.

Mental Health Foundation (1995a) *Mental Health in Black and Minority Ethnic people: Time for Action. The report of a seminar on Race and Mental Health. 'Towards a strategy'.* London: Mental Health Foundation.

Mental Health Foundation (1995b) *Mental Health in Black and Minority Ethnic people. The fundamental facts. The report of a seminar on Race and Mental Health. 'Towards a strategy'.* London: Mental Health Foundation.

Merril, J. *et al.* (1990) 'Asian suicides.' *British Journal of Psychiatry 156,* 748–749.

Mezzich, J.E. *et al.* (1996) *Culture and Psychiatric Diagnosis. A DSM IV perspective.* Washington: American Psychiatric Association.

Miles, R. (1993) *Racism after Race Relations.* London: Routledge.

Miller, C. (2000) 'Citizenship and Inclusion.' *Openmind 105,* 10-11.

Mills, M. (1996) 'Shanti: An intercultural psychotherapy centre for women.' In S. Johnson *et al.* (eds) *Women's Mental Health Services.* London: Routledge.

Millward, D. (1999) 'Cricket fans face first test at immigration.' *www.telegraph.co.uk,* 1453, 18 May.

Milmis Project Group (1995) 'Monitoring Inner London mental illness services.' *Psychiatric Bulletin 19,* 5, 276.

MIND (1999) *Creating Accepting Communities: Report of the MIND enquiry into social exclusion.* London: MIND Publications.

Moodley, P. and Perkins, R. (1991) 'Routes to psychiatric inpatient care in an inner London Borough.' *Social Psychiatry and Psychiatric Epidemiology 26,* 47–51.

Morgan, H. 'Between fear and blindness: The white therapist and the black patient.' *Journal of the British Association of Psychotherapists 4,* 3:1, 48–61.

Morrison, T. (1992) *Playing in the Dark.* Cambridge, MA: Harvard University Press.

Mumford, D. (1992) 'Does Somatisation explain anything?' *Psychiatry in Practice.* Spring 11, 1, 11–14.

NACRO (1989) *Race and Criminal Justice.* London: National Association for the Care and Resettlement of Offenders.

NACRO (1990) *Black people, mental health and the courts: An exploratory study into the psychiatric remand process as it affects black defendants at magistrate's courts.* London: National Association for the Care and Resettlement of Offenders.

NAHAT (1996) *Good practice and quality indicators in primary health care.* Birmingham: NHS Ethnic Health Unit in conjunction with Kensington and Westminster Health Authority NHS Ethnic Health Unit.

Neighbors, H.W., Jackson, J.S., Broman, C. and Thompson, E. 'Racism and the mental health of African-Americans: The role of self and system blame' *Ethnicity and Disease 6,* (1–2): 167–175.

New Caxton Encyclopaedia (1977) *The New Caxton Encyclopaedia,* Vol. 7, p.2249. London: Caxton Publishing.

Nguyen-Van-Tam, J. *et al.* (1996) 'Health care experiences of Vietnamese families in Nottingham.' *Health Trends 27*, 4, 106–110.

Nguyen-Van-Tam, J. and Madeley, R. (1996) 'Vietnamese people in study may have had language difficulties.' *BMJ 313*, 48.

NHS Task Force (1994) *Black Mental Health: A dialogue for change.* London: NHS Management Executive: Mental Health Task Force.

Norton-Taylor, R. (1999) *The Color of Justice.* London: Oberon Books.

NW Thames Regional Health Authority (1994) *Partners in care: Developing health voluntary sector commissioning.* Office for public management. NW Thames regional health authority.

O'Callaghan, E., Sham, P., Takei, N. *et al.* (1998) 'Schizophrenia after prenatal exposure to 1957 A2 influenza epidemic.' *Lancet 337*, 1248–50.

OPCS (1995) *Surveys of Psychiatric Morbidity in Great Britain. Report No. 1. The prevalence of psychiatric morbidity amongst adults aged 16–64 living in private households in Great Britain.* London: OPCS/HMSO.

Owen, D. (1996) 'Size, structure and growth of the ethnic minority populations.' In D. Coleman and J. Salt (eds) *Ethnicity in the 1991 Census. Vol 1. The demographic characteristics of the ethnic minority populations.* London: OPCS/HMSO.

Parker, S. and Kleiner, R. (1966) *Mental Illness in the Urban Negro Community.* New York: Free Press.

Patel, V. *et al.* (1995) 'Concepts of mental illness in medical pluralism in Harare.' *Psychological Medicine 25*, 485–493.

Patton, G.C., Johnson-Sabine, E., Wood, K. and Wakeling, A. (1990) 'Abnormal eating habits in London schoolgirls – a prospective epidemiological study: Outcome at twelve month follow-up.' *Psychological Medicine 20*, 383–394.

Peach, C. (1996) 'Introduction.' In C. Peach, *Ethnicity in the 1991 Census. Vol 2: The ethnic minority populations of Great Britain.* London: ONS/HMSO.

Pelosi, A., McGinnis, E., Elliot, C. and Douglas, A. (1995) 'Second opinions: A right or a concession?' *BMJ 311*, 670–672.

Perera *et al.* (1991) 'Ethnic aspects: A comparison of three matched groups.' *British Journal of Psychiatry 159*, suppl. 13, 40–42.

Pharoah, C. (1992) 'Primary health care: How well are users served.' In *Recent research in services for black and minority ethnic elderly people.* London: Institute of Gerontology, King's College.

Pilgrim, S. *et al.* (1993) *The Bristol Black and Ethnic Minorities Health Survey Report.* Bristol: Department of Sociology and Epidemiology, University of Bristol.

Ponce, D.E. (1998) 'Cultural epistemology and value orientations: Clinical applications in transcultural psychiatry.' In S.O. Okpaku (ed) *Clinical Methods in Transcultural Psychiatry.* Washington: American Psychiatric Association.

Pope, C. and Mays, N. (1993) 'Opening the black box: An encounter in the corridors of health services research'. *BMJ 306*, 315–319.

Popkin, R. (1999) 'Eighteenth Century Racism'. In R. Popkin (ed) *The Pimlico History of Western Philosophy.* London: Pimlico Publishing.

Pouissant, A. (1999) 'They hate. They kill. Are they insane?' *New York Times*, 26 August [op-ed piece].

Power, A. (2000) 'Social Exclusion' *Royal Society Arts Journal 2/4*, 47-51.

Price, H.H. (1934) 'Some considerations about belief.' *Proceedings of the Aristotelian Society 35*, 229–252.

Price, H.H. (1969) *Belief: The Gifford Lectures delivered at the University of Aberdeen in 1960.* London: Allen and Unwin.

Raleigh, V. *et al.* (1990) 'Suicides amongst immigrants from the Indian sub-continent.' *British Journal of Psychiatry 156*, 46–50.

Ramon, S. (1999) 'Social Work.' In K. Bhui and D. Olajide (eds) *Mental Health Service Provision For A Multi-Cultural Society.* London: Saunders.

Ramsay, R., Gorst-Unsworth, C. and Turner, S. (1993) 'Psychiatric morbidity in survivors of organised state violence including torture: A retrospective series.' *British Journal of Psychiatry 162*, 55–59.

Rattansi, A. (1992) 'Changing the subject? Racism, culture and education.' In J. Donald and A. Rattansi (eds) *Race, Culture and Difference.* London: Sage.

Refugee Arrivals Project Annual Report (1994) Room 2005, 2nd floor, Queens Building, Heathrow Airport, Hounslow, Middlesex: Refugee Arrivals Project.

Rex, J. (1961) *Key Problems in Sociological Theory.* London: R.K.P.

Rex, J. (1983) *Race Relations in Sociological Theory.* London: R.K.P.

Richards, H. (1996) 'Managing boundaries and spaces: Leadership in mental health.' *British Journal of Health Care Management 2*, 7, 375–381.

Richardson, J. and Lambert, J. (1985) *The Sociology of Race.* Lancashire: Causeway Press.

Richman, N. (1993) 'Children in situations of political violence.' *Journal of Child Psychololgy and Psychiatry 34*, 8, 1286–1302.

Ridley, C.R. (1995) *Overcoming Unintentional Racism in Counselling and Therapy: A Practitioner's Guide to Intentional Intervention.* Thousand Oaks, CA: Sage Publications.

Ridley, C.R., Chih, D.W. and Olivera, R.J. (2000) 'Training in cultural schemas: An antidote to unintentional racism in clinical practice'. *American Journal of Orthopsychiatry 70*, 1, 65–72.

Ring, J.M. (2000) 'The long and winding road: Personal reflections of an anti-racist trainer.' *American Journal of Orthopsychiatry 70*, 1, 73–81.

Ritchie, J.H, Dick, D. and Lingham, R. (1994) *The Report of the Inquiry into the Care and Treatment of Christopher Clunis.* London: HMSO.

Roberts, G. (1991) 'Delusional belief systems and the meaning of life: A preferred reality?' *British Journal of Psychiatry 159*, suppl. 14, 19–28.

Robertson *et al.* (1996) 'The entry of mentally disordered people to the criminal justice system.' *British Journal of Psychiatry 169*, 172–180.

Robins, D. (1992) 'Nafsiyat: A psychotherapy centre for ethnic minorities.' In *Community Care: Department of Health funded research.* London: HMSO.

Rogers, A., Pilgrim, D. and Lacey, R. (1993) *Experiencing psychiatry: Users' views of services.* London: Macmillan.

Rollock, D. and Gordon, E.W. (2000) 'Racism and Mental Health into the 21st Century: Perspectives and Parameters.' *American Journal of Orthopsychiatry 70*, 1, 5–13.

Rouchy, J.C. (1995) 'Identification and groups of belonging.' *Group Analysis 18*, 2, 129-141.

Royal College of Psychiatrists (2001) *Report of Ethnic Issues Project Group.* Council Report CR92. London: Royal College of Psychiatrists.

Rufford, N. (1999) 'Asylum seekers may be put in transit camps.' *Sunday Times*, 29 August.

Rycroft, C.F. (1968) 'On the defensive function of schizophrenic thinking and delusion-formation.' In C.F. Rycroft (ed) *Imagination and Reality.* London: The Hogarth Press.

Ryle, G. (1963) *The Concept of Mind [1949].* London: Penguin Books.

Sabshin, M., Diesenhaus, H. and Wilkerson, R. (1970) 'Dimensions of institutional racism in psychiatry.' *American Journal of Psychiatry 127*, 787–793.

Sampson, R.J., Raudenbush, S.W. and Earls, F. (1997) 'Neighborhoods and violent crime: A multilevel study of collective efficacy.' *Science 277* (91) 8924.

Sashidharan, S.P. (1993) 'African-Caribbeans and Schizophrenia: the ethnic vulnerability hypothesis revisited.' *International Review of Psychiatry 5*, 129–144.

Sashidharan, S.P. (1994) 'The need for community based alternatives to institutional psychiatry.' *SHARE newsletter*, Issue 7, 3.

Sashidharan, S.P. And Cochrane, R. (1996) *Mental Health and Ethnic Minorities.* NHS Centre for Reviews and Dissemination. CRD Report 5. York: University of York.

Sashidharan, S.P. (1999) 'Alternatives to Institutional Care.' In D. Bhugra and V. Bahl (eds) *Ethnicity: an agenda for mental health.* London: Gaskell.

Sashidharan, S.P. (2001) 'Institutionalised Racism in Psychiatry.' *Psychiatric Bulletin 25*, 244-247.

Scrimshaw, S.C. and Gleason, G.R. (1992) *RAP: Rapid Assessment Procedures: Qualitative methodologies for planning and evaluation of health related programmes.* Boston: INFDC.

Segall, M.H., Dasen, P.R., Berry, J.W. and Pooertingo, Y.H. (1990) *Human Behaviour in a Global Perspective: An Introduction to Cross-Cultural Psychology.* Oxford: Pergamon Press.

Sheehan, J. *et al.* (1995) 'Social deprivation, ethnicity and violent incidents on acute psychiatric wards.' *Psychiatric Bulletin 19*, 10, 597.

Sherwood, R. (1966) *The Psychodynamics of Race: Vicious and Benign Spirals.* Sussex: Harvester Press.

Shrimsley, R. (2000) *www.telegraph.co.uk,* 1781, 10 April.

Simmel, E. (1946) 'Otto Fenichel' *The International Journal of Psycho-Analysis 27*, 67–71.

Simons R. (1985) 'Latah: Paradox.' In C.C. Hughes and R.C. Simons (eds) *Culture-Bound Syndromes.* Dordrecht: D. Reidel.

Simpson, S. (1993) 'Non response to the 1991 census: The effect on ethnic group enumeration.' In *Ethnicity in the 1991 Census. Vol 1. The demographic characteristics of the ethnic minority populations.* London: HMSO.

Sims, A. (1988) *Symptoms in the Mind: An Introduction to Descriptive Psychopathology.* London: Baillière Tindall.

Skellington, R. (1996) *Race in Britain Today.* London: Open University Press and Sage.

Smaje, C. (1995) *Health, Race and Ethnicity: Making sense of the evidence.* London: King's Fund Centre.

Smaje, C. (1996) 'The ethnic patterning of health: Directions of theory and research.' *Sociology of Health and Illness 18,* 139–166.

Sowell, T. (1994) *Race and Culture: A World View.* New York: Basic Books.

Stuart, O. (1996) 'Yes we mean black disabled people too.' In W. Ahmad and K. Atkin (eds) *Race and Community Care.* Buckingham: Open University Press.

Summerfield, D. (1995) 'Addressing human response to war and atrocity: Major challenges in research and practices and the limitations of western psychiatric models.' In R.J. Kleber, C.R. Figley and B.P. Gersons (eds) *Beyond Trauma: Cultural and Societal Dynamics.* New York: Plenum Press.

Sykes, J.B. (1982) *The Concise Oxford Dictionary* (7th edition). Oxford: Clarendon Press.

Tang, M. and Cuninghame, C. (1994) *Focus groups, access to primary health care and the Deptford Vietnamese project.* Save the Children Fund, UK and European Programmes Department, London Division.

Tatla, D.S. (1999) *The Sikh Diaspora.* London: UCL Press.

The Milton S. Eisenhower Foundation and The Corporation for What Works (1998) *The Millenium Breach: Richer, Poorer and Racially Apart.* Washington, DC: The Milton S. Eisenhower Foundation.

Thomas, A. and Sillen, S. (1992) *Racism and Psychiatry.* New York: Brunner/Mazel.

Thomas, H. (1997) *The Slave Trade.* London and Basingstoke: Macmillan.

Thornicroft, G., Davies, S. and Leese, M. (1999) 'Health service research and forensic psychiatry: a black and white case.' *International Review of Psychiatry 11,* 2/3, 250–257.

Trostle, J. (1988) 'Medical compliance as an ideology.' *Social Science and Medicine 27,* 12, 1299–1308.

TUC (1995a) *Black and Betrayed: A Report on black workers' experience of unemployment and low pay in 1994–95.* London: Trades Union Congress.

TUC (1995b) *Race and Social Security: A report on access and discrimination in the benefits system.* London: Trades Union Congress.

Turner, T.H. *et al.* (1992) 'Mentally disordered persons found in public places: Diagnostic and social aspects of police referrals (section 136).' *Psychological Medicine 22,* 765–774.

Tylor, E.B. (1871) *Primitive Culture: Research into the Development of Mythology, Philosophy, Religion, Art and Customs.* London: John Murray.

Tyrer, P. *et al.* (1994) 'The effect of personality on clinical outcome, social networks and adjustment: a controlled trial of psychiatric emergencies.' *Psychological Medicine 24,* 731–740.

UNESCO (1967) *Statement on Race and Racial Prejudice.* Paris: UNESCO.

US Department of Health and Human Services (1985) *Report of the Secretary's Task Force on black and minority health.* Washington, DC: Government Printing Office.

van den Berghe, P.H. (1967) *Race and racism: A Comparative Perspective.* New York: John Wiley.

van Os, J. *et al.* (1996) 'The incidence of mania: Time trends in relation to gender and ethnicity.' *Social Psychiatry and Psychiatric Epidemiology 31*, 129–136.

Victor, P. (1996) 'Driven mad by racial abuse.' *Independent*, 11 December, p.15.

Wade, J.C. (1993) 'Institutional racism: An analysis of the mental health system.' *American Journal of Orthopsychiatry 63*, 535–544.

Watters, C. (1996) 'Representation and realities: Black people, community care and mental illness.' In W. Ahmad and K. Atkin (eds) *Race and Community Care.* Buckingham: Open University Press.

Webb, J. and Enstice. A. (1998) *Fiction, Politics, and Prejudice in Australia: Aliens and Savages.* Sydney: Harper Collins.

Webb-Johnson, A. (1993) *Building on strengths: Enquiry into health activity in the Asian voluntary sector.* London: Confederation of Indian Organisations.

Wellman, D. (2000) 'From evil to illness: Medicalizing racism.' *American Journal of Orthopsychiatry 70*, 1, 28–32.

Werber, R. and Ranger, T. (1996) *Post Colonial Identities in Africa.* London: Zed Books.

Wessley, S. (1991) 'Schizophrenia and African Caribbeans: a case control study.' *British Journal of Psychiatry 159*, 795–801.

Westmayer (1990) 'Working with an interpreter in psychiatric assessment and treatment.' *Journal of Nervous and Mental Disease 178*, (12), 745–749.

Wilson, B. (1992) *Religion in Sociological Perspective.* Oxford: Oxford University Press.

Wilson, M. (1993) *Britain's Black Communities.* NHS Management Executive. London: Mental Health Task Force and King's Fund Centre.

Wilson, M. (1995) *Alternatives in Black mental health. The Sanctuary model.* London: King's Fund Centre.

Wilson, M. and MacCarthy, B. (1994) 'GP consultation as a factor in the low rate of mental health service use by Asians.' *Psychological Medicine 24*, 113–119.

Yee, L. (1996) *Improving support for black carers: A source book of information, ideas and service initiatives.* London: King's Fund.

Young-Bruhl, E. (1998) *The Anatomy of Prejudice.* Cambridge, MA: Harvard University Press.

Contributors

Dr Dinesh Bhugra, Senior Lecturer in Psychiatry, Institute of Psychiatry and Honorary Consultant Psychiatrist, Maudsley Hospital.

Dr Kamaldeep Bhui, Senior Lecturer in Social and Epidemiological Psychiatry, St Bartholomew's and Royal London Medical School and Honorary Consultant Psychiatrist, The Royal London Hospital.

Dr Xavier Coll, Honorary Senior Lecturer and Consultant Child and Adolescent Psychiatrist, Bethel Child and Family Centre, Norfolk Mental Health Care NHS Trust, Norwich.

Dr Edgar Jones, Reader in the History of Medicine and Psychiatry, Department of Psychological Medicine, Guy's, King's and St Thomas' Medical School, London.

Dr Kwame McKenzie, Senior Lecturer in Psychiatry, Royal Free Hospital Medical School and Honorary Consultant Psychiatrist, Haringey Health Care Trust.

Ms Premila Trivedi, Mental Health Service User, SIMBA, (Share in Maudsley Black Action) Maudsley Hospital, London.

Subject Index

Author index

05212160